HOW TO WIN AT GAMBLING

ABOUT THE AUTHOR

Avery Cardoza is the foremost authority on gambling in the world and best-selling author of 21 gaming books and advanced strategies. His company, Cardoza Publishing, founded in 1981, represents the top authors and experts in their fields. More than 75 titles and five million books sold make Cardoza Publishing the largest and most respected seller of gambling books.

In 1995, Cardoza parlayed his winnings into a new company, Cardoza Entertainment, to develop and publish casino simulation software for retail entertainment and internet applications. Their first product, *Avery Cardoza's Casino*, released in early 1997, was a best-seller within two weeks. Featuring 3D interactive dealers, 65 game varieties (of six major games), and more than 2,000 hand enhanced animation frames with full synched sound, *Avery Cardoza's Casino* became the first true casino simulation, and was acclaimed by many as the best simulation ever created. Their follow-up title, *Avery Cardoza's 100 Slots* features 101 slot machines.

Cardoza's life has been unique among all gambling writers or players in that he has counted on his gambling winnings and activities as his only source of income for all his adult life and before. In fact, has never had a 9-5 job. He is the only gambling authority who has always lived by his gambling activities.

He began his gambling career, underage, as a professional blackjack player in Las Vegas - beating the casinos at their own game. At the age of 23, when even the biggest casinos refused him play, Cardoza took his gambling winnings and wrote and published his first book, the best-selling classic, *Winning Casino Blackjack for the Non-Counter*, a revolutionary book that showed non-counting blackjack players a winning method.

Though originally from New York City, where he is occasionally found, Cardoza has used his winnings to pursue a lifestyle of extensive travelling which has included extended sojourns in such exotic locales as Bahia in Brazil, Jerusalem, Tokyo, Greece, Southeast Asia as well as California, New Orleans, and of course, Las Vegas, where he did extensive research into the mathematical, emotional and psychological aspects of winning.

In this book, Cardoza has put it all together; his years of professional play, teaching, research and knowledge into the definitive work on winning at gambling, the standard work every intelligent gambler must have - a book that shows players how to play and how to win at gambling!

HOW TO WIN AT GAMBLING

Avery Cardoza

CARDOZA PUBLISHING

FROM THE WORLD'S BEST-SELLING GAMBLING PUBLISHER
Cardoza Publishing, publisher of **Gambling Research Institute** (GRI) books, is the foremost gaming and gambling publisher in the world with a library of almost 100 up-to-date and easy-to-read books and strategies. These authoritative works are written by the top experts in their fields and with more than 5,000,000 books in print, represent the best-selling and most popular gaming books anywhere.

To Ron Charles

PRINTING HISTORY

First Printing	March 1991
Second Printing	January 1993
2nd Edition	
First Printing	February 1994
New 3rd Edition	
First Printing	July 1997
Second Printing	January 1999

Copyright©1991, 1994, 1997 by Avery Cardoza
- All Rights Reserved -

Library of Congress Catalog Card Number: 97-65217
ISBN: 0-940685-61-2
Author Photo by Ron Charles

TABLE OF CONTENTS

INTRODUCTION

I'm going to show you how to win money at gambling. Whether you're a novice, just starting out, or an experienced veteran, my goal is to show you how to approach gambling like a pro, and how to beat any game you might face.

You'll learn everything you need to know to be adept at gambling; from the rules of the games, the bets involved, and the odds you face, to how the game is played not only in America, but in casinos, gambling parlors and card rooms around the world. And for every game covered here, and there are many, you'll learn the absolute best way, with the odds, to be a winner.

I've packed these pages with winning strategies. Often, I'll show you multiple approaches to beating a particular game. This new expanded edition now covers blackjack, craps, slots, roulette, poker, baccarat, video poker, bingo, horseracing, wheel of fortune, keno, football, baseball, basketball and prizefight betting, Cho Dai Di - an exciting Chinese card game, Let it Ride®, Caribbean Stud Poker, plus money management, and lots more.

This book is about winning and gambling intelligently. That means you must always make the best bets possible, and avoid the sucker bets, and that you must gamble with your head and within your means. Being a winner entails many things, and I'll cover them all here. What you can expect from this book is a straightforward discussion so you how things really are at the tables.

For me, the name of the game is winning. I play to win money. That's my personal motivation. Throughout my adult life, and before, I have supported myself strictly through my gambling activities. My goal in these pages is to make you a player that the casinos and your fellow players respect, the one that plays to win.

I'll now give you a brief preview of the games covered.

In craps, you'll learn bets which give the casino no edge at all, and how to use these wagers to beat the casino. I present eleven different winning strategies from a variety of approaches - single odds and double odds, conservative and aggressive, betting with the dice or against them. This section will make you as good as any craps player out there, for you will be playing against the minimal house edge possible.

In blackjack, you learn how to have a mathematical edge and beat the casino. This thorough section shows how to play against any set of rules and variations and any number of decks so you're ready to play like a pro in any game around the world, be it Las Vegas or the French Riviera. Master charts for a multitude of variations and locales are included for easy strategy reference.

If you're a roulette player, you'll learn the playing rules and differences for both the European and the American game and how to make every bet possible in the game including some little known wagers. I also present three betting systems and an actual strategy for beating the wheel with the odds.

Learn the glamorous and popular European game of baccarat whose odds are so good for the player that casinos sometimes lose money at it during a month of play. There are various styles of play and I'll show how the variations differ and discuss the brand new winning strategies available at baccarat.

Poker players get an in-depth look at the most popular poker games - jacks or better and anything opens, hold 'em, seven card stud - high, low (Razz) and high-low stud and lowball draw poker. You learn how to play and win at each style how to recognize and play good cards, how to read opponent's playing styles, how to bluff out your opponents, and much, much more.

Horseracing is a tremendous gaming passion for many, and this section shows you all about the sport, from the bets available, the types of races run, the odds and the important winning approaches, to 11 winning tips that will help you win at the track.

How would you like to be $50,000 richer? A lucky catch in keno can do the trick, and in this section, I'm going to show you ways to play and bet the game to give you that shot, the odds involved and the payoffs on winning tickets. You'll learn how to play straight, combination, split, way, special, and for you royalty-minded players, how to play the king.

Bingo games are paying bigger and bigger jackpots and have caught on around the world. In this section I'll show you how the game is played, the different winning tickets possible, the division of payoffs, and the giant jackpots in today's games.

Video poker has grown to be a very popular game, and for good reason - astute playing can make one a winner! You'll learn the winning hands and payoffs at all the main variations, how to use the various options, the best strategies to pursue and the best way to play for the giant jackpot.

As a special bonus, I'm introducing Cho Dai Di, a very exciting Chinese card game that's sure to please and thrill those of you who love skill, luck and backstabbing all in one easy-to-play package! I'll show you how to play and score, plus present some winning strategies to get you on the way. I hope you do me the honor and give this section a read - it's a great game and you'll soon be hooked.

Sports betting is like bread and butter for many gamblers; hundreds of millions are wagered on sports events every year. In this section I'll show you how the lines are made, why they exist and how to use inside information to beat the line and make money. Football, baseball, basketball and boxing are all covered - the different types of bets you can make at each, the odds and the payoffs and the best strategies to make you a winner.

I'll also look at the slots, show the different machines available, the straights and progressives, the various odds and how to improve on them, the basics of play and some winning hints.

There is a small section on the wheel of fortune, also called the Big Six. I'll show you the bets available and the odds you face.

In this new edition, I've also included sections on Let it Ride® and Caribbean Stud Poker, two poker-like casino games that have become increasingly popular staples in the casinos in the 1990's.

Both combine table play with bonus payoffs and large "jackpot" possibilities.

Most important of all, I show you how to be a winner. There's more to winning than knowing the odds and the game. You must know how to handle yourself and your bankroll. Money management is the key to all successful gamblers and thus, I've devoted a full chapter specifically addressing the psychological and emotional aspects of beating the casino.

I'll tell you how to keep the game under control, how to minimize losses when you're losing, and when winning, how to turn moderate winning sessions into big winning sessions with a minimum of risk. Finally, I'll show you how to walk away a winner.

There is a lot of information in this book, everything aimed in a positive direction - to make you a more informed and well-rounded gambler. And of course, to make you a winner!

I hope you enjoy my book -   ***Avery Cardoza***

BLACKJACK

INTRODUCTION

Blackjack can be beaten! Once you've finished reading this section and learned the skills presented, you'll find that there will be one major difference between you and 95% of the other players - you'll be a winner at blackjack!

We'll teach you to win without the blind memorization and boring tedium usually associated with learning blackjack. Our computer tested basic strategies are carefully explained so that every play you make is easily learned. In addition, all the winning strategies are presented in easy to read charts.

You'll learn how to beat the single deck game without counting cards. Also shown will be the best way to adjust your play for multiple deck games and variations whether you're a player in the major American gambling centers, Las Vegas, Northern Nevada, Laughlin or Atlantic City, or you're heading for play on cruise ships, in Europe, the Bahamas, the Caribbean or anywhere casinos are found.

You'll receive a wealth of information from this section. We cover the fundamentals of casino blackjack - the rules of the game, the player's options, the variations offered in casinos around the world, how to bet, casino vocabulary, how to play and everything else you'll need to know about playing winning casino blackjack.

So read this section carefully, and you'll be among those players that the casinos fear, and for good reason - you will be a consistent winner at blackjack!

BEGINNERS GUIDE TO CASINO BLACKJACK

Object of the Game

The player's object in casino blackjack is to beat the dealer. This can be achieved in two ways:

1 - When the player has a higher total than the dealer without exceeding 21.

2 - When the dealer's total exceeds 21 (assuming the player has not exceeded 21 first).

In casino blackjack, if the player and the dealer both hold the same total of 21 or less, the hand is a **push**, nobody wins.

Busting or Breaking - Automatic Losers

If the drawing of additional cards to the initial two cards dealt causes the point total to exceed 21, then that hand is said to be **busted**, an automatic loss. Busted hands should be turned up immediately. Once the player has busted, his hand is lost, even if the dealer busts as well afterwards. If the dealer busts, all remaining players automatically win their bets.

Blackjack - Automatic Winner

If the original two card hand contains an Ace with any 10 or face card (J,Q,K), the hand is called a **blackjack**, or **natural**, and is an automatic winner for the player whose bet is paid of at 3 to 2. If the dealer gets a blackjack, all players lose their bets. (The dealer wins only the player's bet, not the 3 to 2 payoff the player receives for a blackjack.) If both the dealer and the player are dealt a blackjack, the hand is a push. Blackjacks should be turned up immediately.

Payoffs

All bets are paid off at even money ($5 bet wins $5), except in cases where the player receives a blackjack which is a 3 to 2 payoff ($5 bet wins $7.50) or when the player exercises an option that allows him to double his bet. In these instances (doubling and splitting), the payoff is equal to the new doubled bet. If a bet is doubled from $5 to $10, a win would pay off $10.

Card Values

Each card is counted at face value. 2=2 points, 3=3 points, 10=10 points. The face cards, Jack, Queen and King, are counted as 10 points. The Ace can be counted as 1 point or 11 points at the player's discretion. When the Ace is counted as 11 points, that hand is called **soft**, as in the hand Ace, 7 = *soft 18*. All other totals, including hands where the Ace counts as 1 point, are called **hard**, as in the hand 10, 6, A = *hard 17*.

The dealer must count his Ace as 11 if that gives him a hand totaling 17 to 21, otherwise he must count the Ace as 1 point. In some casinos the rules dictate that the dealer must draw on soft 17. In these casinos the dealer's Ace will count as 1 point when combined with cards totalling 6 points, and the dealer will have to draw until he forms a hand of at least hard 17.

Dealer's Rules

The dealer must play by prescribed guidelines. He must draw to any hand 16 or below and stand on any total 17-21. As mentioned above, some casinos require the dealer to draw on soft 17. The dealer has no options and cannot deviate from the above-stated rules.

Player's Options

Unlike the dealer, the player can vary his strategy. After receiving his first two cards the player has the following options:

1 · Drawing (Hitting). If the player is not satisfied with his two card total he can draw additional cards. To draw a card, the player scrapes the felt surface with his cards, scraping toward his body. In a game where both the player's cards are dealt face up, he scratches the felt with his index finger or points toward the cards if he desires a hit. A player is not supposed to handle the cards when they're face up.

2 · Standing. When a player is satisfied with his original two card total, and does not wish to draw additional cards, he signals this by sliding his cards face down under his bet. When the cards are dealt face up, the player indicates his decision to stand pat by waving is hand palm down over his cards

3· Doubling Down. This option allows the player to double his original bet, in which case he must draw one additional card to his hand and cannot draw any additional cards thereafter. To double down, the player turns his cards face up, and places them in front of his bet. Then he takes an amount equal to his original bet and places those chips next to that bet, so that there are now two equivalent bets side by side. The dealer will then deal one card face down, usually slipping that card under the player's bet. The bettor may look at that card if he desires.

4 · Splitting Pairs. If dealt a pair of identical value cards, such as 3-3, 7-7, 8-8 (any combination of 10, J, Q, K is considered a pair), the player can split these cards so that two separate hands are formed. To split a pair, the player turns the pair face up, separates them, putting each card in its own place in front of his bet. He then places a bet equal to the original wager behind the second hand. Each hand is played separately, using finger and hand signals to indicate hitting and standing.

If the first card dealt to either split hand has a value identical to the original split cards, that card may be split again (resplit) into a third hand, with the exception of Aces. When the player splits Aces, he can receive only one card on each Ace and may not draw again, no matter what card is drawn.

5 · Doubling Down After Splitting. The player can double down on one or both of the hands resulting from a split according to the normal doubling rules of the casino. This option is offered in all Atlantic City casinos and in certain Nevada casinos. Also found in Australia, Great Britain, various European and Asian casinos and southern Africa.

For example, if a pair of 8s are split, and a 3 is drawn to the first 8 for an 11, the player may elect to double down on that 11. He can place an amount equal to the original bet next to the 11, and will receive only one additional card. If a 2 is drawn to the second 8, the player may double down on that hand as well.

6 · Surrender (Late Surrender). The player can give up his original two card hand and lose one half on his bet after it has been determined that the dealer does not have a blackjack. To surrender, the bettor turns both his cards face up, puts them above his bet, and says "surrender." The dealer will collect the cards and take one half of the bet. This option is offered in only a few Nevada casinos.

7 · Early Surrender. A player option to give up his hand and lose half his bet before the dealer checks for a blackjack. This option originally introduced in Atlantic City is no longer offered because of changes in Atlantic City rules.

8 · Insurance. If the dealer shows an Ace as his upcard, he will ask the players if they want insurance. If any player exercises this option, he is in effect betting that the dealer has a 10-value card as his hole card, a blackjack. To take insurance, he places up to one-half the amount of his bet in the area marked insurance. If the dealer does indeed have a blackjack, he gets paid 2 to 1 on the insurance bet, while losing the original bet. In effect, the transaction is a "standoff", and no money is lost. If the dealer does not have a blackjack, the insurance bet is lost and play continues.

If the player holds a blackjack and takes insurance on the dealer's Ace, the payoff will be even-money whether the dealer has a blackjack or not. Suppose the player has a $10 bet and takes insurance for $5 on his blackjack. If the dealer has a blackjack, the player wins 2 to 1 on his $5 insurance bet and ties with his own blackjack. If the dealer doesn't have a black-jack, the player loses the $5 insurance bet but gets paid 3 to 2 on his blackjack. Either way the bettor wins $10.

Insurance Strategy

Insurance is a bad bet for the following reason:

Making an insurance wager is betting that the dealer has a 10 under his Ace. Since the insurance payoff is 2 to 1, the wager will only be a profitable option for the player when the ratio of 10s to other cards is either equal to or less than 2 to 1.

A full deck has 36 non-tens and 16 tens, a ratio greater than 2 to 1. If the first deal off the top of the deck gives us a hand of 9,7, and the dealer shows an Ace, then we know three cards, all non-tens. Now the ratio is 33 to 16, still greater than 2 to 1, still a poor bet. If you have two 10s for a 20, then the ratio is 35 to 14, an even worse bet.

In a multiple deck game, taking insurance is even a worse bet than in a single deck one.

Insuring a Blackjack

Taking insurance when you have a blackjack is also a bad bet, despite the well-intentioned advice of dealers and other players to always "insure" a blackjack. When you have a black-jack, you know three cards, your 10 and Ace, and the dealer's Ace. The already poor starting ratio of 36 non-tens to 16 tens gets worse, becoming 34 to 15 in a single deck game. Taking insurance when you have a blackjack gives the house an 8% advantage, a poor proposition for the player.

The Play of the Game

The dealer begins by shuffling the cards and offering the cut to one of the players. If refused, it is offered to another player. The dealer then completes the cut, and removes the top card, called the **burn card.** In single and double deck games, the burn card is either put under the deck face up, where all subsequent cards will be placed, or is put face down into a plastic case (procedures vary from casino to casino) to be fol-lowed similarly by future discards.

In games dealt out of a shoe, the burn card will be placed most of the way into the shoe and discards will be put in the plastic case.

Players must make their bets before the cards are dealt.

The dealer deals clockwise from his left to his right, one card at a time, until each player and the dealer have received two cards. The players cards are usually dealt face down in a single or double deck game, though it makes no difference if they are dealt face up as they usually are in a game dealt out of a shoe, for the dealer is bound by strict rules from which he cannot deviate. The dealer deals only one of his two cards face up. This card is called an **upcard**. The face down card is known as the **hole card** or the **downcard**.

If the dealer's upcard is an Ace, he will ask the players if they want insurance. Players that decide to take that option place a bet of up to one-half their wager in front of their bet in the area marked insurance.

If the dealer has a blackjack, all players that did not take insurance lose their original bets. Players that took insurance break even on the play. If the dealer hasn't a blackjack, he collects the lost insurance bets and play continues.

The procedures vary when the dealer shows a 10-value card. In Nevada casinos the dealer must check his hole card for an Ace. If he has a blackjack, it is an automatic winner for the house. All player bets are lost. (Players can't insure against a 10-value card.) If the dealer doesn't have a blackjack, he will face the first player and await that player's decision. Players that hold a blackjack push on the play.

In Atlantic City, the Bahamas and most European games, the dealer will only check the hole card after all the players have acted.

Play begins with the bettor on the dealer's left, in the position known as **first base**.

The player has the option to stand, hit, double down, split (if he has two cards of equal value) and surrender (if allowed). A player can draw cards until he is satisfied with his total or busts, or he can exercise one of the other options discussed previously.

Play then moves to the next player. If any player busts (goes over 21) or receives a blackjack, he must turn over his cards immediately. If a bust, the dealer will collect the lost bet. If a blackjack, the dealer will pay the player 3 to 2 on his bet.

After the last player has acted upon his cards, the dealer will turn his hole card over so that all players can view both of his cards. He must play his hand according to the strict guidelines regulating his play; drawing to 17, then standing. (In some casinos the dealer must draw to a soft 17.) If the dealer busts, all players still in the game for that round of play win automatically.

After playing his hand, the dealer will turn over each player's cards in turn, paying the winners, and collecting from the losers. Once the bettor has played his hand, he shouldn't touch his cards again. He should let the dealer expose his hand which he will do once the dealer has played out his own hand.

When the round has been completed, all players must place a new bet before the next deal.

Casino Personnel

The casino employee responsible for the running of the blackjack game is called the dealer. The dealer's duties are to deal the cards to the players, and play out his own hand according to the rules of the game. He converts money into chips for players entering the game or buying in for more chips during the course of the game, makes the correct payoffs for winning hands, and collects bets from the losers.

The dealer's supervisor - technically called the **floorman**, but more commonly referred to as the **pit boss** - is responsible for the supervision of between 4-6 tables. His job is to make sure the games run smoothly and to settle any disputes that may arise with a player. More importantly, his job is to oversee the exchange of money and to correct any errors that may occur.

Entering a Game

To enter a blackjack game, sit down at any unoccupied seat at the blackjack table, and place the money you wish to gamble with near the betting box in front of you and inform the dealer that you would like to get some chips for your cash. Chips may be purchased in various denominations. Let the dealer know which chips or combination of chips you'd like.

The dealer will take your money and call out the amount he is changing so that the pit boss is aware that a transaction is taking place and can supervise that exchange.

Converting Traveller's Checks and Money Order to Cash

The dealers will accept only cash or chips, so if you bring traveller's checks, money orders or the like, you must go to the area of the casino marked **Casino Cashier** to get these converted to cash. Be sure to bring proper identification to insure a smooth transaction.

Casino Chips

Standard denominations of casino chips are $1, $5, $25, $100, and for the high rollers, $500 and even $1,000 chips can sometimes be obtained. Though some casinos use their own color code, the usual color scheme of chips are: $1=silver, $5=red, $25=green and $100=black.

Betting

Casinos prefer that the players use chips for betting purposes, for the handling of money at the tables is cumbersome and slows the game. However, cash can be used to bet with, though all payoffs will be in chips. To bet, place your chips (or cash) in the betting box directly in front of you. All bets must be placed before the cards are dealt.

House Limits

Placards located at either corner of the table indicate the minimum and maximum bets allowed at a particular table.

Within the same casino you will find minimums raging from $1, $2 and $5 to other tables that require the players to bet at least $25 or $100 per hand. At the $1, $2 and $5 tables, the house maximum generally will not exceed $500 to $1,000 while the $25 and $100 tables may allow the players to bet as high as $3,000 a hand.

There are casinos that will book almost any bet and give high rollers their own private table for large stakes games. If you catch the right night, you might find a *whale*, a high roller, making bets in $10,000 units!

Converting Chips into Cash

Dealers do not convert chips into cash. When you are ready to cash in your chips, take them to the cashier's cage where they'll be changed into cash.

Free Drinks and Cigarettes

Casinos offer their customers unlimited free drinking while playing at the table. In addition to alcoholic beverages, a player can order milk, soft drinks, juices or any other beverages. Cigarettes and cigars are also complimentary. Both drinks and smokes can be ordered through the cocktail waitress.

The Decks of Cards

Nevada casinos use one, two, four, six and sometimes as many as eight decks of cards in their blackjack games. Often, within the same casino, single and multiple deck games will be offered. When one or two decks are used, the dealer holds the cards in his hand. When more than two decks are used, the cards are dealt from a rectangular plastic or wooden device known as a **shoe**. The shoe is designed to hold multiple decks of cards, and allows the cards to be easily removed one at a time by the dealer.

Outside of Nevada, multiple deck blackjack is the norm, and it is rare to see single deck play.

Each deck used in blackjack is a standard pack of 52 cards,

consisting of 4 cards of each value, Ace through King. Suits have no relevance in blackjack. Only the numerical value of the cards count.

Standees

In some areas around the world, most notably Europe and Asia, **standees**, players not occupying a seat and betting spot at the table, are allowed to place bets in the boxes of players already seated. Standees must accept the seated player's decision and are not allowed to advise or criticize the play made.

No Hole Card Rule

The predominant style of play in casinos outside the United States is for the dealer to take his second card after all the players have acted upon their hands. In some cases, the dealer may deal himself the card as in the U.S. casinos, but will not check a 10 or Ace for blackjack until after the bettors have finished playing their hands. The disadvantage to the player is that on hands doubled or split, the additional moneys bet will be lost if indeed the dealer has a blackjack. As you'll see, we adjust our strategies accordingly when playing in no hole card games so as to minimize the effect of this rule.

(In Atlantic City, the game is played in this style, except that when the dealer has a blackjack, the player's additional bets on doubles and splits are returned. Only the original bet will be lost. Thus, it is not a disadvantage to Atlantic City players and playing strategies need not be adjusted for this factor.)

RULES AND VARIATIONS OF THE CASINO CENTERS

Blackjack can be found all over the world, and though basically the same wherever played, the rules and variations vary from country to country, from casino to casino within a country, and sometimes, they even differ within a casino itself.

Nevada Rules

The Las Vegas Strip rules are advantageous to the player and gives one a slight edge on the single deck game if our strategies are followed. The rule exceptions noted in Downtown Las Vegas and in Northern Nevada games are slightly disadvantageous to the player, but these can easily be overcome by using the winning techniques presented later.

Las Vegas Strip Rules

- Dealer must draw on all totals of 16 or less, and stand on all totals of 17-21.
- Player may take insurance on a dealer's Ace.
- Insurance payoffs are 2 to 1.
- Player receives a 3 to 2 payoff on his blackjack.
- Player may double down on any initial two card combination.
- Identical pairs may be split, resplit, and drawn to as desired with the exception of split Aces, on which the player is allowed only one hit on each Ace.

Downtown Las Vegas

Rules are the same as the Las Vegas Strip rules with one exception:
- Dealer must draw to soft 17.

Northern Nevada

Same as Strip rules with two exceptions:
- Dealer must draw to soft 17.
- Doubling is restricted to two card totals of 10 and 11 only.

Atlantic City Rules

The New Jersey Casino Control Commission regulates the rules and variations allowed in Atlantic City casinos, and all Atlantic City clubs must abide by the following guidelines:
- Dealer must draw to all totals 16 or less, and stand on all totals of 17-21.

- Player may take insurance on a dealer's Ace. Insurance payoffs are 2 to 1.
- Player receives a 3 to 2 payoff on his blackjack.
- Player may double on any initial two card combination.
- Identical pairs may be split but not resplit.
- Doubling after splitting allowed.
- Multiple deck games are standard

European Rules

Blackjack is offered in numerous countries around Europe with the rules and variations changing slightly from place to place. However, the following conditions apply in a good many of these places.

- Dealer must draw to all totals 16 or less, and stand on all totals of 17-21.
- Player may take insurance on a dealer's Ace.
- Insurance payoffs are 2 to 1.
- Player receives a 3 to 2 payoff on his blackjack.
- Doubling Down on 9-11 Only
- Standees Permitted
- No Hole Card Rule
- 4-6 Decks Standard
- If player draws a 2 on a A8 double down hand, the total counts as 11, not 21

Rules Around the World

The general variations we present under the European Rules above is probably the most prevalent style of play in casinos around the world. Sometimes you may find double after split permitted as in Great Britain, southern Africa, many European casinos and other places; in Asian and Caribbean casinos, surrender is often allowed - just ask the particular rules before you enter a game.

In our strategy section, we'll show you the best way to play no matter the variation used.

GENERAL STRATEGIC CONCEPTS

The Dealer's Only Advantage

Before we examine the correct strategies of play, it would be instructive to look at a losing strategy. In this strategy, the player will mimic the dealer; he'll draw on all totals 16 or less, and stand on all totals 17-21.

The player doing this figures that, since this strategy wins for the dealer, it must be effective for the player as well. After all, the dealer and the player will get the same number of good hands and the same number of poor hands. And if we draw just as the dealer draws, we must come out even, mustn't we?

No. As a matter of fact, the player will be playing at about a 5 1/2% disadvantage to the house. The "Mimic the Dealer" strategy overlooks one important thing. The player must act upon his hand first.

The dealer's only advantage lies in the fact that once the player has busted, the player's bet is automatically lost, regardless of the outcome of the dealer's hand. While both the dealer and the player will bust equally following these drawing-to-17 guidelines (about 28% of the time), the double bust, where both the dealer and the player bust on the same round, will occur approximately 8% of the time (28% of 28% of the time or 28 x 28). And since the player acted first, this 8% of the time (the double bust) will be the house advantage.

When we adjust for the 3 to 2 bonus the player receives on blackjacks, a bonus the house does not enjoy, we find the house enjoying a 5 1/2% edge over the player that follows the "Mimic the Dealer" strategy.

Overcoming the Disadvantage of Acting First

In the "Mimic the Dealer" strategy we played our hands as if our goal was to get as close to 21 as reasonably possible by using 17 as a cut-off point for drawing. But this losing strategy misstates the goal of the player. In blackjack, the object is to beat the dealer. Our chances of winning are not determined by how close our total approaches 21 as the other strategy assumed, but on how good our total is compared to the dealer's.

We can overcome the disadvantage of having to act first by making judicious use of the options available to us as a player. Not only should we double down, split pairs, hit, stand and surrender (if allowed), but we can use our knowledge of the dealer's exposed upcard to fully capitalize on these options. Needless to say, adjusting our strategy according to this knowledge of the dealer's upcard will vastly improve on the "Get as Close to 21 - Mimic the Dealer" strategy, and completely eliminate the house edge.

To Beat the Dealer
There are two factors that affect our chances of winning; the strength of our total and the strength of the dealer's total. To beat the dealer, we must know how strong our total is compared to the dealer's total so that we know if drawing additional cards or exercising a player option is a viable consideration. In addition, we must be aware of the factors that influence the final outcome of these totals so that we can determine the optimal way to play our hand.

In determining the best way to play our hand, we must know how good our total is as it stands. Do we have the expectancy of winning by standing? If so, can we increase this expectancy by drawing additional cards or by exercising a doubling or splitting option when applicable? If we do not have the expectancy of winning by standing, will the drawing of additional cards or the employment of the doubling or splitting option increase our chance of winning?

Since our object is to beat the dealer, to answer the question "how strong is our total?" We need to ask ourselves if the dealer's expectancy, judged by the information we get from his exposed card, is greater than our total.

Being able to see the dealer's upcard gives us a great deal of information about the strength of the hands that the dealer is likely to make, and we can use that information to our advantage.

Understanding the Dealer's Upcard

Being able to see the dealer's upcard is of great value to the player, for there are two factors - the rules governing the dealer's play of his hand, and the number of tens in a deck of cards (ten factor) - that tell us a great deal about the potential strength of the dealer's hands, and the frequency with which those hands will bust.

Ten Factor

The most striking feature of blackjack is the dominant role that the 10 value cards (10, J, Q, K) play. Each ten and face card is counted as 10 points each in blackjack. Thus, the player is four times more likely to draw a 10 than any other individual card since all the other cards, Aces through nines, consist of only four cards each as opposed to sixteen 10s. Collectively, the 10s constitute just under 1/3 of the deck (16 out of 52 cards).

Because the 10s are such a dominant factor in a deck of cards, it's correct to think of the dealer's hand *gravitating* toward a total 10 points greater than his exposed upcard. When I speak of a hand as gravitating toward a total, I am referring to the tendency of that hand to increase in value by 10 points as a result of the 10 factor. Thus, starting out with an upcard of 9, the dealer will make a hand of 19 thirty-six percent of the time and 19 or better 52% of the time.

The Dealer's Rules and the Ten Factor

Our strategy is based on the fact that the dealer must play by prescribed guidelines from which he cannot deviate. He must draw to all totals 16 or below, and stand on all totals 17-21 (except in casinos that require the dealer to draw to soft 17). All hard totals that exceed hard 21 are automatic dealer losses.

By combining our knowledge of the 10 factor with the above mentioned dealer rules gives us a natural separation of the dealer's upcard into two distinct groupings: 2s through 6s, the dealer "stiff" cards, and 7s through As (Aces), the dealer "pat" cards.

2s through 6s - Dealer Stiff Cards

Whenever the dealer shows a 2, 3, 4, 5 or 6 as an upcard, we know that he must draw at least one additional card regardless of the value of his hole card (unless the dealer has an Ace under his Six and is playing Las Vegas Strip, Atlantic City or European style rules which require the dealer to stand on soft 17). The high concentration of 10s in the deck make it likely that the dealer will expose a 10 as his hole card, giving him a stiff total of 12-16.

Since the dealer must draw to all hard totals 16 or below, the drawing of a 10 (and in some instances, smaller totalled cards) will bust any of these stiff totals. For example, if the dealer shows a 6 and reveals a 10 in the hole, any card higher than a 5 will bust his hand.

Thus, the high concentration of 10 value cards in the deck tells us that the dealer has a good chance of busting when his upcard is a 2, 3, 4, 5 or 6.

7s through As - Dealer Pat Cards

Whenever the dealer shows a 7, 8, 9, 10 or A as an upcard, we know, because of the large number of 10s, that he has a high likelihood of making pat totals 17-21, and conversely, a smaller chance of busting than when he shows a stiff card. This high concentration of 10s makes it likely that the dealer will expose a 10 for an automatic pat hand (17-21). Even when he hasn't a 10 in the hole, combinations such as 89; A7; 99 and so forth, give him an automatic pat hand as well.

UNDERSTANDING THE DEALER'S UPCARD
Dealer Stiff Cards - Advantageous for Player

2	3	4		5	6
Less Advantageous				**More Advantageous**	

Dealer's Upcard of 2 and 3

Though it is favorable for the player when the dealer shows a 2 or 3 as an upcard, we will need to be cautious against these stiff cards, for the dealer will bust less often with these than when he shows the 4, 5 and 6.

Dealer's Upcard of 4, 5 and 6

The dealer is showing the upcards you always want him to hold. The dealer will bust about 42% of the time with these upcards (5% more than the 2,3 and about 18% more than with the pat cards). We will take advantage of these weak dealer upcards by aggressive splitting and doubling.

UNDERSTANDING THE DEALER'S UPCARD
Dealer Pat Cards - Disadvantageous for Player
7   8   9   10   Ace
Moderately Disadvantageous   Very Disadvantageous

Dealer's Upcard of 7 and 8

While the dealer will not bust often with these upcards, they also indicate to us that the dealer's hands gravitate toward the weaker totals of 17 and 18. It is interesting to note that of all the dealer upcards including the stiff cards, the 7 will form the weakest totals.

Dealer's Upcard of 9, 10 and Ace

The 9 and 10 gravitate toward totals of 19 and 20 respectively - tough hands to beat. The Ace is also a powerful dealer upcard, for in addition to forming strong hands, the dealer will bust less with an Ace than with any other upcard.

Against these powerful upcards, we will be very cautious in our doubling and splitting strategies.

Understanding the Player's Hand - Hard Totals

The player's totals can be divided into three distinct groupings: 11 or less, 17-21 and 12-16. We will look at each in turn to see how they affect our strategy.

Player's Hand of 11 or Less - (Hard Totals)

We should always draw to any hard total 11 or less (unless a doubling or splitting option is more profitable). By hitting this hand we have no risk of busting, no matter what we draw, and the drawing of a card can strengthen our total. There is no question about the correct decision; drawing is a big gain.

Player's Hand of 17-21 - (Hard Totals)

We should always stand on these hard totals (17-21), for the risk of busting is too high to make drawing worthwhile. It should be obvious that the chances of improving these high totals are minimal, and the risks of busting very probable. In addition, totals of 19, 20, 21 and, to a lesser extent, 18, are already powerful hands. While hard 17 is a poor player total, the risk of busting by drawing is way too costly to make drawing a viable option. Stand on hard totals of 17-21 against any dealer's upcard.

Player's Hand of 12-16 - (Hard Totals)

With these hands the bulk of our decision making will be exercised, for on these hard totals there are no automatic decisions as on the other player totals. Our hand is not an obvious draw (such as the 11 or less grouping) for the risk of drawing a 10 or other high card and busting is substantial. Our hand is not an obvious stand decision either (such as the 17-21 grouping), for the only times we will win with these weak totals of 12-16 are the times that the dealer busts.

For the Cardoza Non-Counter winning strategies to be effective, you must first know the correct way to play your hands. (The same applies to any player who moves on to any professional counting or non-counting strategy.) Therefore, make sure you understand these basic strategies before going on to the winning techniques of play.

THE OPTIMAL BASIC STRATEGIES

Hitting and Standing - Hard Totals

These strategies are applicable for single and multiple deck games in all casino centers.

General Principles

• When the dealer shows a 7, 8, 9, 10 or A, hit all hard totals of 16 or below (unless doubling or splitting is more profitable - in any case, you will always draw a card).

• When the dealer shows a 2, 3, 4, 5 or 6, stand on all hard totals of 12 or more. Do not bust against a dealer stiff card. Exception - Hit 12 vs. 2, 3.

		HITTING AND STANDING - HARD TOTALS								
		All Casino Centers								
	2	**3**	**4**	**5**	**6**	**7**	**8**	**9**	**10**	**A**
11/less	H	H	H	H	H	H	H	H	H	H
12	H	H	S	S	S	H	H	H	H	H
13	S	S	S	S	S	H	H	H	H	H
14	S	S	S	S	S	H	H	H	H	H
15	S	S	S	S	S	H	H	H	H	H
16	S	S	S	S	S	H	H	H	H	H
17-21	S	S	S	S	S	S	S	S	S	S

H = Hit   S = Stand

(In all our charts, the dealer's upcard is indicated by the horizontal numbers on the top row, and the player's hand is indicted by the vertical numbers in the left column. The letters in the matrix indicate the correct strategy play.)

Conceptual Hitting and Standing Strategy

In the "Understanding the Player's Hand" section we discussed the strategy for hard totals of 11 or less, and for hard totals 17-21.

They will be reiterated briefly here.

11 or less - Draw against all dealer upcards.

17-21 - Stand against all dealer upcards.

Hard Totals 12-16

It is when we hold hard totals 12-16 (stiffs) that the player's big disadvantage of having to go first (the only built-in house advantage) is a costly proposition. If we draw to hard totals and bust, we are automatic losers. But, on the other hand, if we stand, we will win with these weak totals only when the dealer busts.

It is important to realize that the decision to hit or stand with hard totals 12-16 is a strategy of minimizing losses, for no matter what we do, we have a potentially losing hand against any dealer upcard. Do not expect to win when you hold a stiff. However, in order to maximize the gain from our overall strategy, we must minimize the losses in disadvantageous situations (as above), and maximize our gains in advantageous one.

a. Player Totals of 12-16 vs. Dealer Pat Cards 7, 8, 9, 10, A

When the dealer's upcard is a 7 through an Ace, you should expect the dealer to make his hand, for he will bust only about one time in four, a mere 25% of the time. If we stand on our hard totals 12-16, we will win only the times that the dealer busts.

Thus, for every 100 hands that we stand with our stiff totals 12-16 against dealer pat cards, our expectation is to lose 75 of those hands and to win only 25, a net loss of 50 hands. Not an exciting prognosis.

On the other hand, drawing to our stiff totals 12-16 against the dealer pat cards gives us a big gain over standing. By drawing, we will gain an average of 15%. The dealer makes too many hands showing a 7, 8, 9, 10 or Ace, to allow us to stand with our stiffs.

You will bust often when drawing to your stiffs, but do not let that dissuade you from hitting your stiffs against pat cards. The strategy on these plays is to minimize losses. We cannot afford to stand and sacrifice our hand to the 3 out of 4 hands that the dealer will make.

When the dealer shows a 7, 8, 9, 10, or Ace, hit all hard totals 16 or below.

b. Player Totals of 12-16 vs. Dealer Pat Cards 2, 3, 4, 5, 6

The greater busting potential of the dealer stiff cards makes standing with hard player totals of 12-16 a big gain over drawing. While we will win only 40% of these hands (the times that the dealer busts), standing is a far superior strategy to drawing, for we will bust too often drawing to our own stiffs against upcards that will bust fairly often themselves. The times that we would make pat totals by drawing wouldn't guarantee us winners either, for the dealer will often make equal or better totals.

On these plays, our disadvantage of having to go first makes drawing too costly, for once we bust, we automatically lose. Though the dealer will make more hands than bust, our strategy here is to minimize losses so that when we get our good hands, we'll come out an overall winner.

Exception - Hit Player 12 vs. 2, 3

Hitting 12 vs. 2, 3 is the only basic strategy exception to drawing with a stiff total against a dealer's stiff upcard. The double bust factor is not as costly on these plays, for only the 10s will bust our 12. Similarly, the dealer will bust less often showing a 2 or a 3 than with the other stiff cards, 4, 5 and 6.

This is in contrast to the play 13 vs. 2 where the correct strategy is to stand. The additional player busting factor of the 9 makes the player slightly better off by standing, even though the dealer will bust less with a 2 as an upcard. This clearly illustrates the greater importance of the player's busting factor (compared to the dealer's busting factor) when deciding whether to stand or draw with a stiff total 12-16 vs. a dealer stiff upcard.

The combination of the player being less likely to bust (more likely to make his hand) and the dealer being more likely to make his hand (less likely to bust) makes drawing 12 vs 2, 3 the correct strategy play.

Hitting and Standing - Soft Totals

The strategy for hitting and standing with soft totals in Northern Nevada and Europe is identical to the Atlantic City and Las Vegas strategies for both single and multiple deck, except that the Atlantic City and Las Vegas basic strategy players can take advantage of the more liberal doubling rules and will double down on hands that Northern Nevada and European Style rules players cannot.

HITTING AND STANDING - SOFT TOTALS
Northern Nevada & Europe · Single and Multiple Deck

	2	3	4	5	6	7	8	9	10	A
A2-A6	H	H	H	H	H	H	H	H	H	H
A7	S	S	S	S	S	S	S	H	H	H
A8-A9	S	S	S	S	S	S	S	S	S	S

H = Hit   S = Stand

HITTING AND STANDING - SOFT TOTALS
Atlantic City & Las Vegas · Single and Multiple Deck

	2	3	4	5	6	7	8	9	10	A
A2-A5	H	H	D*	D	D	H	H	H	H	H
A6	D**	D	D	D	D	H	H	H	H	H
A7	S	D	D	D	D	S	S	H	H	H
A8	S	S	S	S	S	S	S	S	S	S
A9	S	S	S	S	S	S	S	S	S	S

H = Hit   S = Stand   D = Double

*Do not double A2 or A3 vs. 4 in a multiple deck game.

**Do not double A6 vs. 2 in a multiple deck game.

Conceptual Hitting and Standing - Soft Totals
Player's Hand of A2, A3, A4, A5

Unless the player is able to double down, he should always draw a card to these hands. Standing is a poor option, for these totals will win only when the dealer busts. The player has nothing to lose by drawing (no draw can bust these totals), and may improve his total. Players that stand on these hands might just as well give the casinos their money. Draw on A2-A5 against all dealer upcards.

Player's Hand of A6, A7, A8, A9

The decision to hit or stand with soft totals 17 or higher necessitates a closer look at the strength of these totals. Unlike hard totals of 17 or more, drawing is a viable option with these soft totals. Since we have the option of counting the Ace as 1 point or 11 points, the drawing of a 10, or for that matter, the drawing of any other card, will not bust our soft totals. While we have no risk of busting, we do have the risk of drawing a weaker total, and therefore must ask the question, "How strong is our total?"

For soft totals, we want to know:
· What are our chances of winning by standing?
· What are the chances of improving our hand by drawing additional cards?

Player's Hand of Soft 17 (A6)

A standing total of 17 is a weak hand against all dealer upcards, including the dealer stiff cards, and in the long run is a losing total. The only time we will win with this total is when the dealer busts. Otherwise, at best we have a push.

Always draw on soft 17 no matter what the dealer shows as an upcard. (In Las Vegas, Atlantic City, and other locations where allowed, the correct strategy may be to double down. See doubling section.) This standing total is so weak that attempting to improve our hand by drawing is always a tremendous gain against any upcard.

When a casino requires the dealer to draw to soft 17, it is a disadvantageous rule to the player. Though the dealer will sometimes bust by drawing to a soft 17, in the long run he will make more powerful totals and have more winners. It affects the player the same way.

Player's Hand of Soft 18

Against dealer stiff totals of 2, 3, 4, 5 and 6, standing with our 18 is a smart strategy move (unless playing Las Vegas or Atlantic City doubling rules where doubling will often be a big player gain). We have a strong total against these weak dealer upcards.

Stand against dealer upcards of 7 and 8, for our 18 is a solid hand. Against the 7, we have a winning total, and against the 8, we figure to have a potential push, as these dealer upcards gravitate toward 17 and 18 respectively. We do not want to risk our strong position by drawing.

Against the powerful dealer upcards of 9, 10, Ace, our standing total of 18 is a potentially losing hand. Normally you would think that hitting a soft 18 is only a fair total. We are not chancing a powerful total but rather attempting to improve a weak situation.

As a matter of fact, for every 100 plays (at $1 a play) that we draw rather than stand on soft 18 vs. 9 and 10, we will gain $9 and $4 respectively. You must realize that 18 vs. 9, 10, Ace is not a winning hand and since our 18 is a soft total, we have a chance to minimize losses by drawing.

Player's Hand of Soft 19 and 20

These hands are strong player totals as they stand.

Doubling Down

Doubling down is a valuable option for it gives the player a chance to double his bet in advantageous situations. The only drawback to the doubling option is that the player must receive one card and gives up the privilege to draw additional cards should that card be a poor draw. To determine if the doubling option will be profitable, we must weigh the benefits of doubling our bet against the drawbacks of receiving only one card.

One of the most important factors to consider when contemplating the doubling option is the 10 factor. We are more likely to draw a 10 on our double than any other card value. Thus, doubling on a total of 11, where the drawing of a 10 gives us an unbeatable 21, is a more powerful double than an initial two card total of 9, where the drawing of 10 gives us a strong total of 19, not as powerful as the 21.

On the other hand, we would not double any hand of hard 12 or more, for the drawing of a 10 would bust our total, and we would have an automatic loser at double the bet.

The 10 factor is also an important strategic consideration, for it affects the dealer's busting potential. We double more aggressively against the weakest of the dealer stiff cards, the 4, 5 and 6, and less aggressively against the other stiff cards, the 2 and 3. The only times we will double against the dealer pat cards are when our doubling totals of 10 and 11 are powerful themselves.

Doubling Down - Single Deck Basic Strategy
A. Northern Nevada - The player is restricted to doubling down on two card totals of 10 and 11 only.

DOUBLING DOWN
Northern Nevada · Single Deck

	2	3	4	5	6	7	8	9	10	A
10	D	D	D	D	D	D	D	D		
11	D	D	D	D	D	D	D	D	D	D

D = Double Down   Blank = Do Not Double Down

B. Las Vegas - The player may double down on any initial two card combination.

DOUBLING DOWN
Las Vegas · Single Deck

	2	3	4	5	6	7	8	9	10	A
62										
44/53				D	D					
9	D	D	D	D	D					
10	D	D	D	D	D	D	D	D		
11	D	D	D	D	D	D	D	D	D	D
A2			D	D	D					
A3			D	D	D					
A4			D	D	D					
A5			D	D	D					
A6	D	D	D	D	D					
A7		D	D	D	D					
A8										
A9										

D = Double Down   Blank = Do Not Double Down

Multiple Deck Basic Strategy

A. Northern Nevada - The player is restricted to doubling down on two card totals of 10 and 11 only.

DOUBLING DOWN
Northern Nevada · Multiple Deck

	2	3	4	5	6	7	8	9	10	A
10	D	D	D	D	D	D	D	D		
11	D	D	D	D	D	D	D	D	D	

D = Double Down   Blank = Do Not Double Down

B. European Style - The player may double down on totals of 9, 10 and 11 only. The no hole card rules accounts for the less frequent doubling against the dealer's 10 than you see with the Atlantic City and Nevada casinos.

DOUBLING DOWN
European Style Rules · Multiple Deck

	2	3	4	5	6	7	8	9	10	A
9		D	D	D	D					
10	D	D	D	D	D	D	D	D		
11	D	D	D	D	D	D	D	D		
A8										

D = Double Down   Blank = Do Not Double Down

C. Atlantic City and Las Vegas - The player can double down on any initial two card combination. These strategies are good for all multiple deck games in Atlantic City and Las Vegas.

DOUBLING DOWN
Atlantic City & Las Vegas · Multiple Deck

	2	3	4	5	6	7	8	9	10	A
8										
9		D	D	D	D					
10	D	D	D	D	D	D	D	D		
11	D	D	D	D	D	D	D	D	D	
A2				D	D					
A3				D	D					
A4			D	D	D					
A5			D	D	D					
A6		D	D	D	D					
A7		D	D	D	D					
A8										
A9										

D = Double Down   Blank = Do Not Double Down

Conceptual Doubling - Hard Totals (11, 10, 9, 8)

These strategies are applicable to single and multiple deck games in all casino centers. Where multiple deck strategies differ from the single deck, an asterisk will denote the strategy change, and that change will be indicated.

Doubling 11*

This is the strongest doubling hand for the player and should be doubled against all the dealer upcards in a single deck game. If we draw a 10 value card on our double, we will have a 21, the strongest hand we can have. At best, the dealer can tie us.

*Do not double 11 vs. Ace in multiple deck games. In no hole card rules games, do not double against the 10 or Ace. Hit instead.

Doubling 10

This is the second strongest doubling hand for the player and should be doubled against the dealer's 2 through 9. Our hard 10 gravitates toward a 20, an overwhelmingly strong hand against these dealer upcards.

Do not double 10 against the dealer's 10 or Ace. Doubling our hard 10 against the dealer's 10 is not a potential winner as before (against the dealer's 2 through 9), for the dealer's hand gravitates toward a 20 as well, and our possible 20 is not powerful enough to compensate for the low busting probabilities of the dealer's Ace. Giving up the option to draw an additional card should the first card be a poor one is too costly on these plays.

Note: In Northern Nevada, only hard 10 and 11 can be doubled down.

Doubling 9

Double 9 against 2 through 6 only*. The high busting potential of the dealer stiff cards (2-6) makes the 9 a profitable double down. We cannot double down against any of the pat cards (7-Ace) for our win potential when we do draw the 10 (for a total of 19) is not strong enough to compensate for the times when we when we draw a poor card and cannot draw again.

*Do not double 9 vs. 2 in a multiple deck game.

Doubling 8

Doubling 8 vs. 5, 6 is a valid play in a single deck game*. Our 8 gravitates toward an 18, only a fair total. However, the very high busting potential of the dealer 5 and 6 make this double a slight gain. Our 8 is not strong enough to make doubling against the other dealer upcards a good play.

* Do not double 8 against any upcard in a multiple deck game.

Conceptual Doubling - Soft Totals

The high concentration of 10s play a different role in soft doubling than in hard doubling, for instead of having a positive effect on our chances of making a good total, the drawing of 10 will not even give us a pat hand on many of these doubles.

Doubling with soft totals is generally a gain against the weak dealer upcards. The 10 factor will figure strongly in the dealer's chances of busting, while the drawing of small and medium cards will often improve our hand to a competitive total.

Doubling A2, A3, A4, A5

Double A2, A3, A4 and A5 against the dealer's 4, 5 and 6*. The very high busting probabilities of the dealer 4, 5 and 6 makes doubling with our A2 to A5 profitable for the player. Again, the drawing of a 10 value card does not help our total, but the high dealer busting factor gives us an edge.

We do not double against the 2 and 3, because the dealer will make just too many hands with these upcards. The same is more strikingly true with the dealer pat cards, 7 through Ace.

* Do not double A2 vs. 4, A3 vs. 4 in a multiple deck game.

Doubling A6

Double A6 vs. dealer 2, 3, 4, 5 and 6*. The A6 is a more powerful double than the A2-A5, for the drawing of a 10 to the A6 will at least give us a pat total and a potential push against a dealer's 17. This "push" factor enables us to gain by doubling against the dealer's 2 and 3 despite the fact that they will make more dealer pat totals than with the weaker upcards 4, 5 and 6.

* Do not double A6 vs. 2 in a multiple deck game.

Doubling A7

Double A7 vs. 3, 4, 5 and 6. Our soft 18 is only a fair total and drawing an additional card won't risk the destruction of a powerful total such as a 19 or 20.

Soft 18 is a strong double against the weaker dealer stiffs 4, 5 and 6, but differs from the soft 17 in that we do not double against the 2. A standing total of 18 vs. a 2 is a stronger winning hand and we do not want to risk the weakening of this hand by doubling and having to draw a card.

Doubling A8, A9

We have two very strong totals here and do not want to risk our excellent chances of winning by attempting to double.

Splitting Pairs

Splitting can do two valuable things. It can turn one poor total into two stronger hands, such as splitting a hard 16 (8-8) into two hands of 8 each, and it effectively doubles our bet.

The decision to split requires a closer look at our hand vs. the dealer's hand, for we must balance the standing total of our hand against the two proposed split hands, and see if the split and resultant doubling of our bet increases our expectation of winning.

Here's our thought process:

How strong is our total as it stands?

Is the hand too powerful a total as it stands to risk breaking up? If not, we can consider the split.

How strong are the two proposed split totals?

Thinking in terms of the 10 factor, we want to see if our split totals gravitate toward strong totals relative to the strength of the dealer's upcard, or if the split totals represent an improvement over the hard standing original hand.

And finally,

Does splitting either increase our chances of winning or reduce our rate of loss?

These factors are our guides in seeing if a split produces a gain for us.

Splitting Pairs - Single Deck Basic Strategy

These strategies are applicable to all Northern Nevada and Las Vegas single deck games.

Note that single deck blackjack is rare or nonexistent outside the Nevada casinos. Multiple deck blackjack is the predominant style of play in casinos around the world.

SPLITTING PAIRS
Northern Nevada & Las Vegas · Single Deck

	2	3	4	5	6	7	8	9	10	A
22		spl	spl	spl	spl	spl				
33			spl	spl	spl	spl				
66	spl	spl	spl	spl	spl					
77	spl	spl	spl	spl	spl	spl				
88	spl	spl	spl	spl	spl	spl	spl	spl	spl	spl
99	spl	spl	spl	spl	spl		spl	spl		
AA	spl	spl	spl	spl	spl	spl	spl	spl	spl	spl

spl = Split   Blank = Do Not Split
Do not split 44, 55, 10s.   Always split 88, AA

Multiple Deck Basic Strategy

A. Las Vegas and Northern Nevada Multiple Deck - The standard game allows pair splitting on any two cards but does not allow doubling after splitting. (If the particular game allows doubling after splitting, use the chart following this one.)

SPLITTING PAIRS
Las Vegas & Northern Nevada · Multiple Deck

	2	3	4	5	6	7	8	9	10	A
22			spl	spl	spl	spl				
33			spl	spl	spl	spl				
66		spl	spl	spl	spl					
77	spl	spl	spl	spl	spl	spl				
88	spl	spl	spl	spl	spl	spl	spl	spl	spl	spl
99	spl	spl	spl	spl	spl		spl	spl		
AA	spl	spl	spl	spl	spl	spl	spl	spl	spl	spl

spl = Split   Blank = Do Not Split
Do not split 44, 55, 10s.   Always Split 88, AA

B. Atlantic City (and selected Nevada casinos where doubling down after splitting is permitted) - Because of the doubling after splitting rule, the player will split pairs more aggressively so that he can take advantage of good doubling situations that may arise as a consequence of the split.

SPLITTING PAIRS
Atlantic City · Multiple Deck

	2	3	4	5	6	7	8	9	10	A
22	spl	spl	spl	spl	spl	spl				
33	spl	spl	spl	spl	spl	spl				
44					spl	spl				
66	spl	spl	spl	spl	spl					
77	spl	spl	spl	spl	spl	spl				
88	spl	spl	spl	spl	spl	spl	spl	spl	spl	spl
99	spl	spl	spl	spl	spl		spl	spl		
AA	spl	spl	spl	spl	spl	spl	spl	spl	spl	spl

spl = Split   Blank = Do Not Split
Do not split 55, 10s.   Always split 88, AA

C. European Style - Players will split less aggressively than the Atlantic City (and certainly the Nevada) casinos due to the no hole card rule. This chart assumes that doubling after splitting is not allowed.

D. European Style - Doubling After Splitting Allowed - Many international casinos allow doubling after splitting, and in those instances the player will double more aggressively than Nevada, but less aggressively than Atlantic City due to the no hole card rule.

SPLITTING PAIRS
European Style Rules · Multiple Deck

	2	3	4	5	6	7	8	9	10	A
22			spl	spl	spl	spl				
33			spl	spl	spl	spl				
66		spl	spl	spl	spl					
77	spl	spl	spl	spl	spl	spl				
88	spl	spl	spl	spl	spl	spl	spl	spl		
99	spl	spl	spl	spl	spl		spl	spl		
AA	spl	spl	spl	spl	spl	spl	spl	spl	spl	

spl = Split   Blank = Do Not Split
Do not split 44, 55, 10s.

SPLITTING PAIRS
European Style Rules · Doubling After Splitting Allowed

	2	3	4	5	6	7	8	9	10	A
22	spl	spl	spl	spl	spl	spl				
33	spl	spl	spl	spl	spl	spl				
44				spl	spl					
66	spl	spl	spl	spl	spl					
77	spl	spl	spl	spl	spl	spl				
88	spl	spl	spl	spl	spl	spl	spl	spl		
99	spl	spl	spl	spl	spl		spl	spl		
AA	spl	spl	spl	spl	spl	spl	spl	spl	spl	

spl = Split   Blank = Do Not Split
Do not split 55, 10s.

Conceptual Splitting

We will examine the decision to split 99 first, for it is a good example of the thinking process involved in splitting. First of all, we should note that this hand totaling 18 is only "fair," not a powerful total like a 19 or 20.

Splitting 9s - Dealer shows a 2, 3, 4, 5, 6

Split 99 against these dealer stiff cards. Our 18 is a winner, but splitting the hand into two halves of 9 each is a big gain. Each starting hand of 9, because of the 10 factor, gravitates toward strong player totals of 19. The high busting potential of the dealer stiff cards gives us an excellent opportunity to maximize our gain in an advantageous situation.

Splitting 9s - Dealer shows a 7

Stand with 99 vs. dealer 7. We figure the dealer for a 17. Our standing total of 18 is a stronger total and a big potential winner. While splitting 9s will also produce a positive expectation of winning, the risking of our fairly secure 18 against the 7 for two strong but chancy totals reduces the gain. We have the dealer beat. Stand.

Splitting 9s - Dealer shows an 8

Splitting 99 against the dealer's 8 is a big gain. Against the dealer's 8, we figure our 18 to be a potential push. However, by splitting the 18 into two separate hands of 9 each, we hope to turn our potential push into two possible winners. (Each 9 gravitates toward a total of 19, one point higher than the dealer's 18.)

Splitting 9s - Dealer shows a 9

Splitting 99 vs. the dealer's 9 is also a big gain. Against the 9, our 18 is a losing total, but splitting the 18 into two totals of 9 each reduces our potential loss. Rather than one losing total of 18, we will have two hands gravitating toward potential pushes.

Splitting 9s - Dealer shows a 10 or Ace

Do not split 99 against the dealer's 10 or Ace. Our split hands of 9 each gravitate toward good totals, but against these more powerful dealer upcards, splitting would be a poor play. We do not want to make one loser into two.

Splitting 22 and 33

Split 22 vs. dealer 3 through 7*
Split 33 vs. dealer 4 through 7*

The high busting probabilities of the dealer 4, 5 and 6 makes the 22 and 33 good splits. We split 22 vs. 3 and not 33 vs. 3, because of the lower player busting factor of our split hands of 2 each. The drawing of a 10 gives us another chance to improve on our 2, for correct basic strategy is to draw 12 vs. 3, while the drawing of a 10 on our 3 forces us to stand.

We do not split 22 or 33 vs. the dealer's 2, because the dealer's 2 does not bust often enough to make splitting a profitable play.

Splitting 22 and 33 vs. 7 seems unusual at first, for this play seems to exceed our normal strategic boundaries of making aggressive plays against the weak dealer stiff cards. Though the 7 is a pat card and will make a lot of pat hands, the 7 will also make the weakest totals, only gravitating toward a total of 17. Our starting totals of 2 and 3 will make hands of 18 or better about one-half the time. Splitting 22 and 33 against the dealer's 7 will not make us money (because of the high busting factor of our hands), but they will produce a moderate gain over drawing to these hands.

Do not split 22 and 33 against the 8, 9, 10 or Ace. We do not want to make one loser into two losers.

*Nevada multiple deck exception - Do not split 22 vs. 3.

*Atlantic City multiple deck exception (and games with doubling after splitting allowed) - Split 22 and 33 vs. 2 through 7.

Splitting 4s

Do not split 44*. The hard total of 8 gravitates toward a total of 18, a far better position than two weak starting totals of 4 each. Against the dealer stiff cards, 2 through 6, we have a big gain by drawing to our 8. While the drawing of 10 will not give us an overwhelmingly strong total, an 18 is far better than drawing the same 10 to a split 4. We do not want to hold two weak hands of 4 each against the dealer pat cards, especially the dealer's 7 and 8, where we have a good starting total of 8.

*Atlantic City exception (and games with doubling after splitting allowed) - Split 44 vs. 5 and 6.

Splitting 55

Never split 55. 55 by itself is an excellent starting total of 10. You do not want to break up this powerful player total into two terrible hands of 5 each. (Our 10 is an excellent doubling hand against dealer upcards of 2 through 9.)

Splitting 66

Split 66 against dealer stiff cards 2 through 6 only*. Our hard total of 12 is not very favorable, nor are the split hands of 6 and 6 too promising either. We have a losing hand either way against all dealer upcards. However, we want to minimize our losses.

Against the dealer stiff cards 2, 3, 4, 5 and 6, our split hands of 6 and 6 will sometimes draw cards to give us some pat totals 17-21.

Of course, we will often end up with stiff totals on the split pair (by the drawing of a 10 or other sufficiently large card) and be forced to stand. But the high dealer busting factor makes splitting 66 against the dealer stiffs a slight gain.

Obviously we will not split 66 against the dealer pat cards. We don't need two hands of 16 against a card that will bust only one time in four.

*Nevada multiple deck exception - Do not split 66 vs. 2.

*Atlantic City multiple deck (and games with doubling after splitting allowed) - No exceptions. Split 66 vs. 2-6.

Splitting 77

Split 77 against dealer upcards of 2, 3, 4, 5, 6 and 7. Against the dealer stiff cards 2 through 6, two playable hands of 7 and 7 are preferable to one stiff total of 14. Splitting 77 is not a strong split, for these totals only gravitate toward a 17, but the high busting rate of the dealer stiff cards makes this split a big gain.

Splitting 77 against the dealer's 7 is also an excellent split, for we are taking one losing total of 14 into two potential pushes of 17 each.

We do not split 77 vs. the dealer's 8, 9, 10, Ace, for we do not want to take one poor total of 14 into two hands gravitating toward a second best total of only 17.

Splitting 88

Split 88 against all dealer upcards. Against the dealer's 2 through 8, we are taking one terrible hand of 16 into two playable totals of 8 each. There is a tremendous gain on all these plays.

Splitting 88 against the dealer's 9, 10, A are the strangest of the basic strategy plays. Using all of the intuitive knowledge we have developed, at first glance we would reason that this is a poor split, for we are making two losers out of one. However, more is involved in this play.

First, you must realize that the player hand of 16 is the worst total possible. While splitting this 16 into two hands of 8 and 8 is not a winning situation against the strong dealer upcards of 9, 10 and A, it is an improvement over our very weak total of hard 16. Bear with this unusual play, for computer simulation studies have played out the hand millions of times for both drawing and splitting, and found that the player loses less by splitting 88. Realize that although the split is weak, it does produce a gain over drawing to our easily bustable 16.

In games employing the no hole card rule, do not split 8s against the dealer's 10 and Ace. With the possibility of the dealer getting a blackjack, we don't need more money out on this hand. Hit instead.

Splitting 10,10

Do not split 10s. The hard total of 20 is a winning hand against all dealer upcards. Splitting 10s against any dealer upcard is a terrible play, for you are taking one "solid" winning hand into two good but uncertain wins. Too often, the splitting of 10s will draw low cards, in effect destroying a great hand.

Splitting AA

Split AA against all dealer upcards. Each Ace is a powerful starting total of 11 points. If we draw the 10, our 21 can't be beat. Splitting AA is a tremendous gain against all dealer upcards.

In no hole card rule games, we will not split Aces when the dealer shows an Ace. The high likelihood of the dealer getting a blackjack when he already has an Ace is too costly for us to double our bet. Draw instead.

MASTER CHART
Northern Nevada · Single Deck

	2	3	4	5	6	7	8	9	10	A
7/less	H	H	H	H	H	H	H	H	H	H
8	H	H	H	H	H	H	H	H	H	H
9	H	H	H	H	H	H	H	H	H	H
10	D	D	D	D	D	D	D	D	H	H
11	D	D	D	D	D	D	D	D	D	D
12	H	H	S	S	S	H	H	H	H	H
13	S	S	S	S	S	H	H	H	H	H
14	S	S	S	S	S	H	H	H	H	H
15	S	S	S	S	S	H	H	H	H	H
16	S	S	S	S	S	H	H	H	H	H
A2	H	H	H	H	H	H	H	H	H	H
A3	H	H	H	H	H	H	H	H	H	H
A4	H	H	H	H	H	H	H	H	H	H
A5	H	H	H	H	H	H	H	H	H	H
A6	H	H	H	H	H	H	H	H	H	H
A7	S	S	S	S	S	S	S	H	H	H
A8	S	S	S	S	S	S	S	S	S	S
A9	S	S	S	S	S	S	S	S	S	S
22	H	spl	spl	spl	spl	spl	H	H	H	H
33	H	H	spl	spl	spl	spl	H	H	H	H
66	spl	spl	spl	spl	spl	H	H	H	H	H
77	spl	spl	spl	spl	spl	spl	H	H	H	H
88	spl	spl	spl	spl	spl	spl	spl	spl	spl	spl
99	spl	spl	spl	spl	spl	S	spl	spl	S	S
AA	spl	spl	spl	spl	spl	spl	spl	spl	spl	spl

H = Hit   S = Stand   D= Double   spl = Split

Do not split 44, 55 (double on 55) and 10s.
Always split 88 and AA

MASTER CHART
Las Vegas · Single Deck

	2	3	4	5	6	7	8	9	10	A
7/less	H	H	H	H	H	H	H	H	H	H
62	H	H	H	H	H	H	H	H	H	H
44/53	H	H	H	D	D	H	H	H	H	H
9	D	D	D	D	D	H	H	H	H	H
10	D	D	D	D	D	D	D	D	H	H
11	D	D	D	D	D	D	D	D	D	D
12	H	H	S	S	S	H	H	H	H	H
13	S	S	S	S	S	H	H	H	H	H
14	S	S	S	S	S	H	H	H	H	H
15	S	S	S	S	S	H	H	H	H	H
16	S	S	S	S	S	H	H	H	H	H
A2	H	H	D	D	D	H	H	H	H	H
A3	H	H	D	D	D	H	H	H	H	H
A4	H	H	D	D	D	H	H	H	H	H
A5	H	H	D	D	D	H	H	H	H	H
A6	D	D	D	D	D	H	H	H	H	H
A7	S	D	D	D	D	S	S	H	H	H
A8	S	S	S	S	S	S	S	S	S	S
A9	S	S	S	S	S	S	S	S	S	S
22	H	spl	spl	spl	spl	spl	H	H	H	H
33	H	H	spl	spl	spl	spl	H	H	H	H
66	spl	spl	spl	spl	spl	H	H	H	H	H
77	spl	spl	spl	spl	spl	spl	H	H	H	H
88	spl	spl	spl	spl	spl	spl	spl	spl	spl	spl
99	spl	spl	spl	spl	spl	S	spl	spl	S	S
AA	spl	spl	spl	spl	spl	spl	spl	spl	spl	spl

H = Hit   S = Stand   D= Double   spl = Split

Do not split 44, 55 (double on 55) and 10s.
Always split 88 and AA

We just looked at the strategies for single deck blackjack in Nevada. Let's now see how the multiple deck game is different.

The Difference Between Single and Multiple Deck Blackjack

The greater number of cards used in a multiple deck game makes the removal of particular cards less important for composition change purposes and, as a result, our doubling and splitting strategies are less aggressive.

For example, the removal of three cards (5,3,5) creates a favorable imbalance for the player in a single deck game and makes a 53 double vs. the dealer's 5 a profitable play. Not only will these cards be poor draws for the player's double but they're three cards the dealer needs to improve his hand. The effective removal of these three cards gives the player a better chance of drawing a 10 on his 8 and, at the same time, increases the dealer's chance of busting. In a single deck game, 53 vs. 6 is a favorable double.

However, the removal of these three cards are barely felt in a multiple deck game. There are 29 other 3s and 5s in a four deck game as compared to only five in a single deck. Thus, no favorable imbalance has been created, and the double down is not a correct play. This lack of sensitivity to particular card removal accounts for nine strategy changes in the multiple deck game from the single deck strategies we just presented.

Except for these nine changes in the doubling and splitting strategies, multiple deck basic strategy is identical to the single deck basic strategy. In a multiple deck game:

> 1- Do not double hard 8 vs. 5; hit instead
> 2- Do not double hard 8 vs. 6; hit instead
> 3- Do not double hard 9 vs. 2; hit instead.
> 4- Do not double hard 11 vs. Ace; hit instead.
> 5- Do not double A2 vs 4; hit instead.
> 6- Do not double A3 vs. 4; hit instead.
> 7- Do not double A6 vs 2; hit instead
> 8- Do not split 22 vs. 3; hit instead
> 9- Do not split 66 vs. 2; hit instead

MASTER CHART
NORTHERN NEVADA · MULTIPLE DECK

	2	3	4	5	6	7	8	9	10	A
7/less	H	H	H	H	H	H	H	H	H	H
8	H	H	H	H	H	H	H	H	H	H
9	H	H	H	H	H	H	H	H	H	H
10	D	D	D	D	D	D	D	D	H	H
11	D	D	D	D	D	D	D	D	D	H
12	H	H	S	S	S	H	H	H	H	H
13	S	S	S	S	S	H	H	H	H	H
14	S	S	S	S	S	H	H	H	H	H
15	S	S	S	S	S	H	H	H	H	H
16	S	S	S	S	S	H	H	H	H	H
A2	H	H	H	H	H	H	H	H	H	H
A3	H	H	H	H	H	H	H	H	H	H
A4	H	H	H	H	H	H	H	H	H	H
A5	H	H	H	H	H	H	H	H	H	H
A6	H	H	H	H	H	H	H	H	H	H
A7	S	S	S	S	S	S	S	H	H	H
A8	S	S	S	S	S	S	S	S	S	S
A9	S	S	S	S	S	S	S	S	S	S
22	H	H	spl	spl	spl	spl	H	H	H	H
33	H	H	spl	spl	spl	spl	H	H	H	H
66	H	spl	spl	spl	spl	H	H	H	H	H
77	spl	spl	spl	spl	spl	spl	H	H	H	H
88	spl	spl	spl	spl	spl	spl	spl	spl	spl	spl
99	spl	spl	spl	spl	spl	S	spl	spl	S	S
AA	spl	spl	spl	spl	spl	spl	spl	spl	spl	spl

H = Hit   S = Stand   D= Double   spl = Split

Do not split 44, 55 10s
Always split 88, AA

MASTER CHART
LAS VEGAS · MULTIPLE DECK

	2	3	4	5	6	7	8	9	10	A
7/less	H	H	H	H	H	H	H	H	H	H
8	H	H	H	H	H	H	H	H	H	H
9	H	D	D	D	D	H	H	H	H	H
10	D	D	D	D	D	D	D	D	H	H
11	D	D	D	D	D	D	D	D	D	H
12	H	H	S	S	S	H	H	H	H	H
13	S	S	S	S	S	H	H	H	H	H
14	S	S	S	S	S	H	H	H	H	H
15	S	S	S	S	S	H	H	H	H	H
16	S	S	S	S	S	H	H	H	H	H
A2	H	H	H	D	D	H	H	H	H	H
A3	H	H	H	D	D	H	H	H	H	H
A4	H	H	D	D	D	H	H	H	H	H
A5	H	H	D	D	D	H	H	H	H	H
A6	H	D	D	D	D	H	H	H	H	H
A7	S	D	D	D	D	S	S	H	H	H
A8	S	S	S	S	S	S	S	S	S	S
A9	S	S	S	S	S	S	S	S	S	S
22	H	H	spl	spl	spl	spl	H	H	H	H
33	H	H	spl	spl	spl	spl	H	H	H	H
66	H	spl	spl	spl	spl	H	H	H	H	H
77	spl	spl	spl	spl	spl	spl	H	H	H	H
88	spl	spl	spl	spl	spl	spl	spl	spl	spl	spl
99	spl	spl	spl	spl	spl	S	spl	spl	S	S
AA	spl	spl	spl	spl	spl	spl	spl	spl	spl	spl

H = Hit   S = Stand   D= Double   spl = Split

Do not split 44, 55 10s
Always split 88, AA

Atlantic City Multiple Deck

The blackjack games offered in Atlantic City differ from the Nevada games in several ways. For one thing, all the Atlantic City games are dealt as multiple deck games. They do not offer single deck games as in Nevada. Doubling allowed after splitting is standard in Atlantic City as opposed to Nevada, where only a few casinos offer this option. Resplitting of pairs is not allowed in Atlantic City. Nevada casinos generally allow the player to resplit pairs as often as they wish.

To protect against collusion between the player and the dealer, the dealer does not check his hole card for a blackjack (as is standard in Nevada) until all the players have finished playing their hands. This safeguard does not affect the player's chances of winning, for if the dealer does indeed have a blackjack, any additional money the player wagered on a doubled or split hand will be returned. Only the original bet loses.

Another difference is that all player hands are dealt face up in Atlantic City. No casinos allow the player to physically handle the cards. The player must employ hand signals to convey his strategy intentions to the dealer. (Single and double deck games in Nevada are generally face down games where the player can handle his cards, while multiple deck games are played similarly to the Atlantic City face up game.)

The Atlantic City basic strategy is the same as Nevada multiple deck strategy except for more frequent pair splitting due to the player being allowed to double after splits.

European No Hole Card Rules

These strategies are for multiple deck play and take into account that players may only double on totals of 9, 10 and 11, and also will double and split less aggressively when the dealer shows a 10 or Ace due to the no hole card rule.

In no hole card games that allow the player to double after splitting, the player will split more aggressively to take advantage of this favorable option and we'll also show that strategy in a master chart.

MASTER CHART
ATLANTIC CITY · MULTIPLE DECK

	2	3	4	5	6	7	8	9	10	A
7/less	H	H	H	H	H	H	H	H	H	H
8	H	H	H	H	H	H	H	H	H	H
9	H	D	D	D	D	H	H	H	H	H
10	D	D	D	D	D	D	D	D	H	H
11	D	D	D	D	D	D	D	D	D	H
12	H	H	S	S	S	H	H	H	H	H
13	S	S	S	S	S	H	H	H	H	H
14	S	S	S	S	S	H	H	H	H	H
15	S	S	S	S	S	H	H	H	H	H
16	S	S	S	S	S	H	H	H	H	H
A2	H	H	H	D	D	H	H	H	H	H
A3	H	H	H	D	D	H	H	H	H	H
A4	H	H	D	D	D	H	H	H	H	H
A5	H	H	D	D	D	H	H	H	H	H
A6	H	D	D	D	D	H	H	H	H	H
A7	S	D	D	D	D	S	S	H	H	H
A8	S	S	S	S	S	S	S	S	S	S
A9	S	S	S	S	S	S	S	S	S	S
22	spl	spl	spl	spl	spl	spl	H	H	H	H
33	spl	spl	spl	spl	spl	spl	H	H	H	H
44	H	H	H	spl	spl	H	H	H	H	H
66	spl	spl	spl	spl	spl	H	H	H	H	H
77	spl	spl	spl	spl	spl	spl	H	H	H	H
88	spl	spl	spl	spl	spl	spl	spl	spl	spl	spl
99	spl	spl	spl	spl	spl	S	spl	spl	S	S
AA	spl	spl	spl	spl	spl	spl	spl	spl	spl	spl

H = Hit   S = Stand   D = Double   spl = Split

Do not split 55, 10s
Always split 88, AA

MASTER CHART
EUROPEAN NO HOLE CARD STYLE · MULTIPLE DECK

	2	3	4	5	6	7	8	9	10	A
7/less	H	H	H	H	H	H	H	H	H	H
8	H	H	H	H	H	H	H	H	H	H
9	H	D	D	D	D	H	H	H	H	H
10	D	D	D	D	D	D	D	D	H	H
11	D	D	D	D	D	D	D	D	H	H
12	H	H	S	S	S	H	H	H	H	H
13	S	S	S	S	S	H	H	H	H	H
14	S	S	S	S	S	H	H	H	H	H
15	S	S	S	S	S	H	H	H	H	H
16	S	S	S	S	S	H	H	H	H	H
A2	H	H	H	H	H	H	H	H	H	H
A3	H	H	H	H	H	H	H	H	H	H
A4	H	H	H	H	H	H	H	H	H	H
A5	H	H	H	H	H	H	H	H	H	H
A6	H	H	H	H	H	H	H	H	H	H
A7	S	S	S	S	S	S	S	H	H	H
A8	S	S	S	S	S	S	S	S	S	S
A9	S	S	S	S	S	S	S	S	S	S
22	H	H	spl	spl	spl	spl	H	H	H	H
33	H	H	spl	spl	spl	spl	H	H	H	H
66	H	spl	spl	spl	spl	H	H	H	H	H
77	spl	spl	spl	spl	spl	spl	H	H	H	H
88	spl	spl	spl	spl	spl	spl	spl	spl	H	H
99	spl	spl	spl	spl	spl	S	spl	spl	S	S
AA	spl	spl	spl	spl	spl	spl	spl	spl	spl	H

H = Hit   S = Stand   D= Double   spl = Split

Do not split 44, 55 10s

MASTER CHART
European No Hole Card: Doubling After Splitting Allowed

	2	3	4	5	6	7	8	9	10	A
7/less	H	H	H	H	H	H	H	H	H	H
8	H	H	H	H	H	H	H	H	H	H
9	H	D	D	D	D	H	H	H	H	H
10	D	D	D	D	D	D	D	D	H	H
11	D	D	D	D	D	D	D	D	H	H
12	H	H	S	S	S	H	H	H	H	H
13	S	S	S	S	S	H	H	H	H	H
14	S	S	S	S	S	H	H	H	H	H
15	S	S	S	S	S	H	H	H	H	H
16	S	S	S	S	S	H	H	H	H	H
A2	H	H	H	H	H	H	H	H	H	H
A3	H	H	H	H	H	H	H	H	H	H
A4	H	H	H	H	H	H	H	H	H	H
A5	H	H	H	H	H	H	H	H	H	H
A6	H	H	H	H	H	H	H	H	H	H
A7	S	S	S	S	S	S	S	H	H	H
A8	S	S	S	S	S	S	S	S	S	S
A9	S	S	S	S	S	S	S	S	S	S
22	spl	spl	spl	spl	spl	spl	H	H	H	H
33	spl	spl	spl	spl	spl	spl	H	H	H	H
44	H	H	H	spl	spl	H	H	H	H	H
66	spl	spl	spl	spl	spl	H	H	H	H	H
77	spl	spl	spl	spl	spl	spl	H	H	H	H
88	spl	spl	spl	spl	spl	spl	spl	spl	H	H
99	spl	spl	spl	spl	spl	S	spl	spl	S	S
AA	spl	spl	spl	spl	spl	spl	spl	spl	spl	H

H = Hit   S = Stand   D = Double   spl = Split

Do not split 55, 10s

Player's Options
Use these strategies where the following variations are permitted:

Doubling Down Permitted After Splitting

A standard option in Atlantic City, Great Britain and many casinos around the world, but offered only in a few Nevada casinos. It allows the player to double down on one or more of the hands resulting from a split according to the standard doubling rules of the casino. This option allows us to split more aggressively so that we may take advantage of good doubling situations that can arise as a consequence of the split. This option is favorable to the player.

Our Hand		Single Deck	Multiple Deck
22	split against	2-7	2-7
33	split against	2-7	2-7
44	split against	4-6	5-6
66	split against	2-7	2-6
77	split against	2-8	2-7

Late Surrender (Surrender)

A player option to forfeit his hand and lose half his bet after it has been determined that the dealer does not have a blackjack. This option is favorable to the player.

Our Hand		Single Deck	Multiple Deck
16*	surrender against	10, A	9,10, A
15	surrender against	10	10
77	surrender against	10	-

* Do not surrender 88 (split)

Early Surrender

A player option to forfeit his hand and lose half his bet before the dealer checks for a blackjack. An extremely valuable option for the player. No longer offered in Atlantic City.

Dealer's Upcard		Player's Totals
A	early surrender with	5-7, 12-17
10	early surrender with	14-16
9	early surrender with	16*

*Do not early surrender 88 (split).   Do not surrender soft totals.

THE WINNING EDGE

The removal of cards during play and the continued dealing from a deck depleted of these used cards creates a situation in blackjack where the odds of receiving particular cards or combinations of those cards constantly change during the course of the game. Computer studies have found that the removal of certain cards during play gives the player an advantage over the house, while the removal of others gives the house an advantage over the player.

Therefore, as cards are removed from play, the player's chances of winning constantly change. Sometimes the depleted deck of cards will favor the house and sometimes the player. By learning to analyze a depleted deck of cards for favorability, and capitalizing on this situation by betting more when the remaining cards are in your favor, you can actually have an edge over the casino.

The heart of all winning systems at blackjack is based on this theory - Bet more when you have the advantage, and less when the house has the advantage. This way, when you win, you win more, and when you lose, you lose less. Beginning with an even game (playing accurate basic strategy), this "maximize gain, minimize loss" betting strategy will give the player an overall edge on the house.

How do we determine when we have the edge? Computer studies have determined that 10s and Aces are the most valuable cards for the player, while the small cards, 2 through 7, are the most valuable cards for the house, 8s and 9s being relatively neutral. Off the top of the deck, with all cards still in play, the player has an even game with the house - neither side enjoys an advantage*.

The odds shift in favor of the player when there is a higher ratio of 9s, 10s and As in the deck than normal, and shift in favor of the house when there is a higher ratio of small cards, 2 through 7, than normal. All counting systems base their winning strategies on keeping track of the ratio of high cards to low cards. The systems vary in complexity from the very simple to the very complicated, all being based on the same principle - betting more when there is a higher proportion of high cards in the deck.

However, there are many blackjack players that wish to have an edge over the house but are loathe to learn counting systems. For the player that desires to win without counting cards, the Cardoza School of Blackjack has developed some simple but effective techniques.

The Cardoza Non-Counter's Edge

The system is simple. All you need to know is that high cards favor us and the small cards favor the house. When there are more high cards in the deck than normal, you will bet more. But you need not count cards. All you need to do is to keep your eyes open and watch the cards, just as you probably do anyway.

---

*Assuming the player plays perfect basic strategy, and that the game is a single deck game with the favorable Las Vegas Strip rules. If the particular game has less liberal rules (Northern Nevada) or is a multiple deck game, the house will enjoy a slight initial edge.

Here are 5 easy guidelines for the non-counter to have an edge:

1. When a great many small cards have been played in the first round, it is to the player's advantage. Bet 3 or 4 units instead of your normal 1 or 2 unit bet. (If $5 is your standard bet, then $15 is considered a 3 unit bet)

Example - The following cards have been played. You had an 8, 5, 6, the player to your left had 10, 6, 2, another player had 10, 6, 5 and the dealer had a 10, 7. A disproportionate number of small cards have been played, meaning the remaining cards are richer in high cards - to the player's advantage. So you bet more.

2. If on succeeding rounds, you estimate that there are still a disproportionate number of high cards remaining, continue to bet at a higher level than your minimum or neutral bet. Through practical experience, you will be able to improve on your estimation abilities.

3. If the cumulative distribution of cards seems to be fairly normal after a round of play, bet your neutral or minimum bet (1 or 2 units, whatever your preference is). If, however, you notice that no Aces have appeared, increase your bet by one unit. Your potential to get a blackjack has increased. While the dealer's chances of getting a blackjack has increased as well, he only gets paid even-money; you get paid 3 to 2.

4. On the other hand, if a disproportionate number of high cards appear in the first round, then place your minimum 1 unit bet, for the house has an edge. And if on succeeding rounds you judge that there is still a disproportionate number of small cards remaining, continue to place your minimum bets.

5. If the cumulative distribution of cards appears to be normal and you notice that more Aces have appeared than what you normally would expect (one Ace for every 13 cards is the normal composition), you want to downgrade your bet to one unit if you had been making 2 unit bets.

To sum up, when there are more 10s and Aces remaining in the deck than normal, increase your bet. When there are fewer 10s and Aces than normal (meaning more small cards than normal), decrease your bet. Every time the deck is shuffled, start your estimation of favorability over again.

The Power of Our Advantage

The Cardoza Non-Counter strategy gives the player an advantage powerful enough to give the $5-$20 bettor close to a $100 profit expectancy in a heavy weekend of play in a single deck game, and the $25-$100 bettor a $500 expectancy of winning. Now that you have the winning edge on the house, time will work to your advantage. The longer you play, the more money you can expect to make.

The Cardoza Non-Counter strategy is most effective in single deck games, and less so in double decks, due to the fewer number of cards compared to four deck or more games. The advantage of this strategy is that you can win with much less mental effort than the counting systems require. Obviously we cannot win as much without counting cards, but we will win.

The strategy is less effective in four, six and eight deck games where the overall number of the cards is less susceptible to composition changes from just a few cards being removed.

For multiple deck players, the news is not all bad though, for the basic strategies that we have presented in this book will bring you very close to an even game against the casino. Should you ever decide to improve your game further by learning a professional strategy, you must know these basic strategies anyway. They are 100% correct for single and multiple deck games, and the absolute best available.

Readers desiring to further their edge over the house and make more money playing blackjack, must learn a professional counting or non-counting system. We have developed several casino-tested strategies for use under actual playing conditions. The first and most powerful, the Cardoza Base Count Strategy is surprisingly easy to use, but for those players intimidated by counting, we have developed a new strategy that gives non-counting players the mathematical edge over the casino in multiple deck games. This strategy, more than 15 years in development, is our own research and is only available through Cardoza Publishing. (See the ads in the back of the book for information on buying these pro-level strategies.)

Getting the Most Out of the Cardoza Non-Counter Strategy

For those players that will be playing in Nevada, or other areas where there is a choice, it will be to your advantage to play in a single deck game rather than a multiple deck one for the following two reasons:

1. The single deck game is inherently more favorable.

2. The Cardoza Non-Counter strategy is most effective in a single deck game because the single deck game is highly sensitive to composition changes.

For those players who are accessible only to multiple deck games, you have two choices if you want to have the mathematical advantage over a multiple deck game. Choice number one is to purchase the *Cardoza Non-Counter Multiple Deck* Strategy discussed above. This will give you an edge of about 1/2 - 1%. Serious players who want to work just a little harder for the maximum edge possible, 1-3% over the casino, must learn the *Cardoza Base Count Strategy.* (*See back pages.*) However, before anything else, you must learn the material in this book. These basic strategies are the foundation for any winning approach.

Bet Range

I recommend a bet range of 1-4 units. Thus, if $5 is your standard bet, your maximum bet should not exceed $20. This is an important guideline to adhere to for several reasons:

• Your advantage will rarely be large enough to warrant a bet larger than 4 units. We have bankroll limitations to consider, and do not want greed to be our downfall. Keep in mind that blackjack is a slow grind for the good players.

• Raising your bets in advantageous situations to a range greater than 1-4 will attract undue attention to you as a skillful player, and the casino may begin to shuffle every time you make a large bet, in effect shuffling away advantageous situations.

• You do not want to have one extremely large losing bet destroy an otherwise good session at the table.

• The losing of a huge bet will generally have a very detrimental effect on your confidence, your concentration and your ability to think clearly. You will be surprised at how fast this can affect your physical and psychological frame of being.

• The ranging of your bets from 1 unit in disadvantageous situations to 4 units in highly advantageous situations is a wide enough bet spread to maximize your gains while at the same time minimizing your risk.

Tipping

Tipping, or **toking**, as it is called in casino parlance, should be viewed as a gratuitous gesture by the player to a dealer he feels has given him good service. Toking is totally at the player's discretion, and in no way should be considered an obligation. It is not the player's duty to support casino employees.

If you toke, toke only when you're winning, and only to dealers that are friendly and helpful to you. Do not toke dealers that you don't like or ones that try to make you feel guilty about not tipping. Dealers that make playing an unpleasant experience for you deserve nothing.

The best way to tip a dealer is to place a bet for the dealer in front of your own bet, so that his chances of winning that toke are tied up with your hand. If the hand is won, you both win together; if the hand is lost, you lose together. By being partners on the hand, you establish camaraderie with the dealer. Naturally, he or she will be rooting for you to win. This is the best way to tip, for when you win, the dealer wins double - the tip amount you bet plus the winnings from that bet.

Cheating

It is my belief that cheating is not a problem in the major American gambling centers, though I would not totally eliminate the possibility. If you ever feel uncomfortable about the honesty of a game, stop playing. Though you probably are being dealt an honest game, the anxiety of being uncomfortable is not worth the action.

Do not confuse bad luck with being cheated, or a dealer's mistake as chicanery. Dealers have a difficult job and work hard. They are bound to make honest mistakes. If you find yourself shorted on a payoff, bring it immediately to the dealer's attention and the mistake will be corrected.

Bankrolling

The following bankroll requirements have been prepared to give the player enough capital to survive any reasonable losing streak, and be able to bounce back on top.

In the following table, flat betting refers to betting the same amount every time. When ranging bets from 1-4, the player needs a larger bankroll, for more money is bet.

BANKROLL REQUIREMENTS		
Hours to Play	**Bet Range**	**Bankroll Needed**
10	Flat	50 units
20+	Flat	100 units
10	1-4	150 units
20+	1-4	200 units

If you plan on playing for an extended weekend's worth of play (20 hours or more) at $5-$20 a hand, you should bring $1,000 with you, while if you are only planning to play 10 hours at those stakes, $750 will give you a fairly safe margin.

This does not mean that you will lose this money playing $5-

$20. Using the Cardoza Non-Counter betting strategy, you will have an edge on the house in a single deck game, and your expectancy is to win money every time you go*. However, it is important that the reader be aware that losing streaks occur, and the losing of $500-$600 is a possibility, though admittedly small. If the thought of losing amounts comparable to this during a downswing scares you, then you should not play $5-$20 a hand, for you are betting over your head.

Again, bet within your financial and emotional means, and you will never regret a single session at the tables.

If you have a definite amount of money to play with and want to figure out how much your unit size bet should be, simply take your gambling stake and divide it by the amount of units you need to have.

Thus, if you bring $500 with you, and plan to play for 10 hours ranging your bets from 1-4, divide $500 by 150 units (see chart: bankroll needed column) and you will wager about $3 a hand. Betting more than $3 as a unit would be overbetting, and leaving yourself vulnerable to the risks discussed earlier.

Table Bankroll

How much money should you bring to the table?

My recommendation is that your bring 30 units to the table each time you play. If playing $5 units, bring $150; if $2 units, bring $60. $25 bettors should bring $750. $100 bettors should sit down with $3,000.

You can bring less if you want. If flat betting, 15 units will suffice. If your bet range is from 1-4, 20 units will do the trick. However, do not bring more money to the table. 30 units is enough to cover normal swings, and you never want to lose more than that in any one sitting.

---

* If playing a multiple deck game, the house will enjoy only a slight advantage over the player if following our strategies. You must learn the Cardoza Non-Counter Multiple Deck Strategy (for non-counters) or The Cardoza Base Count Strategy (for counters) to enjoy an edge over the casino in a multiple deck game.

SUMMARY

Blackjack is a game of skill that can be beat. However, to win, you must learn the game properly. Take you time reading this section and practicing your skills at home.

Learn your basic strategies perfectly, apply the Cardoza Non-Counter betting strategy and pay careful attention to the advice offered in the money management section and you will have the knowledge and skills to be a consistent winner at the 21 tables!

CRAPS

INTRODUCTION

Craps is the most exciting of the casino games, one perfectly tuned to the temperament of action players, for it offers the bettor opportunities to win large sums of money quickly. But big money can be lost just as fast unless the player is conversant with the best bets available and knows how to use them in a coordinated strategy.

You'll learn everything you need to know about craps - from the rules of the game, how to bet and how to play, to the combinations of the dice and the casino vocabulary. You'll learn the best percentage bets to make and how to use them in winning strategies, and how to bankroll and handle your cash so that you'll manage your money like a pro.

We present winning strategies for players betting with the dice, and for players against the dice, and show the best ways conservative and aggressive players alike can bet their money so that losing streaks are kept to the bare minimum and winning streaks can be taken all the way to the bank!

You'll learn 11 winning strategies in all, enough to keep the excitement level high, and when things are going right, the profits rolling. So whether you're a beginner, new to craps, or an experienced player with decades of experience under your belt, you'll find this chapter to be an indispensable guide on how to play and win at craps!

So let's get on with it, and let the dice roll!

BEGINNER'S GUIDE TO CASINO CRAPS

The Table

The standard casino craps table is rectangular in shape and depending upon the particular size of the casino's table, is built to accommodate between 15 to 24 players. The sides of the table are several feet above the layout where the bets are made, giving the players an edge to lean on, and giving the dice walls to carom off.

The Layout

The craps layout is divided into three distinct sections. The two end sections, which are identical, are areas around which the players cluster, and where the majority of bets are made. Each end area is run by one of the standing dealers.

The middle area is flanked on either side by a boxman and stickman. This area contains the proposition, or center bets, and is completely under the jurisdiction of the stickman.

The layout is a large piece of green felt with various imprints marking the plethora of bets possible. All action is centered on the layout. Bets are placed, paid off and collected on this felt surface. And, of course, it is on the layout where the dice are thrown.

Layouts around the world are basically the same, though some clubs may have slight variations, but none of these need concern us, for the game of craps is basically the same whatever casino you play in. The minor variations that do occur, concern bets whose odds are so poor that we wouldn't want to make them anyway.

The Dice

The game of craps is played with two standard six sided dice, with each die numbered from 1 to 6. The dice are manufactured so that they fall as randomly as possible, with a 5 being just as likely to fall on one die as a 3. However, we'll see later that combining two dice together creates some combinations that are more likely to appear than others, and this is the basis of the odds in craps.

Players

Only one player is needed to play craps, while as many as can fit around a craps table are the maximum. When the action is hot and heavy, bettors will be lined up shoulder to shoulder, screaming, yelling and cajoling, for the dice to come through and make them winners.

Below is a standard craps layout.

THE LAYOUT

Casino Personnel

The average craps table is manned by a crew of four casino employees - one stickman, who stands at the center of the table, two dealers, who stand on the opposite side of the stickman at either end of the table, and a boxman who is seated between the two standing dealers and directly across from the stickman.

Let's look at the function of each crewman in turn.

The Stickman

The **stickman's** main responsibility is the handling of the dice, a task he performs with a flexible, hooked stick. When a new shooter is coming-out, the stickman will offer him a cache of dice to choose from, and after two have been selected, will return the remaining dice to his box.

After each roll of the dice, the stickman will announce the number thrown and bring the dice back to the center of the table. Usually, he will supply additional information about its consequences.

If a 7 is thrown on the come-out roll, he may announce, "7, winner on the pass line."

If instead, a 2, 3 or 12 is rolled on the come-out, he may say, "Craps, line away." When a shooter sevens-out, the stickman might exclaim, "7 out, line away."

A good stickman is a show in himself, and by the excitement he generates, makes the game more lively and colorful for both the players and the dealers. And from the casino's standpoint, happy players tend to bet heavier and wilder than they normally would.

The dice will be returned to the shooter after the dealers have finished making payoffs.

The stickman is also responsible for the proposition, or center bets made in the middle of the layout. He will place all proposition bets directed his way into their proper location on the layout.

If these bets are winners, the stickman will direct the dealers to pay off the winning players, and if the bets are losers, he will collect the lost bets and push them over to the boxman.

The Dealers

There is a dealer located on either side of the boxman, and his main responsibility is to handle all the monetary transactions and betting on his end of the table. He pays off winning bets and collects losing ones, converts cash into chips, and will change chips into higher or lower denominations for the player.

Though the player can make many of the bets himself, there are wagers such as the place bets and certain free-odds bets which must be given to the dealer to be placed.

Each standing dealer has a **marker buck**, a plastic disk used to indicate the established point. If a player is coming-out, beginning his roll, the marker buck will be lying on its black side, labeled "**off**," and if a point is established, the dealer will flip the marker buck to the white side, marked "**on**," and place it in the appropriately numbered box to indicate the point. It is with the dealers that the player will have most of his contact and to whom he can address his questions.

The Boxman

The **boxman** sits between the two dealers and across from the stickman, and from this central position, supervises the running of the craps table. His job is not only to watch over the casinos bankroll, most of which sits right in front of him in huge stacks, but to make sure the dealers make the correct payoffs so that neither the player nor the house gets shorted.

He is responsible for settling any disputes that may arise between the players and the dealers. Generally, the benefit of the doubt will be given to the player on any disputed call. If the dice leave the table for any reason, the returned dice are brought directly to the boxman for inspection. He will check the logo and coded numbers on the dice to make sure they haven't been switched, and will inspect the surfaces for imperfections that may influence the game. If, for any reason, the boxman feels suspicious of the returned dice, he will remove them from play and have the stickman offer the shooter a new pair.

When one boxman is on duty, he will supervise one end of the table while the stickman watches the other.

However, when the action is fast, and stacks of chips are riding on each roll of the dice, a second boxman will often be added to the crew to help watch the table. In these cases, the boxmen will sit next to each other behind the chips, each being responsible for one end of the table.

In addition to the boxmen, there are other supervisors, called floormen and pit bosses, who watch over the action from behind the boxman in the area known as the pit.

The Pit

Craps tables are arranged in a pattern so that a central area, known as the **pit**, is formed in the middle. The tables are arranged around the pit so that the boxmen and standing dealers have their backs to the pit area, and so that the floormen, standing inside the pit, can easily watch over all of the craps tables.

Floormen

The **floormen** spend their entire shift on their feet, and are responsible for supervising a particular table or group of tables in the pit.

In addition to these supervisory capacities, they deal with players that have established credit lines. If a player requests credit, the floorman checks to see if his credit is good, and if verified, authorizes the dealer to give the requested chips. At the same time, or soon afterwards, he will bring the player an IOU to sign, acknowledging the credit transaction.

The Pit Boss

The **pit boss**, under whose authority the floormen work, is in the charge of the entire craps pit. He's rarely in contact with the players, unless a high roller is playing, whereby he may come over and introduce himself or offer the roller some comps.

Entering a Game

To enter a craps game, slip into a space by the rail of the craps table. After catching the dealer's attention, place your cash on the layout and inform him of the denomination of chips you would like. The dealer will take your money, and give it to the boxman who will supervise the exchange.

Converting Traveller's Checks and Money Orders to Cash

The dealers will accept only cash or chips at the table, so if you bring traveller's checks, money order or the like, you must go to the area of the casino marked **Casino Cashier** to get these converted to cash. Be sure to bring proper identification to insure a smooth transaction.

Casino Chips

Chip denominations run in $1, $5, $25, $100 and $500 units. $1 chips are generally referred to as **silver**, $5 chips as **nickels**, $25 chips as **quarters**, and $100 chips as **dollars**. Unless playing at a 25¢ minimum craps table, $1 chips are the minimum currency available.

Betting

Casinos prefer that the player uses chips for betting purposes, for the handling of money at the tables, is cumbersome and slows the game. However, cash can be used to bet with, though all payoffs will be in chips.

House Limits

The house limits will be posted on placards located on each corner of the table. They will indicate the minimum bet required to play and also the maximum bet allowed.

Minimum bets range from $1 and $5 per bet, to a maximum of $500, $1000 or $2,000 a bet. Occasionally, 25¢ minimum craps tables may be found as well. If special arrangements are made, a player can bet as much as he can muster in certain casinos. The Horseshoe Casino in Las Vegas is known to book any bet no matter the size.

In 1981, a man walked into the Horseshoe and placed a bet for $777,777. He bet the don't pass, and walked out two rolls later with one and a half million dollars in cash!

Converting Chips into Cash

Dealers do not convert your chips into cash. Once you've bought your chips at the table, that cash is dropped into a dropbox, and thereafter unobtainable at the table. When you are ready to convert your chips, take them to the cashier's cage where they'll be changed into cash.

Free Drinks and Cigarettes

Casinos offer their customers unlimited free drinking while gambling at the tables. In addition to alcoholic beverages, a player can order milk, soft drinks, juices or any other beverages. This is ordered through and served by a cocktail waitress.

Cigarettes and cigars are also complimentary and can be ordered through the cocktail waitress.

Tipping

Tipping, or **toking**, as it is called in casino parlance, should be viewed as a gratuitous gesture by the player to the crew of dealers he feels has given him good service. Tipping is totally at the player's discretion, and in no way should be considered an obligation.

If you toke, toke only when you're winning, and only if the crew is friendly and helpful to you. Do not toke dealers that you don't like or ones that try to make you feel guilty about not tipping. Dealers that make playing an unpleasant experience for you deserve nothing.

Tips are shared by the crew working the craps table. Though the usual tip is to make a proposition bet, with the exclamation "one for the boys," a better way to toke the crew would be to make a line bet for them, so they can have a good chance of winning the bet. Dealers prefer this type of tip for they too are aware how poor the proposition bets are. This is also better than just handing over the toke, for if the bet is won, the dealer wins double for the tip - the amount bet for him plus the winnings from that bet.

Play of the Game and the Come-Out Roll

When a new player is to throw the dice, the stickman will empty his box of dice and push them across the layout with his stick. After this player, known as the **shooter**, selects two dice of his choice, the stickman will retrieve the remaining dice and return them to his box. In a new game, the player closest to the boxman's left side will receive the dice first, and the rotation of the dice will go clockwise from player to player around the craps table.

The shooter has no advantage over the other players except perhaps the psychological edge he may get throwing the dice himself. He is required to make either a pass or don't pass bet as the shooter, and in addition, can make any other bets allowed.

There are a wide variety of bets the players can make, and these bets should be placed before the shooter throws the dice. Players can bet with the dice or against them at their preference, but in either case, the casino will book all wagers.

Play is ready to begin. The shooter is supposed to throw the dice so that they bounce off the far wall of the table. If the throw does not reach the far wall, the shooter will be requested to toss harder on his next throw, and if he persists in underthrowing the dice, the boxman may disallow him from throwing further. This policy protects against cheats that can manipulate unobstructed throws of the dice.

The first throw is called the **come-out roll**, and is the most significant roll in craps. It marks the first roll of a shoot, and can either become an automatic winner or loser for players betting with the dice, called **right bettors**, or those betting against the dice, called **wrong bettors**, or establish a point with which the shooter hopes to repeat before a 7 is thrown.

The come-out roll works as follows. The throw of a 7 or 11 on the come-out roll is an automatic winner for the pass line bettors, players betting that the dice will win, or *pass*, while the throw of a **craps**, a 2, 3 or 12 is an automatic loser. For the don't pass bettors, those betting against the dice, the come-out roll works almost exactly opposite to the pass line bet. A come-out roll of a 7 or an 11 is an automatic loser, a 2 or a 3 an automatic winner, while the 12 (in some casinos a 2 instead) is a standoff.

If the come-out roll is an automatic decision, a 2, 3, 7, 11 or 12, the affected players will have their bets paid or collected, and the following roll will be a new come-out roll.

Any other number thrown, a 4, 5, 6, 8, 9 or 10, becomes the **point**, and the dealers will indicate this by flipping their respective marker bucks to the white side marked "on," and move the disk into the rectangular numbered boxes corresponding to the point number thrown.

The shoot will continue until either the point is repeated, a winner for the pass line bettors and a loser for the don't pass bettors, or until a seven is thrown, known as **sevening-out**, a loser on the pass line and winner on the don't pass. In either case, the shoot will have been completed, and the following roll will be a new come-out roll, the start of a new shoot.

Once a point is established, only the 7 and the point are consequential rolls for the pass and don't pass bettors, also called **line bettors**. All other rolls are neutral throws for these bets.

There are many other bets available to the player as we will discuss later, some that can be made only after a point is established, and others that can be made at any time during a shoot. So while the line bettors may not be affected by a particular throw, the dealers may be paying off or collecting chips on other affected wagers while the shoot is in progress.

The shooter can continue throwing the dice until he sevens-out, whereupon, after all the bets are settled on the layout, the stickman will present his collection of dice to the next player in a clockwise rotation. Even though the shooter may **crap-out** (the throw of a 2, 3 or 12) on his come-out roll, a losing roll for the pass line bettors, the shooter does not have to yield the dice. It is only when he throws a 7 before his point repeats, sevens-out, that the dice must be relinquished.

The Come - Out Roll Capsulated

The come-out roll occurs when:
- A new shooter takes the dice.
- The shooter throws a 2, 3, 7, 11 or 12 on the come-out roll, an automatic winner or loser for the line bettors.
- After a point is established, the shooter either repeats that point or sevens-out

---

Betting Right or Wrong

Betting right or wrong are only casino terms used to designate whether a player is betting with the dice, **betting right**, or betting against the dice, **betting wrong**, and are in no way indicative of a correct or incorrect way of playing. As we shall see, both ways of betting are equally valid.

UNDERSTANDING THE ODDS

Knowing how to figure the possible combinations that can occur when two dice are thrown is essential to understanding the basics of craps - the bets, the odds and the payoffs. You'll be surprised at how simple the odds really are, and will find craps to be a more rewarding experience once you learn these fundamentals.

Craps is played with two dice, individually called die, and each die is a near perfect six sided cube, guaranteed to be within 1/10,000 of an inch accurate.

Each die has six equally possible outcomes when thrown - numbers one through six. The two dice thrown together have a total of 36 possible outcomes, the six combinations of one die by the six combinations of the other. The chart below shows these combinations. Notice how certain totals have more possibilities of being thrown, or are more probable of occurring by the random throw of the two dice.

COMBINATIONS OF THE DICE

NUMBERS COMBINATIONS

2... **ONE**

3... **TWO**

4... **THREE**

5... **FOUR**

6... **FIVE**

7... **SIX**

8... **FIVE**

9... **FOUR**

10... **THREE**

11... **TWO**

12... **ONE**

You can see by the chart that the 7 is more likely to be thrown than any other number, having six possible combinations. Next in frequency are the 6 and the 8, five outcomes each, then the 5 and the 9, four outcomes, the 4 and the 10, three outcomes apiece, the 3 and the 11, two outcomes, and finally, the 2 and the 12, one combination each.

A Shortcut to Remembering the Odds

Notice the symmetry of combinations on either side of the 7. The 6 and 8 have equal possibilities of being thrown, just as the 5 and 9, 4 and 10, 3 and 11, and 2 and 12 do.

If you take rolls of 7 and below and subtract one from that number, you arrive at the correct number of combinations for that roll. Thus, there are four ways to roll a 5 (5-1), six ways to roll a 7 (7-1) and one way to roll a 2 (2-1).

For numbers greater than the 7, match that number with the corresponding symmetrical number on the other side of the 7, and subtract one. Thus, to find the combinations of the 8, you match it with the 6 (which has an equal likelihood of occurring), and subtracting one, you get five combinations.

Figuring the Odds of Rolling a Specific Number

To figure the odds of rolling any particular number, divide the number of combinations for that particular number into 36, the total number of combinations possible.

Let's say the 7. There are six ways to roll a 7. Dividing the six combinations into 36, the total number of combinations, we find the odds of rolling a 7 on any one roll is one in six (6/36 reduced to 1/6), or equivalently, 5 to 1. The chart below shows the odds of rolling a number on any one roll.

ODDS OF ROLLING THE NUMBERS			
	Combinations	Chance of Being Rolled	Expressed in Odds
2 or 12	1	1/36	35 to 1
3 or 11	2	2/36	17 to 1
4 or 10	3	3/36	11 to 1
5 or 9	4	4/36	8 to 1
6 or 8	5	5/36	6.2 to 1
7	6	6/36	5 to 1

The listing of two numbers together such as the 5 or 9 is done to abbreviate. The odds apply to either the 5 or the 9, not to both together.

Understanding The Terminology
Correct Odds, House Payoff and Edge

The house advantage or edge is the difference between the player's chances of winning the bet, called the **correct odds**, and the casino's actual payoff, called the **house payoff** or simply, the **payoff**. For example, the correct odds of rolling a 7 are 5 to 1. Since the house will pay only 4 to 1 should the 7 be thrown, they maintain an edge of 16.67 percent on this wager.

To play craps intelligently and better understand the choices available to him, the player must first and foremost be aware of the house advantage on every bet he will ever make, for that, in the long run, determines the player's chances of winning.

Five for One, Five to One

Sometimes on a layout you will see payoffs represented as *for* instead of the usual *to*, such as 9 for 1. This means that the payoff will be a total of nine units, eight winning chips along with your original bet, a house subterfuge to increase its edge over the player. The usual 9 to 1 payoff means nine winning chips and your original bet returned, for a total of 10 units.

Beware of any payoffs with the *for*. As a rule, this type of bet has poor odds to begin with and we wouldn't want to make it anyway, with the to or the for.

The Bets

Craps offers the player a wide variety of possible wagers, with each bet having its own characteristics and inherent odds. Some bets, which we will refer to as **sequence bets**, may require a series of rolls before the outcome is determined, while the outcome of others, called **one-roll bets**, is determined on the very next roll.

Some bets are paid off by the house at **even-money**, for every dollar wagered, the player wins a dollar, while other bets have payoffs as high as 30 to 1. However, as you will see, generally the higher the house payoff, the worse the odds are for the player.

And the odds of the bet, that is, the mathematical house return on every dollar wagered, is the most important concern of the player. To have the best chances of winning, the player must avoid all the sucker bets, and make only the best bets available to him.

A. MOST ADVANTAGEOUS BETS

The bets presented in this section have the lowest built-in house edge of all the bets in craps, and one bet, the free-odds bet, gives the house no advantage whatsoever. These bets, the pass, don't pass, come, don't come and the free-odds bets, are the most important bets a player can make, and are the foundation of our winning strategies.

The Line Bets - Pass and Don't Pass

These even-money bets can only be made on a come-out roll, before a point is established, and give the house an edge of only 1.4 percent. And when backed by the free-odds wagers, the overall house edge drops to 0.8 percent in a single odds game and to 0.6 percent in a double odds game.

Pass Line

Players making pass line bets are wagering that the dice will **pass**, or win, and are called right bettors. Pass line bets are also referred to as **front line bets**, and are made by placing the wager in the area marked *pass line*.

On the come-out roll, a throw of a 7 or 11 is an automatic winner for the pass line bettors while the throw of a craps, a 2, 3 or 12 is an automatic loser. If any other number is thrown, the 4, 5, 6, 8, 9 or 10, then that number is established as the point, and the shooter must repeat the point before a 7 is thrown for pass line bettors to win. The throw of a 7 before the point repeats is a loser for pass line bettors, called **sevening-out**, and the dealers will collect the lost bets.

Once the point is established, only the 7 and the point number affect the pass line bettor. All other numbers have no bearing on the bet and can be considered neutral throws.

Let's look at three progressions to see how the pass line bet works.

1. The come-out roll is a 5, establishing 5 as the point. The following roll is a 2, a neutral throw, for a point has already been established. An 8 is then thrown, still having no bearing on the outcome, and then a 5. The point was repeated, or made, before the seven was thrown, and the pass line bettors win their bets.

2. The come-out roll is a 7, an automatic winner for the pass line bettors, and they are paid off by the dealers. Since the progression has been completed, the following roll will be another come-out roll.

3. Here is a losing proposition. The come-out roll is a 9, establishing 9 as the point. The shooter then rolls a 6, then a 12, and then an 11. All three rolls are neutral since a point is already established. The following roll is a 7. Since the 7 was rolled before the 9, the shooter's point repeated, pass line bettors lose and the dealer will collect their bets. A new come-out roll will ensue.

PASS LINE CAPSULATED

Payoff: Even - Money   **House Edge**: 1.4%
Automatic Winners - 7 or 11 on the come-out roll.
Automatic Losers - 2,3, or 12 on the come-out roll.
If a point is established on the come-out roll, the pass line bettor:
Wins - by the point repeating before the 7 is thrown.
Loses - by the roll of a 7 before the point repeats.

Don't Pass

Players betting don't pass are called wrong bettors, and are betting against the dice. Don't pass bets are also called **back line bets** and are made by placing the wager in the area marked *don't pass*.

On the come-out roll, a throw of a 2 or 3 is an automatic winner for the don't pass bettors, while a 7 or an 11 is an automatic loser. The 12 is a standoff between the back line bettor and the house. (In some casinos the 2 is the standoff and the 12 is the automatic winner. Either way it makes no difference, for there is only one way to throw the 2 or 12.)

Once the point is established, don't pass bettors win by having the 7 thrown before the shooter repeats his point, and lose by the point being repeated before the shooter sevens-out. Here are some progressions to illustrate the don't pass wager.

1. The come-out roll is a 6, establishing 6 as the point. The following rolls are a 5 (no bearing on the outcome), then a 12 (still no bearing) and then a 7. Since the 7 was rolled before the 6 repeated, don't pass bettors win.

2. The come-out roll is a 3, an automatic winner for the don't pass bettor.

3. The come-out roll is a 4, establishing 4 as the point. A 3 is then rolled (neutral), and then a 4, a loss for the back line bettors since the point repeated before the 7 was rolled.

DON'T PASS LINE CAPSULATED

Payoff: Even-Money   **House Edge**: 1.4%
Automatic Winners - 2 (or 12) and 3 on the come-out roll.
Automatic Losers - 7 or 11 on the come-out roll.
Standoff - 12 (or 2 in some casinos) on the come-out roll.
If a point is established on the come-out roll don't pass bettors:
Win - by the throw of a 7 before the point repeats.
Lose - by the point repeating before the 7 thrown.

Come and Don't Come Bets

The come and don't come bets work according to the same rules as the pass and don't pass bets except that the come and don't come bets can only be made after a point is established. The line bets, on the other hand, can only be placed on a come-out roll, before a point is established.

The advantage of these bets are that they allow the player to cover more points as a right or wrong bettor at the same low 1.4% house edge. And like the line bets, the overall house edge drops to 0.8% when backed by single odds, and 0.6% when backed by double odds.

Come bets are made by putting the chips into the area marked *come*, while don't come bets are placed in the *don't come* box. Won bets are paid at even-money

Come Bets

We follow the play of the come bets just as we would with the pass line bets. A 7 or 11 on the first throw following the placing of the bet is an automatic winner, while a 2, 3 or 12 in an automatic loser.

Any other number thrown, the 4, 5, 6, 8, 9 or 10, becomes the point for that come bet, called the **come point**, and the dealer will move the bet from the come box into the large rectangular numbered boxes located at the top of the layout to mark the come point.

Once the come point is established, the bet is won if the come point repeats before the shooter sevens-out, and lost if the 7 is rolled before the point repeats. All other throws are inconsequential on this bet. Won bets will be paid off and removed from the layout.

The bettor can make continuous come bets until all the points are covered if he desires. Thus, it is possible for the throw of a 7 to simultaneously wipe out several established come bets. On the other hand, a hot shooter rolling point numbers can bring frequent winners to the aggressive come bettor.

Let's follow a progression where the right bettor makes both pass line and come bets.

Player Bets: $5 on the pass line.
The come-out roll is a 5, establishing 5 as the point.
Player Bets: $5 on the come.
The roll is an 8, establishing 8 as the come point. The dealer moves the $5 come bet to the rectangular box marked 8 to indicate that 8 is the point for that come bet. In effect, the player has two points working, the 5 and the 8, and decides to make another come bet.
Player Bets: $5 on the come.
The roll is a 6. The dealer moves this new come bet to the 6, the come point for this bet. The other two points are not affected by this roll.

Player Bets: The player has three points established, the 5, 6 and 8, and makes no more bets at this time.

The roll is a 5, a $5 winner on the pass line. It is paid off and removed from the layout, leaving the player with two come points, the 6 and 8.

Player Bets: $5 on the pass line. Since the next roll is a come-out roll and the player wants to cover another point, he bets the pass.

The roll is a 10, establishing 10 as the point.

Player Bets: No additional bets at this time.

The roll is a 2 (neutral on all established bets), then an 8 is thrown, a $5 winner on the come point of 8, and that bet is paid off and removed. The following roll is not a come-out roll, for the come point was made, not the pass line point, the 10.

Player Bets: Wishing to establish a third point, $5 is bet on the come.

The roll is a 7. While the 7 is a $5 winner for the new come bet, it is a loser for the two established points, and they are removed from the layout by the dealer.

The roll of the 7 cleared the layout, and the following roll will be a new come-out roll.

Don't Come Bets

Like the don't pass wager, a 7 or 11 on the first roll following a don't come bet is an automatic loser and the 2 and 3 are automatic winners, 12 being a standoff. (In casinos where the 2 is a standoff and the 12 a winner on the don't pass, the same will hold true for the don't come bets.)

If a 4, 5, 6, 8, 9 or 10 is thrown, establishing a point for the don't come bet, the dealer will move the chips behind the appropriate point box to mark the don't come point. Don't come bettors now win by having the 7 thrown before that point is made. Other numbers, as with the don't pass bets, are neutral rolls. Only the 7 and the come point determine the bet.

Let's follow a progression where the wrong bettor makes both don't pass and don't come bets.

Player Bets: $5 on the don't pass.

The roll is a 10, establishing 10 as the point.

Player Bets: Continuing to bet against the dice, the player now makes a $5 bet on the don't come.

The roll is a 2, a $5 winner on the new don't come bet, and that bet is paid off and removed.

Player Bets: $5 on the don't come.

The roll is a 6. The dealer moves the bet from the don't come area to the upper section of the box numbered 6 to indicate that 6 is the point for this don't come bet. The player now has two points working, the 10 and 6, and decides to establish a third point.

Player Bets: $5 on the don't come.

The roll is a 10, a $5 loser on the don't pass since the point repeated before a 7 was thrown. The don't come point of 6 is unaffected, and the new don't come bet is moved to the 10 box, since 10 is the come point for the new don't come wager.

Player Bets: The player decides not to make any more bets, being content with his bets on points 6 and 10, unwilling to place more bets on the layout. If he were to make another bet against the dice, he would bet don't pass for the next throw is a come-out roll.

The roll is 7, winner on both established come points; they are paid off and removed. The next roll will be a new come-out.

Free-Odds Bets

Though not indicated anywhere on the layout, the free-odds bets are the best bets a player can make at craps, and are an indispensable part of the winning strategies. The **free-odds** bets are so named, for, unlike the other bets at craps, the house has no advantage over the player. Hence, the term *free-odds*.

However, to make a free-odds bet, the player must first have placed a pass, don't pass, come or don't come wager, and in a sense, is backing those bets, for the free-odds bet can only be made in conjunction with these wagers. When backed by single odds, the overall odds of the pass, don't pass, come and don't come bets drop to 0.8%, and where double odds are allowed and utilized, the overall odds drop to only 0.6% against the player. These are the best odds a player can get at craps.

Free-Odds - Pass Line

Once a point is established on the come-out roll, the pass line bettor is allowed to make an additional bet, called a **free-odds bet**, that his point will be repeated before a 7 is thrown. This bet is paid off at the correct odds, giving the house no edge, and is made by placing the chips behind the pass line wager and just outside the pass line area.

PASS LINE AND FREE-ODDS BET

When single odds are allowed, the player can bet up to the amount wagered on his pass line bet, and in certain instances he can bet more. And when double odds are allowed, the player can bet twice his pass line bet as a free-odds wager.

Though the player can bet less than the permissible amount on the free-odds wager and is allowed to reduce or remove this bet at any time, he should never do so, for the free-odds bets are the most advantageous bets in craps, and should be fully taken advantage of.

Following is a table which shows the correct odds of the point repeating before a 7 is thrown and the house payoff. Note how the house takes no percentage advantage on these bets since the payoff is identical to the correct odds.

ODDS OF POINT REPEATING BEFORE A SEVEN		
Point Number	**Correct Odds**	**House Payoff**
4 or 10	2 to 1	2 to 1
5 or 9	3 to 2	3 to 2
6 or 8	6 to 5	6 to 5

The odds presented in this table are easy to figure for the only numbers that affect the free-odds bet are the point number, which is a winner, and the 7, which is a loser. All other throws are inconsequential.

There are three ways to roll a winning 4 or 10, and six ways to roll a losing 7, thus 2 to 1 is the correct odds on points 4 or 10. A 5 or 9 can be rolled four ways each against the same six ways of rolling a 7, thus the correct odds are 3 to 2 against the 5 or 9. A 6 or 8 can be made by five combinations, and again, since there are six ways to roll a losing 7, the correct odds are 6 to 5 against the 6 or 8.

Special Allowances - Single Odds Game

To make the payoffs easier, most casinos will allow the player to make a single odds bet greater than his pass line (or come) bet in the following instances.

a. With a pass line bet such as $5 or $25 and the point being a 5 or 9, the casino will allow the player to make an odds bet of $6 and $30 respectively behind the line. If the bet is won, the 3 to 2 payoff on the $6 free-odds bet would be $9, and on the $30 bet, $45.

If the player wasn't allowed this special allowance, he would be unable to get the full correct odds on the $5 or $25 free-odds bet since the $1 or more minimum craps tables do not deal in half dollars.

b. With a three unit bet such as $3 or $15, and the point being a 6 or 8, the casino will allow a five unit free-odds bet behind the line. This allows the player to take full advantage of the 6 to 5 payoff on points 6 and 8. In the above examples, $5 and $25 free-odds bets would be permitted, and if won, would pay the player $6 and $30 respectively.

A three unit bet translates to $3 for the $1 bettor, $15 for the $5 bettor, $30 for the $10 bettor, and so on. Any bet that can be divisible by three can be considered a three unit bet and be backed by the special allowance single odds bets.

A $30 bet on the pass line can be backed by only $30 if the point is a 5 or 9 since the 3 to 2 payoff can be made on this amount, but if the point is a 6 or an 8, can be backed by $50 (five unit special allowance).

If uncertain about the amounts you are allowed to back your pass line bet with, check with the dealer, and he will let you know the permissible wager.

THREE UNIT BET · SINGLE ODDS SPECIAL ALLOWANCE

Basic Three Unit Bet	6 or 8 as Point
$3	$5 ($6)
$15	$25 ($30)
$30	$50 ($60)
$45	$75 ($90)
$75	$125 ($150)
$300	$500 ($600)

The first column, Basic Three Unit Bet, is what our standard pass and come bet is, while the second column shows the special allowance permitted when the point is 6 or 8. Numbers in parenthesis indicate the amount paid if the single odds bet is won.

Note that this is only a partial listing of the basic three unit bets, and many more are possible for the player that wants to bet in different ranges than shown.

No special allowances are allowed when the 4 or 10 are points for they are easily paid off at 2 to 1, no matter the amount wagered.

On bets smaller than $5 with the point being a 6 or 8, single odds bets will not be able to receive the full 6 to 5 payoff, and will be paid off at even-money only, for again, the craps tables do not stock units smaller than $1 chips.

On bets larger than $5 but in unequal multiples of $5, the free-odds bet will be paid to the highest multiple of $5 at 6 to 5, and the remainder will be paid at even-money. Thus, a $12 odds bet on the 8 will yield a payoff of only $14, $12 on the first $10 (at 6 to 5), and even-money on the unequal remainder of $2.

When the free-odds bets do not receive their full payoff, the bet works to the disadvantage of the player. Therefore, we recommend that pass and come wagers be made in multiples of $3, for this allows the player to take full advantage of the special allowances and lowers the overall house edge for the single odds game below 0.8 percent.

Double Odds - Pass Line

Double odds work just like single odds except that the player is allowed to bet double his pass line bet as a free-odds wager. If $10 was bet on the pass line and a 5 was established as the point, the double odds game would allow the player to bet $20 as a free-odds wager and receive the same correct 3 to 2 odds on that point, instead of only being allowed a $10 free-odds bet as in the single odds game.

When combined with the pass line bet, double odds brings the overall house edge down to only 0.6%, the best odds a player can get at craps. Therefore, when there is a choice of playing a single or double odds game, choose the latter, for you should take advantage of every favorable option allowed.

If you're uncertain whether double odds are allowed, just ask the dealer, and he will let you know.

Special Allowances - Double Odds Game

One special allowance to keep in mind on the double odds game. With a two unit bet on the pass line and the point a 6 or 8, double odds casinos will allow the player to wager five units as a free-odds bet. Thus, with a $10 bet (two $5 unit chips), and the point a 6 or 8, a $25 double odds bet would be allowed. If won, the 6 to 5 payoff would bring $30 in winnings (six $5 chips, an easier payoff for the casino).

We recommend that players bet in multiples of two for it permits us to take advantage of the special five unit allowance when the point is a 6 or an 8. Any bet that can be divisible by two can be considered a two unit bet and be backed by the special five unit allowance if the point is a 6 or an 8.

TWO UNIT BET · DOUBLE ODDS SPECIAL ALLOWANCE

Basic Two Unit Bet	6 or 8 as Point	4, 5, 9 or 10 as Point
$2	$5 ($6)	$4
$10	$25 ($30)	$20
$20	$50 ($60)	$40
$30	$75 ($90)	$60
$50	$125 ($150)	$100
$200	$500 ($600)	$400

*The Basic Two Unit Bet is our standard pass and come bet. The third column is the normal double odds allowance for points 4, 5, 9 and 10.

Numbers in parenthesis indicate the amount paid if the double odds bet is won at 6 to 5 payoff). Other two unit bets than the ones shown in this chart are possible.

Let's see how this would work.

$15 is bet on the pass line, and the come-out roll is a 6. Taking advantage of the special five unit allowance, $25 is wagered as a free-odds bet behind the line. (This bet is placed by the player.)

If the shooter throws a 7 before the point repeats, the player loses the $15 pass bet and the $25 free-odds bet, but should the point be rolled before the 7, $15 will be won on the pass line bet and $30 on the odds bet ($25 paid at 6 to 5).

If the game was a double odds game, the player could have backed the $15 pass bet with a $30 free-odds bet. And if the point was a 6, the free-odds bet would pay $36 if won ($30 at 6 to 5 = $30).

Free-Odds - Don't Pass

Once the point is established, don't pass bettors are allowed to make a free-odds bet that a 7 will be rolled before the point repeats. The bet is paid off at correct odds, the house enjoying no edge, and is made by placing the free-odds bet next to the don't pass wager in the don't pass box.

DON'T PASS AND FREE-ODDS BET

Since the odds favor the don't pass bettor once the point is established, there being more ways to roll a winning 7 than any point number, the don't pass bettor must *lay odds*, that is, put more money on the free-odds bet than he will win.

Let's say the point is a 4. The don't pass bettor's chances of winning the bet are now 2 to 1 in his favor. There are only three ways to roll a 4, a loser, against the six combinations of a 7, a winner. Therefore, the don't pass bettor must bet $20 to win $10 when the point is a 4 (or 10).

(On the other side of the bet, pass line bettors are receiving 2 to 1 odds, for their bet is the underdog, having only three winning chances against six losing combinations.)

To lay odds as a don't pass bettor, the allowable free-odds bet is determined by the *payoff*, not the original bet. Using the above example of a $10 bet on the don't pass with 4 established as the point, the don't pass bettor in a single odds game is allowed up to a $10 win on the free-odds bet. Since the odds are 2 to 1 in his favor, the don't pass bettor must lay $20 to win $10. If it was a double odds game, meaning the player could win $20 on his original $10 bet, than at 1 to 2 odds, $40 would have to be staked for a potential win of $20.

The odds the don't pass bettor must lay are exactly opposite the odds pass line bettors take on the same points. Below is a table showing the free-odds bets from the wrong bettors position.

ODDS OF ROLLING A SEVEN BEFORE POINT REPEATS

Point Number	Correct Odds	House Payoff
4 or 10	1 to 2	1 to 2
5 or 9	2 to 3	2 to 3
6 or 8	5 to 6	5 to 6

Note how the house has no percentage advantage on these bets since the payoff is identical to the correct odds.

Like the free-odds bets for right bettors, don't pass free-odds wagers can be removed or reduced at any time, but since these are the player's best bets, it should not be done.

Let's look at a quick example to see how the free-odds bet works for the don't pass bettor.

$10 is bet on the don't pass, and the come-out roll is a 9. The wrong bettor bets $15 behind the line as a free-odds bet, the maximum allowed in a single odds game. He stands to win $10 on the free-odds bet if the 7 is rolled before the 9 repeats, in addition to $10 on his don't pass bet.

Should the point be rolled before the 7, the $15 free-odds bet and $10 don't pass bet will be lost. If double odds were allowed, $20 would be the maximum allowable free-odds win. At 2 to 3 odds, the don't pass bettor would have to lay $30 to win $20.

Wrong Bettors Special Allowances - Single Odds Game

The casino makes a special provision for don't pass bettors when the point is a 5 or 9 and an odd figure such as $5 is wagered. Since the craps tables do not deal in half dollars, the player is allowed to make a free-odds bet of $9 behind the line in this instance, and if the bet is won, will get paid $6 ($9 at 2 to 3).

Whenever the point is 5 or 9 and the original bet is unequal, the house will allow the player to bet more than the straight single odds. Ask the dealer the exact amount allowed in those instances; the rules may vary from casino to casino.

Free-Odds: Come and Don't Come

Once a come point is established, the bettor can take odds (or lay odds for don't come bettors) and get the same advantageous payoffs, 2-1 on points 4 and 10 (1-2 for wrong bettors), 3-2 on the 5 and 9 (2-3 for wrong bettors), and 6-5 on the 6 and 8 (5-6 for wrong bettors).

The house has no advantage on these free-odds wagers, and like the line bets, the overall house edge on the come or don't come bets teamed with single odds drops to 0.8%, and with double odds, to 0.6%.

The same special allowances apply for the come bets. In a single odds game; a three unit bet can be backed by five units if the point is 6 or 8, while a free-odds bet on points 5 and 9 can be backed by additional chips if the original come bet is uneven. In the double odds game, a two unit wager can be backed by five units if the point is a 6 or 8.

However, the odds bets on the come and don't come bets are placed differently than line bets. Rather than being made by the player, the odds bets are given to the dealer with the instruction, "odds on the come," or "odds on the don't come."

The dealer will place the odds bet in the appropriate box atop the come point, but slightly offset, so that the odds bet can be differentiated from the come bet.

COME, DON'T COME AND FREE-ODDS BETS

4	5	SIX	8	NINE	10

don't come and free-odds bet

come and free-odds bet

COME

Dealer will place free-odds bet atop original bet but offset to distinguish from come or don't come bet.

The only other difference is with the come bet. While the come bet itself is working on the come-out roll, the odds bet on that come bet is not. Let's say the player had $15 bet on the come point of 6 and had that bet backed by $25 free-odds. A come-out roll of a 7 would of course be a loser for the $15 come bet, as that bet is always working, but since the free-odds bet was off, the $25 single odds wager would be returned to the player.

If a 6 was rolled instead, a winner for the come bet, the player would only win the $15, and be returned the $25 odds bet.

Though it is standard procedure for the free-odds bet backing the come wager to be off on the come-out roll, the player can request the odds bet to be "on" by informing the dealer that the "odds are on for the come bet," and then, of course, the odds bet is subject to the normal rules.

The odds on the don't come bets, as with the pass and don't pass wagers, are always working.

Let's look at some betting sequences to illustrate how the free-odds bets on come and don't come wagers work in conjunction with the line bets.

Right Bettors (Pass and Come Bets)

Player A is a right bettor, he likes betting with the dice. His standard betting unit is $15 (3 units of $5) and this allows him to take advantage of the special free-odds allowances when the points are 5 and 9, and 6 and 8.

Single Odds Game

Player Bets: $15 on the pass line.

The come-out roll is an 8, establishing 8 as the point.

Player Bets: $25 odds bet behind the 8 (5 unit special allowance bet). $15 on the come.

The roll is a 4, establishing the 4 as a come point. Dealer moves Player A's bet from the come line to the box marked 4.

Player Bets: $15 odds bet on the 4. The dealer places the wager on the come bet but at a tilt to show it's an odds bet. Player A decides to make another $15 come bet.

The roll is an 11. The new come bet is an automatic winner for $15. The other bets are unaffected.

Player Bets: $15 more on the come.

The roll is a 4, a winner on that come point. Player A wins $15 on the come bet and $30 (2 to 1 payoff) on the free-odds bet. The new $15 come bet is moved to the place box of 4, to indicate that it's a come point.

Player Bets: $15 odds on the come point of 4.
                $15 more on the come.

Player A now has a $15 pass line bet backed by $25 odds on the point of 8, a $15 come bet backed by $15 odds on the point of 4, and a new $15 come wager.

The roll is an 8, a winner on the pass line. Player A gets paid $15 on the pass line bet and $30 on his odds bet (6 to 5 odds) and these bet are removed from the layout. The new come bet is moved to the 8 box, the come point for that last bet. A new come-out roll will follow since the point was made.

Player Bets: $15 on the passline.

$25 odds bet on his come point of 8.

The roll is a 7, a $15 winner on the new passline bet, but a loser for the two come points of 4 and 8. Since the odds bets were off on the come-out roll, the $15 odds on the 4 and $25 odds on the 8 are returned to the player, leaving the player with only a $30 loss on the come points themselves, but a $15 winner on pass line bet.

Player A won $120 in bets and lost only $30 for a net win of $90.

Wrong Bettors (Don't Pass and Don't Come Bets)

Player B is a wrong bettor, he prefers to bet against the dice. His standard betting unit is $20 because it's easier to figure the laying of odds with bets in multiples of $10.

Single Odds Game

Player Bets: $20 on the don't pass.

The come-out roll is a 6, establishing the 6 as a point.

Player Bets: $24 free-odds bet behind the 6 (laying 5 to 6 odds). $20 on the don't come.

The roll is a 3, craps, a winner on the new don't come bet. The other bets are unaffected. The winning bet is removed from the layout.

Player Bets: $20 on the don't come again.

The roll is a 10, and the dealer moves the don't come bet above the box marked 10 to indicate the come point for the don't come bet.

Player Bets: $40 free-odds on the come point of 10 (laying 1 to 2 odds). The dealer places the odds bet atop the original bet but at a tilt so the bet can be a distinguished from the don't come bet. $20 bet in the don't come box.

The roll is a 9, establishing 9 as the come point for the new don't come bet. Player B now has bets against three points, the 4, 9 and 10. The roll of any of those point numbers is a loss for

Player B on that particular number rolled, while the throw of a 7 will be a winner on all.

Player Bets: $30 free-odds on the 9, and decides not to make any more come bets.

The roll is a 6, a loser on the don't pass. Player B loses that $20 bet and the $24 odds bet behind it. Since the point was made, the next roll is a new come-out roll. All bets for the wrong bettor will be working.

Player Bets: $20 on the don't pass.

The roll is an 8, establishing 8 as the come point on the new don't pass bet.

Player Bets: $24 odds on the come point of 8, and decides not to make any further bets at this time.

The roll is a 7, a simultaneous winner on all the don't pass, don't come and odds bets. Player B wins $20 per wrong bet plus the $20 odds behind each bet for a $40 win per point. With three points covered, the total win on that 7 was $120.

Player B won $140 in bets and lost only $44 for a net win of $96.

THE REST OF THE BETS

With the exception of the place bet of 6 and 8, none of the bets presented in this section, which include the remainder of the bets possible at craps, are recommended for play. The house edge over the player on these bets is too large to be incorporated into a winning strategy, and the bettor making these bets will soon find himself drained of significant portions of his bankroll.

In fact, the majority of bets listed here are sucker bets, wagers that give the house an edge so exorbitant that the player stands no more than a slim chance of winning. Just because a bet is exotic looking and available doesn't mean that it should be bet on. To do well at craps, all bets with prohibitive odds must be avoided.

The bets listed in this section are discussed anyway so that the player has a full understanding of all the bets possible at craps, and so that the player is never tempted to make these poor wagers.

Place Bets

The **place bets** are among the most popular wagers in craps, and are a bet that a particular point number, whichever is wagered on, the 4, 5, 6, 8, 9 or 10, is rolled before a 7 is thrown. The player can make as many place bets as he wants, and some players do, covering all the numbers with place bets.

However, this is not recommended strategy, for as we will see, with the exception of the place bets of 6 and 8, the other place bets, the 4, 5, 9 and 10, are poor wagers, and will have no role in our winning strategies.

Place bets are made by giving the dealer the desired wager, and telling him, for example, "to place the 9," or any such statement that indicates the player wants to make a place bet on the 9.

Though place bets can be made at any time, they are not working, or are "**off**" on the come-out roll, unless the player requests them to be "**on**" (working).

The player can also request his place bets to be off for a limited series of throws, and may increase, reduce or remove them at any time prior to a roll.

HOUSE PAYOFFS ON PLACE BETS			
Bet	**Payoff**	**Correct Odds**	**House Advantage**
4 or 10	9 to 5	2 to 1	6.67%
5 or 9	7 to 5	3 to 2	4.00%
6 or 8	7 to 6	6 to 5	1.52%

To get the full payoffs on the place bets, the player should make his bets in the proper multiples. On place bets of 4 and 10, and 5 and 9, the bets should be made in multiples of $5 since the payoffs are 9 to 5 and 7 to 5 respectively. On the 6 and 8, the bet should be in multiples of $6 (7 to 6 payoff).

Excess bets in unequal multiples will be paid off at even-money only and work to the disadvantage of the player. For example, a $10 bet on the 6 will be paid as follows. The first $6 will get the full 7 to 6 odds for $7, while the remaining $4 gets paid at even-money, or $4, for a total win of $11. The last $4, paid off at only even-money, is a terrible payoff, and makes the entire bet a poor one.

Unless the player makes the place bets of 6 or 8 in multiples of $6 to insure full payoffs, the bet should not be make. Also, bets less than $5 on the 4, 5, 9 and 10, and less than $6 on the 6 and 8, will be paid of at only even-money.

To summarize, do not make place bets of 4 or 10, or 5 and 9, for the house edge is too high.

The place bets of 6 and 8 have playable odds of 1.52 percent and can be used in an aggressive maximize gain strategy, though some players may prefer to stick with the line, come and don't come bets backed by free-odds, the best bets of all.

Big 6 and Big 8

The **Big 6** and **Big 8** are bets that a particular number bet on, the 6 or 8, is thrown before a 7 is rolled. These bets can be made at any time, and are bet by putting the wager into the box marked Big 6 or Big 8.

These bets work just like the place bets of 6 and 8 except that the house only pays even-money on a won bet as opposed to the 7 to 6 payoff he would receive had he made the superior place bet on 6 or 8 instead.

Let's look at the correct odds. There are five ways to throw a winning 6 (or 8, if that is bet), and six ways to throw a losing 7, making the correct odds 6 to 5. The house pays only even-money on a won bet in Nevada, giving them a whopping 9.90% advantage. This makes the Big 6 and Big 8 terrible bets in Nevada, especially when they are compared to the 1.52% odds of the 6 and 8 place bets.

(The Big 6 and Big 8 bets were formerly offered in Atlantic City and were paid off at 7 to 6, like the place bets of 6 and 8. However, the New Jersey gaming commission approved the removal of the Big 6 and Big 8 wager, and they are no longer offered there.)

Buying the 4 or 10

This is an option the casino gives the player when betting on a place number, and though it reduces the odds on the 4 or 10 from 6.67 percent to 4.76 percent, the buy bet is still a poor one and should not be made.

But here's how it works.

To **buy** the 4 or 10, you must give the house a 5% commission on your bet. Once you've bought a number, the house will pay off the bet at the correct odds. Thus, your payoff will be 2 to 1, the correct odds, rather than 9 to 5 as is usually the payoff for these place bets.

A five percent commission on $20 would be $1. For any bet smaller than $20, the commission would still be $1 since the craps tables generally carry no smaller units. In these cases, the house edge on your buy bet would be much larger than 4.76 percent. If you buy the 4 and 10 at $10 each, for a total of $20, the commission would only be 5 percent of the two bet total, or $1.

Like the place bets, buy bets are not working on the come-out roll, unless you instruct the dealer that the bet is on. They are also similar to the place bets in that they can be increased, reduced or removed at any time prior to the roll. Note that an increased buy bet is subject to the 5 percent commission on the additional wager.

Some casinos will keep the 5 percent commission if you decide to remove an established bet or charge an additional 5 percent if you win your bet and decide to let it ride.

Buying the 5, 6, 8, 9

Theoretically, you can buy these numbers as well, but since the commission is 5 percent, and the house edge on all these place bets is less than that, there is no advantage in buying these numbers.

Lay Bets

The **lay bet** is the opposite of a buy bet, and is used by wrong bettors who are wagering that the 7 will be thrown before the point or points they bet against is rolled. While the bet is paid off at correct odds, it costs the bettor 5 percent commission on the projected win to get this payoff, and is therefore, a poor bet.

Lay bets, which can be bet at any time, are made by giving the dealer your chips along with the required 5 percent commission on the projected win. The dealer will place the bet above the point number covered (in the area where the don't come bets are placed) and place a buy button on top to distinguish the lay bet.

To receive the full value on the lay bet of 4 or 10, the bettor would have to wager at least $40 to win $20 (1 to 2 odds). The 5 percent commission on the projected win of $20 would be $1. Any bet smaller than the $40 lay bet on the 4 or 10 would still be charged the minimum $1 commission (craps tables do not generally deal in currency smaller than $1 chips) making the house edge greater than the 2.44% advantage already built into this wager.

The 5 and 9 lay bets would require a minimum wager of $30 for the player to get the maximum value. The potential $20 win (laying odds at 2 to 3) would be charged $1 commission. Again, a bet smaller than the projected win of $20 would still be charged the minimum $1 commission, and raise the overall house edge on the bet.

The 6 and 8 bets would require a wager of $24 at 5 to 6 odds on a projected win of $20 to get full value from the commission.

HOUSE ALLOWANCE ON LAY BETS

Points	House Advantage
4 or 10	2.44%
5 or 9	3.23%
6 or 8	4.00%

The lay bet can be added to, reduced or removed altogether at any time.

The player is advised not to make lay bets. We get much better odds with the wagers in the previous section, "The Most Advantageous Bets."

Field Bet

The **field bet** is a one roll wager that the next throw of the dice will be a number listed in the field box, the 2, 3, 4, 9, 10, 11 or 12. If one of the numbers not listed is rolled, the 5, 6, 7 or 8, then the bet is lost.

The field bet can be made at any time and is done by placing the wager in the area marked "Field".

At first glance, the bet seems attractive. There are seven winning numbers listed in the field box, and two of these numbers, the 2 and the 12, pay double if they are rolled. In some casinos, the 2 or 12 pays triple. The other winning numbers, the 3, 4, 9, 10 and 11 pay even-money. But let's look closer.

The losing numbers, the 5, 6, 7 and 8, are the most frequently rolled numbers, and make up a total of 20 losing combinations. (Four ways to roll a 5, five ways to roll a 6, fives ways to make an 8, and six ways to roll a 7 = 20). Adding up all the other numbers gives us a total of only 16 winning combinations. The 2 to 1 bonus on the 2 and the 12 is actually worth one more combination each for a total of 18 winning units, and where the 12 (or 2) is paid at 3 to 1, we get a total of 19 winners.

However, there are 20 combinations that will beat us, giving the house an edge of 5.55% when the 2 and 12 are paid at 2 to 1, and 2.7% when one is paid at 2 to 1 and the other at 3 to 1.

In either case, the house advantage is much larger than other bets available at craps, and the player should not make field bets.

Proposition, or Center Bets

The **proposition**, or **center bets**, as they are sometimes called, are located at the center of the layout, and are made by either giving the chips to the dealer who will pass them along to the stickman, or, as with the hardways bet or craps-eleven bet, can sometimes be tossed directly to the stickman.

The central area of the layout is under the complete domain of the stickman, and though he will physically handle the placing and removing of bets in this area, it is with the dealer that the player will generally make his bets and receive his payoffs.

The proposition bets are the worst bets a player can make at craps and should never be made. The house advantage rages as high as 16.67 percent on some of these wagers. However, these bets are listed and their odds explained so that the reader will be fully conversant with all the wagers possible at craps.

Any Seven

This bet, which is that the following roll of the dice will be a 7, is paid off by the house at 4 to 1 (5 for 1), and is among the worst bets a player can make.

There are six ways to throw a 7 out of 36 possible combinations, making the odds one in six of throwing a 7 on any one roll, or equivalently, 5 to 1. Since the player is paid off at only 4 to 1, the house maintains an exorbitant edge of 16.67 percent over the player.

Don't even make this bet in your dreams.

Any Craps

This bet, located at the bottom of the center layout and along its sides, is a bet that the following roll will be a craps - a 2, 3 or 12.

There are four ways to roll a winner. The 2 and 12 account for one way each, while there are two ways to roll a three. The other 32 combinations are losers, making the correct odds 8 to 1. The house only pays 7 to 1; an 11.1 percent house edge.

2 or 12

This is a bet that the next roll of the dice will come up a 2, or a 12 if you bet that number, and is paid off by the house at 30 to 1.

Of the 36 possible combinations of the dice, there is only one way of rolling a 2 or a 12, making the correct odds 35 to 1 against rolling either number. With only a 30 to 1 payoff, the house enjoys a hefty 13.69 percent advantage.

Sometimes a casino may only pay off at 30 for 1 (29 to 1), giving them an edge of 16.67 percent. This should make no difference to us for we won't go near that bet in either case.

3 or 11

This is a wager that the following roll will be a 3, or an 11, whichever you place your money on, and the house payoff is 15 to 1.

Since there are only 2 ways to roll either number out of a possible 36 combinations, the correct odds are 17 to 1 (34 losers, 2 winners). The house edge is 11.1 percent. Where the payoff is 15 for 1 (14 to 1), this edge jumps to 16.67 percent.

Horn Bet

It takes four chips or multiples thereof to makes this bet. The horn bet is a four way bet that the next roll will be a 2, 3, 11 or 12, in effect combining four poor bets together. The house pays off the winning number at the normal payoffs (15 to 1 for the 3 or 11, and 30 to 1 for the 2 or 12), and deducts the other three losing chips from the payoff.

This sucker bet combines four losing wagers for a combined house edge of 11.1 percent, or 16.67 percent with the poorer payoffs discussed earlier. Never make this bet.

Hop Bet

This one roll wager, which does not appear on the layout, is generally made on a combination of the dice not otherwise offered on the one roll bets, such as 2, 3. If the bet is a pair such as 5, 5, the player will get the same payoff as the casino gives on the 2 or 12 bet (30 to 1 or 29 to 1). If the bet is a non-pair, such as 4, 5, which has two ways to win (4, 5; 5, 4), the payoff will be the same as on the 3 or 11 bet (15 to 1 or 14 to 1).

To make a hop bet, give your bet to the dealer or stickman, and call out for example "Hop 54", if the 5, 4 is the hop bet you wish to make.

With the more generous payoff, hop bets give the casino an edge of 13.39%; otherwise the edge is 16.67%. In either case, consider the bet a donation. Never make these bets.

Craps-Eleven (C-E)

The stickman will constantly exhort the player to make this horrendous bet, which is an appeal to bet the Any Craps and 11 bet simultaneously - the circles with the "C" and "E" on the layout. We don't want to go near either bet by itself let alone together. Save your money for the show.

Hardways

Whenever the numbers, 4, 6, 8 or 10 are rolled as doubles, the roll is said to be thrown **hardways** or **hard**. A throw of 22 is said to be *4, the hardway* or *hard 4*, and similarly with 33, 44 and 55 for hard 6, 8 and 10 respectively.

Rolling the 4, 6, 8 and 10 in other combinations is called **easy** such as 6, 4; *10 the easy way*.

Betting hardways is betting that the particular number you

choose comes up hard before it comes up easy or before a 7 is thrown. Let's look at the odds involved.

Hard 4 and Hard 10

There is only one way to throw a hard 4 (22) or hard 10 (55), and eight ways to lose - six ways to roll a seven, and two ways to throw a 4 or 10 the easy way (13, 31, 64 and 46).

The correct odds should be 8 to 1 but the house only pays 7 to 1 for an advantage of 11.1 percent. As with the other center bets, this bet is greatly disadvantageous to the players and should never be made.

Hard 6 and Hard 8

There are a total of 10 losing combinations - the 6 ways to roll a 7, and 4 ways to roll a 6 or an 8 the easy way. (There are a total of 5 ways to throw the 6 or 8, and subtracting the hardway, it leaves 4 other combinations). There is only 1 way to throw the 6 or 8 the hardway.

The correct odds of this hardway bet is 10 to 1 but the house only pays 9 to 1, giving them a commanding edge of 9.09% percent. Don't make this bet.

WINNING STRATEGIES

The underlying principle of all our winning strategies is to make only the best bets available, those with the lowest odds, for this gives us the best chances of winning. When used as we suggest, the overall house edge will be only 0.8 percent in a single odds game and 0.6 percent in a double odds one. We will never make any bet which gives the house an advantage greater than 1.52%, and in fact, the majority of our money will be placed on bets in which the house has no advantage whatso-ever!

We'll play aggressively when winning, so that our winning sessions will be big, and when the dice go against us, we'll reduce our bets or even stop betting altogether. This will maxi-mize our profits and minimize our losses, a smart money management technique that can put winnings in our pocket. And we'll follow the guidelines in the money management chapter, so that once we're winning big, we'll leave big winners.

This winning strategies chapter is divided into two main sections, one for right bettors, and the other for wrong bettors. The reader is reminded that betting right or wrong are equally valid approaches to winning, with equivalent odds, and that the choosing of either method is merely a matter of personal style.

Within each approach, right and wrong betting, we'll present the best strategies for the single and double odds game, and also the best methods for conservative and aggressive bettors to follow.

The **Basic Conservative** methods presented are formulated for the cautious bettor, one who wants to get the best odds possible, but not risk substantial sums, while the **Aggressive** methods are more suited for the heavier bettor, one who is willing to risk more to win more.

The two methods, Basic Conservative and Aggressive, though, are equally powerful. The choice of one or the other depends solely on a player's bankroll considerations and financial temperament.

A. Winning Strategies: Betting with the Dice

In this section we're going to show how the right bettor, using sound principles of play can lower the house edge to the lowest possible figure, 0.8 percent in a single odds game and 0.6 percent in a double odds one.

Using our methods, the majority of the right bettors wagers will be made on the free-odds bets, wagers that the house not only has no advantage whatsoever, but which if won, will pay the player more than he bet!

We'll use only the best bets in our basic strategies - the pass line, come and free-odds wagers, bets which give the player the best chances of winning. Built-in to the strategies are methods to turn winning sessions into big winning sessions without any risk of big losses.

I. Basic Conservative Method - Right Bettors Single Odds Strategy. Our standard bet will be in increments of three units so that we can take advantage of the special free-odds allowances should the points be 6 or 8, whereupon we can back our pass line or come bet by five units, or points 5 or 9, where we can bet extra if the original bet is uneven such as $15, where $20 would be permitted as a free-odds wager.

This allows maximum usage of the free-odds bets, wagers the house has no edge on, and brings the overall house advantage down to the barest minimum possible in a single odds game.

These are the guidelines of our basic conservative strategy:

• We will make three unit pass line and come bets until we have two points established, and back both those bets with the maximum single odds allowed.

• Every time a point repeats, whether as a come or pass line point, we will make another three unit pass line or come bet so that we continue to have two points working for us. If a 2, 3, 11 or 12 declares a winner or a loser on the new pass line or come bet, we will follow with another bet until we get that second point established and then take the maximum single odds allowed on that point.

• If the shooter sevens-out, clearing the board of all bets, we'll begin the progression again with a new pass line bet.

II. Aggressive Method - Right Bettors/Single Odds Strategy. Rather than playing only two points as in the Basic Conservative method, this strategy immediately attempts to establish three points. Otherwise, the strategies are equivalent.

We begin by making a pass line bet. After a point is established, we will make a free-odds bet behind the pass line and a three unit come bet. When the come point is established, we will back that point with the maximum single odds allowed, and place yet another come bet backing that too with free-odds.

Once three points are established, we'll stop betting. Every time a point repeats and is paid off, we'll make another bet, so that at all times during a shoot we strive to have three points working for us. If the come point is made, we'll place another come bet. If it's the pass line, then we'll make another pass line bet. Like always, we'll back all our bets with the maximum single odds allowed.

If the shooter sevens-out, we'll start the sequence over again.

With three points covered, the bettor using this Aggressive method can make a lot of money when the shooter starts rolling numbers, especially when he utilizes our strategies for maximizing winning sessions.

III. Maximizing Profits - Methods For Right Bettors. The way to win big at craps is to play winning streaks aggressively so when points start repeating, our profits will mount quickly. The beauty of these strategies is that, while we give ourselves the opportunity of making huge profits, we never incur the risk of taking a devastating loss, for we'll only increase our bets when winning.

We won't start playing more aggressively until we're ahead by at least 20 units as Basic Conservative players and 25 units as Aggressive players. For $1 bettors making standard bets of $3, that means $20 and $25 respectively, for $5 bettors making standard bets of $15, that means $100 and $125, while for $25 chip players betting $75 a play, it means $500 and $625 respectively.

Theoretically, we could increase our bet size before this time, but that leaves or bankroll vulnerable to bad runs of luck. The concept is to play aggressively on their money, not ours.

We wait until all our points are established and working before increasing our bets.

Let's say we're betting $15 as our basic three unit bet ($5 units), and have already established the pass line point with single odds on the 8, and two come points with single odds on the 5 and 10. We now have three points working for us, the basic plan for the Aggressive Method, and see that we're already ahead 27 units.

Our strategy now works as follows. Every time a point repeats and we get paid off, instead of re-establishing an additional come or pass line point at the basic three unit bet, we increase that bet by three units to six units, and back the new bet with maximum single odds. Thus, on a six unit bet, points 4 and 10 can be backed by six units, 5 and 9 by six units, and 6 and 8 by ten units.

(If the bet is uneven on points 5 and 9, more than six units can be bet as a free-odds wager, but if the bet is even and can be paid at 3 to 2, the special allowance wouldn't apply.)

Let's say points 8 and 10 have repeated and we have made six unit bets on the new pass and come wagers. The new points thrown are 9 on the come bet and a 10 on the pass line. So as it stands, we have six unit bets on the 9 and 10 (both bets backed by the full odds) and three units on the come point of 5. Should the 10, our pass line point repeat, our new bet would be six units, for our other point, the 5, still has only a three unit bet on it. Do not increase bets to higher levels (in this example, above 6 units) until all the points have been brought up to the same bet size.

If the streak continues and all the basic pass and come bets have been brought up to six unit bets, begin to reestablish won points by making pass and come bets in units of nine, and of course, backing all these bets with the maximum single odds allowed. Increase bets in this fashion for as long as the streak continues.

This steady progressive increase of bets allows us to maximize the profits resulting from a hot roll while protecting us against a sudden seven-out making serious inroads into our winnings.

IV. Maximizing Profits: The Texas Roll Method. As an alternate and more aggressive way of increasing won bets, the bettor could increase each won bet by three units regardless of how many units were already placed on the other points. Thus, a bet that repeated twice in a row, could have a nine unit bet on it while the other points were covered by only three units each.

Our bet increases are in units of three so that we can continue to take advantage of the special three unit single odds allowances.

Do NOT begin new progressions (once a shooter sevens-out) at a level higher than three units. This is very important. A bettor that continues to bet in amounts higher than his initial standard three unit wager is susceptible to a short losing streak wiping out his hard earned gains in a matter of a few bad shoots. We will only bet more aggressively during a hot streak, and will not try to anticipate one occurring.

Once we've had our one great shoot we'll never give the casino a chance to get our winnings back. We'll return to our basic three unit bet. If things go poorly, we'll call it quits soon afterwards, a huge winner. If the shooter gets hot again, we'll start increasing our bets and winnings, always ready for the next big kill.

This is smart money management, the key to success for winners.

V. Double Odds Strategies. Whenever the bettor has a choice, he should always choose a double odds game over a single odds game, for the additional allowance of the free-odds bet drops the overall house edge from 0.8 percent to 0.6 percent when using our methods.

The playing strategies we will pursue in the double odds game are identical to the single odds game except that we will bet in units of two instead of three as recommended in the single odds game to take advantage of the special five unit free-odds allowance when the point is 6 or 8. Basic Conservative bettors should establish two points with maximum double odds on each, while Aggressive bettors will want to cover three points.

Follow the procedures for the single odds methods substituting only the two unit basic bet for the three unit bets, and making double odds bet instead of single odds.

VI. Maximizing Profits - Double Odds Game. Again our strategy here will follow that of the single odds game except we'll be increasing our bets by two units instead of three. Basic Conservative bettors will not begin increasing bets until they've accumulated 20 units in profits, and Aggressive bettors will need 25 units.

Remember to take advantage of the special allowances when the point is a 6 or 8. A four unit bet can be backed by 10 units in the double odds game, and a six unit bet by 15.

When eventually the shooter sevens-out, ending our winning streak, we'll start the next progression again at two units, ready to capitalize on another hot roll should one develop.

B. Winning Strategies: Betting Against the Dice

Though the odds of winning are equivalent to the right betting strategies, 0.8 percent in a single odds game and 0.6 percent in a double odds game, very few craps players bet against the dice. Many bettors feel uncomfortable about having to lay odds, putting more money on their free-odds bet than they will win should the bet be won, but as stated earlier, the free-odds wagers give the house no edge betting right or wrong.

However, players that bet wrong don't mind giving the odds, for the roll of a 7, their winner, will occur more often than any point number, and they'll have frequent winners. In addition, should a point be repeated, a losing roll for wrong bettors, only one bet will be lost. The other points covered by the wrong bettor are still in play.

On the other side of the dice, the right bettors fear the 7, for when it is thrown, all their established points and free-odds bets are lost.

We will apply the same principles of play as right bettors. We'll make only the best bets available to us, those that reduce the house edge to the lowest possible figure - the don't pass, the don't come and free-odds bets.

VII. Basic Conservative Method - Wrong Bettors/Single Odds Strategy. Our standard bet will be in even increments of two units. Bets such as $15 or $25 are difficult to work with when the point is a 5 or 9 and 2 to 3 odds should be laid. Betting in other unit sizes is equally valid, but the player will find it easiest to work in multiples of $10.

These are the guidelines of our Basic conservative strategy:

1. We will make two unit don't pass and don't come bets until we have established bets against two points, and back both those bets with maximum free-odds.

2. Should a point repeat, a loser for us, we will make another don't come or don't pass bet, so that we can continue to have bets working against two points. If a 2, 3, 11 or 12 determines a winner or loser on a new don't pass or don't come bet, we will follow with another bet until we get that second point established, and then we'll play the maximum single odds against that point.

3. Stop establishing don't pass and don't come bets if a second point repeats. This is an important safeguard to protect us against bad losing streaks.

4. If a 7 is thrown, a winner on all our bets, we'll begin the progression again with our two unit don't pass bet.

5. Follow the recommendations in the Maximizing Profits section for advice on how to increase winnings when the dice are going our way.

As cautious bettors, we'll limit ourselves to a coverage of only two points and strictly follow the safeguard recommended in step three.

VIII. Aggressive Method - Wrong Bettors Single Odds Strategy. Our Aggressive strategy follows the same guidelines as the Basic-Conservative method except that we will cover three points during a shoot instead of two, and will stop making additional don't pass and don't come bets if three points repeat, instead of two as advised in the Basic Conservative method. We'll use the same bets - the don't pass, don't come and free-odds bets, and enjoy the same low 0.8 percent house edge in a single odds game.

We begin by making a don't pass bet, and backing that with the maximum single odds once the point is established. Then, we'll make two successive don't come wagers, or as many as necessary, until two points are established, and will back those bets with maximum single odds as well. Once we have bets established against three points, we'll stop betting.

Should a 2, 3, 11 or 12 be rolled before all the points are established, we'll make another don't come bet until that third point is set. And we'll strictly adhere to our safeguard. If a third point repeats, we'll stop making additional bets during the cycle, and just ride out the unlucky streak. We never want to bet into a losing streak.

When the shooter sevens-out, a winner on all our bets, we'll start our cycle again, establishing three points with the maximum single odds.

IX. Maximizing Profits - Methods for Wrong Bettors. The safest and most effective way of winning big at craps is to increase bets only during cold runs*, when the dice are going *our* way. The concept is to parlay winnings into big winnings. We do this by increasing bets only during a winning cycle, when the dice have already won for us, and never after a losing bet. Players and systems that attempt to regain lost money by increasing their bets only court disaster, for this type of desperate betting leaves one vulnerable to huge losses, and that's bad money management.

* *Cold* runs favor the wrong bettor.

We won't start playing more aggressively until we're ahead by at least 20 units as a Basic-Conservative player and 25 units as an Aggressive method player. This gives us the opportunity to make big profits when the dice are with us, while protecting us against ever getting hurt by a bad run. And as a matter of fact, if the basic wrong betting safeguards and the stop-loss advice in the money management section are adhered to, we'll never take a crippling loss. But we're always ready to win big.

Unlike the right bettors strategies where bets are increased during a cycle, we will wait until the shooter sevens-out, a winner for us, before we begin to play more aggressively. Once you're ahead the aforementioned amounts, and the previous betting cycle was a winning one, increase the basic bet by two units.

If all our points were covered by two unit basic bets, we'll now cover the points by four unit basic bets, and if after the shooter sevens-out, we have emerged winners again, we'll continue to bet into the winning streak, and up our bet by another two units, to six units. We'll continue to increase bets by two units as long as the streak continues, all the time backing the bets with the maximum single odds allowed.

If the basic bet was $10 (two units of $5), the next basic bet will be $20, and then $30 and so on.

Anytime a sequence has been a losing one, begin the following shoot at the original two unit basic bet. In the example above, we would begin again at $10. Smart money management dictates that we only increase bets during a winning streak.

All the time during a shoot, we'll follow the safeguards outlined in the strategies. Basic Conservative method bettors will stop establishing points should two points be repeated, and Aggressive method bettors will hold their bets if a third point repeats.

X. Double Odds Strategy - Wrong Bettors. Whenever possible, the wrong bettor should play a double odds game over a single odds game, for it lowers the overall house edge from

0.8% to 0.6%. And we always want to play with the best odds we can get - the lower the house edge, the greater our chances of winning.

By nature, the double odds strategies are more aggressive than the single odds games, and are more in tune for players whose temperament demands hotter action. For example, if the point is a 4 and $10 is bet on the don't pass, the single odds bettor would wager $20 (laying 1 to 2) as a free odds bet while the double odds bettor covers that some point with a $40 wager (also laying 1 to 2).

The double odds bettor lays more to win more and therefore needs a larger bankroll than his single odds counterpart. Therefore, to play this strategy, the double odds bettor must feel comfortable with the larger bet levels.

Our double odds strategies are identical to the single odds methods, except that we're playing double odds instead of single odds. We'll begin by making a two unit don't pass bet, and backing that bet by double odds once a point is established. If $10 is the line bet, $40 will be the double odds bet if the point is 4 or 10 (laying 1 to 2), $30 if the point is 5 or 9 (laying 2 to 3), and $24 if the point is 6 or 8 (laying 5 to 6).

Basic Conservative bettors will follow with a don't come bet and lay double odds on both points while Aggressive Strategy bettors will make two more don't come bets backed by the full double odds, or as many don't pass or don't come bets as needed until three points are covered and then backed by free odds bets.

Like the single odds strategies, the Basic Conservative players attempt to keep two points working at all times while the Aggressive Strategy players strive for three working points. When points repeat, new don't pass or don't come bets are made to reestablish another, but should a second point repeat for Basic Conservative players or a third point for Aggressive Strategy players, then we'll curtail all new betting until the shooter sevens-out, a winner on our remaining bets.

We employ this stop-loss as a safeguard to protect against

one really bad shoot wiping out our table stakes. However, should the dice start blowing profits in our direction, we're immediately ready to capitalize on the situation.

We start the next come-out roll fresh, with a two unit don't pass wager, always ready for the streak that will mint chips for us.

XI. Double Odds Strategy - Maximizing Gains. It is recommended that the bettor increase his wagers cautiously when playing a double odds game. The mushrooming effect of double odds can rapidly increase the outlay of money on the table, so we want to be conservative in our increases. For example, a $10 bettor may want to increase bets by only $5, since each $5 increase could call for an additional double odds bet of $20 if the point were a 4 or 10. The player must use his own discretions for bet increases, possibly one unit per winning cycle.

We'll use the same principles outlined in the single odds Basic Conservative strategy for increasing bets. We'll increase only during a winning streak and not before we're up at least 20 units, and for Aggressive Strategy players, we'll leave ourselves a cushion of 25 units before increasing our wagers.

BANKROLLING

The amount of money necessary to withstand the normal fluctuations common to craps vary according to the type of strategy you employ (right or wrong betting), the aggressiveness of your approach (Basic Conservative or Aggressive), and your expected playing time.

We'll discuss the single session bankroll first for the various strategies, and then present the type of bankroll the player will need for longer sessions at the craps table.

SINGLE SESSION BANKROLL · RIGHT BETTORS
Single & Double Odds Game

Approach (Points Covered)	Units Needed for a Single Cycle	Table Bankroll Needed
Basic-Cons. (2 Points)	14	100
Aggressive (3 points)	21	150

Bankroll Needed: Basic Conservative Strategy

In the single odds game, Basic Conservative bettors will cover two points through pass and come bets and back both points with the maximum single odds allowed. Since the standard line bet will be three units, and the single odds bet backing the pass and come wagers will be between three to five units, we can expect each point to require a total of six to eight units to be fully covered, or about 14 units to fully cover each cycle of two points.

In the double odds game, our standard line bet of two units will be backed with the maximum double odds allowed, or about four to five units for a total of six to seven units per point. Fully covering a cycle of two points will require about 14 units, the same as the single odds game.

Bankroll Needed: Aggressive Strategy

Aggressive strategy bettors will need roughly 21 units to fully cover their three points in a single or double odds game.

To play safe, and give himself sufficient funds, the bettor should have enough of a table stake for about seven betting cycles. The Table Bankroll Needed columns in the above charts are computed by multiplying the units needed for a single cycle by seven, and then adding a few units as extra padding.

SINGLE SESSION BANKROLL · WRONG BETTORS
Single Odds Game

Approach (Points Covered)	Units Needed for a Single Cycle	Table Bankroll Needed
Basic-Cons. (2 Points)	10	75
Aggressive (3 points)	15	115

SINGLE SESSION BANKROLL · WRONG BETTORS
Double Odds Game

Approach (Points Covered)	Units Needed for a Single Cycle	Table Bankroll Needed
Basic-Cons. (2 Points)	16	125
Aggressive (3 points)	24	175

Bankroll Needed: Single Odds Game - Wrong Bettors

The standard betting size for both Basic Conservative players and Aggressive Strategy players is two units in our strategies*. Our free odds wager in the single odds game will vary from just over two units on the 6 or 8 (laying 5 to 6), to three units on the 5 or 9 (laying 2 to 3), to four units on the 4 or 10 (laying 1 to 2) for an average of about three units per single odds bet. In addition to the two unit don't pass or don't come bet, that adds up to five units per point.

Basic conservative bettors will need 10 units, two points times five units, for each betting cycle, while Aggressive Strategy bettors will need 15 units for a round, three points each covered by approximately five betting units.

*For players that bet in unit sizes other than two units, they can figure the table stake needed by estimating the number of units needed for one full cycle of play, and multiplying that number by seven.

Bankroll Needed: Double Odds Game - Wrong Bettors

The standard betting size for either strategy here is two units, and we'll back each point by about six units, for a total of about eight units needed to fully cover each point in a double odds game. Basic Conservative bettors playing two points will need 16 units for a betting cycle while Aggressive Strategy players, who cover three points, need about 24 betting units.

In a double odds game, a two unit bet on the 4 or 10 gets backed by eight units, on the 5 and 9 gets backed by six units, and on the 6 or 8 gets backed by a little under five units, for an average of six units per double odds bet.

Total Bankroll

The longer one plans on playing craps, the larger one's bankroll must be to cover the inevitable fluctuations. The following bankroll requirements have been formulated to give the player enough capital to survive any reasonable losing streak, and be able to bounce back on top.

TOTAL BANKROLL REQUIREMENTS · RIGHT BETTORS
Single and Double Odds Games

Approach (Points Covered)	Single Session Stake	One Day Bankroll	Weekend Bankroll
Basic-Cons. (2 points)	100	300	500
Aggressive (3 Points)	150	450	750

TOTAL BANKROLL REQUIREMENTS · WRONG BETTORS
Single Odds Games

Approach (Points Covered)	Single Session Stake	One Day Bankroll	Weekend Bankroll
Basic-Cons. (2 points)	75	225	375
Aggressive (3 Points)	115	350	675

TOTAL BANKROLL REQUIREMENTS · WRONG BETTORS Double Odds Games			
Approach (Points Covered)	Single Session Stake	One Day Bankroll	Weekend Bankroll
Basic-Cons. (2 points)	125	375	625
Aggressive (3 Points)	175	525	875

The bankroll needed for a full day's session should be about three times that of a single session, and the weekend's bankroll should be about five times that of a single session. Players should never dip into their pockets past these levels for we never want to get beat bad at the tables.

These bankroll levels give us sufficient room to take some losses and still have enough of a bankroll to play confidently and wait for a hot streak to turn the tables on the casino and make us winners.

This does not mean the player must have all the money out on the table when playing, but that that money should be readily available in his pocket in case it's needed.

As you will see later in the minimizing losses section, we will never use all our table stake in any one session but will restrict our losses should luck go against us. This way we'll never get hurt by an unlucky session.

If you arrive at the casinos with a definite amount of money to gamble with, and want to figure out how much your unit size bet should be, simply take your gambling stake and divide it by the amount of units you need to have for the particular strategy you want to play.

If you bring $1,000 with you and were to spend a day using the right bettors Basic Conservative strategy in a single odds game, you would divide $1,000 by 300 units, the number in the *Total Bankroll* column, for a basic unit bet of roughly $3 ($3,33). Since right bettors wager in units of three in our single odds strategy, the standard pass or come bet would be about $10.

If you were to play the Aggressive Strategy, you would divide $1,000 by 450 units, for a basic unit bet of $2 ($2.22). Three unit bets would come out to the rough equivalent of betting $5 or $6 on the pass line or come bet, $5 being a good choice in the single odds game for we could use the special odds bet allowance when the point is a 6 or an 8.

Similarly, a player who likes to bet against the dice and has brought $1,500 for a single day's gambling would bet in $10 units if playing the Aggressive Strategy in a single odds game. We divide $1,500 by 350 for the rough equivalent of $5 ($4.29), and since our strategies call for bets in increments of two units, the standard don't come or don't pass wager will be $10.

However, we advise against the player overdoing it at the craps tables, for though we have reduced the house edge to the lowest possible amount, and give the player the best chances of winning, that small house edge can grind out the bettor over extended sessions of play.

Minimizing Losses

Here are some simple guidelines that, if followed, will save you a lot of money. You'll notice that our stop-loss limits are less than the recommended single session table stakes.

Stop - Loss Limits

Right bettors: Limit your table losses to 70 units for Basic Conservative bettors, and 100 units for Aggressive bettors. If betting $5 chips ($15 standard line bet), never lose more than $350 and $500 respectively in any one session; if $1 chips ($3 standard line bet), then $70 for Basic Conservative bettors and $100 for Aggressive bettors.

Wrong bettors: Wrong bettors should limit their table losses to the same levels as right bettors in single and double odds games.

Do not dig in for more money, and you can never be a big loser. Take a break, try again later. You never want to get into a position where losing so much in one session totally demoralizes you.

Bet Within Your Means
Never increase your bet range beyond your bankroll capabilities. In other words, always bet within your means.

Do Not Increase Bets When Losing
Never increase your bet size to catch up and break even. Raising it will not change the odds of the game, nor will it change your luck. What it will do is make your chances of taking a terrible beating frighteningly high. Do not get into a position where losing so much in one session destroys any reasonable chance of coming out even. You can't win all the time. Rest a while, you'll get them later.

Protecting Wins
Once winning, the most important thing in craps is to walk away a winner. Read the money management section carefully so that you can use the strategies here to maximum advantage.

BACCARAT

INTRODUCTION

This glamorous game is steeped in centuries of European tradition and while a mainstay and important game on the continent, is only just beginning to catch on in the American casinos.

Bettors are not only attracted to baccarat's leisurely style of play and the very low casino odds the game offers the player, but to the exciting new winning approach, card counting, which has proved so successful for blackjack players.

In its different varieties, baccarat can be found in casinos around the world. The version played in the United States originated in Cuba in the 1950s and is called **American** or **Nevada style baccarat** though U.S. casinos simply refer to it as **baccarat**. Elsewhere in the world this version is known as **punto banco**.

In Europe, **chemin de fer** and **baccarat banque** are quite popular, while **mini-baccarat**, a smaller version of punto banco is found more and more in casinos in the U.S. and around the world.

Baccarat is a simple game to play even for beginners, for the dealer or croupier, directs all the action according to fixed rules. As you'll see, the game is quite easy to play and in no time at all, you'll be ready to take your place at the tables and enjoy all that baccarat has to offer.

Let's move on now and see what the game is all about!

THE BASICS OF BACCARAT

The Layout

Baccarat is played on a specially constructed layout which allows players to choose either of the two betting spots, **Banker** or **Player** to make their wager. The regulation tables normally have betting spots for 12-14 players, with each player having a corresponding number spot, 1 through 12, or 14 as the case may be, to place his or her bets.

Bets on the Player position can be placed immediately in front of the player, in the numbered area, while bets on the Banker position, go in the numbered slots indicated by "**bank**."

The mini-baccarat layout has space for about seven players. As on the regulation table, each spot is numbered, and bets on either of the betting positions are placed in front of the bettor.

THE BACCARAT LAYOUT

Casino Personnel

The game is generally manned by three dealers. One dealer is in charge of the game and his function is to run the show. He or she will direct the play, telling players what to do - when they need a draw and when the cards should be dealt. The other two dealers handle the betting, collecting lost bets from the losers, making payoffs on won hands and keeping track of the commissions owed.

Card Values

Cards valued 2 to 9 are counted according to their face value, a 2 equals 2 points, an Ace equals one point, and a 7 equals 7 points. The 10, Jack, Queen, and King, have a value of 0 points. They have no effect when adding up the points in a hand. Points are counted by adding up the value of the cards. However, hands totaling 10 or more points, have the first digit dropped so that no hand contains a total of greater than 9 points. For example, two nines (18) is a hand of 8 points and a 7 5 (12) is a hand of 2 points. A hand of a 3 and a 4 would simply be valued at 7 points.

The suits have no value in baccarat.

The Object of Baccarat

A player has the choice of betting Banker or Player, and the object of the game is for the position chosen to beat the other hand. The hand closer to the total of 9 is the winner. The worst score is zero, called **baccarat.** A tie is a standoff or push, neither hand wins.

Betting Limits

The casino limits on minimum and maximum bets will be posted by the table, and as long as these guidelines are followed, a player may bet whatever desired. Higher limits than those posted can often be arranged.

Table de Banque Card

Like roulette, serious baccarat players like to keep track of the winning progressions and can do so on cards provided by the casino and called, a **Table de Banque** card. These cards provide a convenient place to record wins by either the Banker or Player position, and keep the systems players on track for the game.

The Play of the Game

Baccarat is normally played with eight decks of cards dealt out of a shoe, though a mini-baccarat table may use only six decks. Each deck is a standard 52 card deck containing thirteen cards, ace through king, in each of the four suits, though as we mentioned above, the suits have no bearing in the game.

There are two opposing sides, the Player and the Banker, and no matter how many players are betting in a game, only two hands will be dealt; one for the Banker position and one for the Player position, except in the baccarat banque version, where there are two Player positions instead of one.

A bettor may choose either side to bet on and does so by placing the wager in the Banker or Player's position, whichever is chosen, corresponding to his or her numbered seat. After the betting is done, each side will be dealt two cards.

In Nevada style baccarat (punto banco), the players deal the cards. The shoe rotates counterclockwise around the table with each player having his or her turn at it. There is no advantage in dealing and a player may refuse the deal, in which case the shoe will be offered to the next player in turn.

The player acting as dealer will slide the first card face down to the **caller**, the dealer who controls the pace and runs the game, and slip the second card, also face down, under the front corner of the shoe. Likewise, the third card will go face down to the caller, and the fourth one, like the second, goes face down under the shoe.

Each side now, the Player position represented by the caller's cards, and the Banker position, represented by the two cards under the shoe, has two cards.

The caller will pass the two cards dealt to him to the bettor with the highest wager on the Player's position. After examining the cards, the bettor will flip them back to the caller who then will announce the total.

The dealer will now take the Banker's cards from under the shoe and pass them along to the caller who will announce their total as well.

Hand Values

A dealt total of 8 or 9 points is called a **natural**, and no additional cards will be drawn. It is an automatic win unless the opposing hand has a higher natural (a 9 vs. an 8), or the hand is a tie.

A natural of 8 points is called **le petit**, a total of nine, **le grande.**

On all other totals, 0 through 7, the drawing of an additional card depends strictly on established rules of play. There is never more than one card drawn to a hand in any case.

The player need not be familiar with the rules for drawing on the third card for the caller will direct the action and request that a third card be drawn if the rules require it. Just follow the caller's instructions - as easy as that!

The Player's hand will be acted upon first, and then the Banker's. Despite the different variations of baccarat, the third card rules for draw are consistent for games around the world.

The two card total of the Player's hand determines whether a third card should be drawn and is regulated by the following rules:

PLAYER RULES

Two Card Total	Player's Action
0-5*	Draw a Card
6 or 7	Stand
8 or 9	Natural. Banker cannot draw.

*In chemin de fer and baccarat banque, the player has the option to stand or draw on a point total of 5 points only.

After the Player's hand has been acted upon, it is the Banker's turn. Whether the Banker position receives a card depends upon two variables. In some cases, it depends upon his two card total, and other times, it depends upon the card that the

Player position has drawn.

If the Banker hand is 0, 1 or 2, a card is drawn, while with hands of 7, 8 and 9, no cards are drawn. The other Banker totals of 3, 4, 5 and 6 are drawn upon depending upon what card the Player position has drawn.

Rules for drawing or standing can be broken up as follows.

Situation 1 - Either the Player or the Banker has a natural 8 or 9. It is an automatic win for the hand with the natural. If both hands have naturals, the higher natural wins. (A natural 9 beats a natural 8.) If the naturals are equal, the hand is a tie.

Situation 2 - If the Player has a 0-5, Player must draw another card; if a 6-7, the Player must stand.

Situation 3 - If Player stands, than Banker hand follows the same rules as the Player - it must draw on totals of 0-5, and stand on 6-7.

Situation 4 - If Player draws, Banker must draw or stand according to the value of the third card dealt as show below in the Banker Rules chart. (Note that the banker always draws on totals of 0-2, unless of course, the Player has a natural.)

BANKER RULES		
Banker Total	Bank Draws When Giving Player This Card	Bank Does Not Draw When Giving Player This Card
0-2	0-9	
3	0-7, 9*	8
4	2-7	0-1, 8-9
5	4*, 5-7	0-3, 8-9
6	6-7	0-5, 8-9
7	Banker Always Stands	
8-9	A Natural - Player Can't Draw	

*In punto banco and mini-baccarat, the drawing of a third card is mandatory, while in chemin de fer, it is an optional draw or stand.

PAYOFFS AND ODDS

The winning hand in baccarat is paid at 1 to 1, **even money**, except in the case of the Banker's position where a 5% commission is charged on a winning hand. Commission is charged because of the inherent edge the Banker position has over the Player position.

During actual play, this commission is kept track of on the side by use of chips, and won bets at the Banker position are paid off at even money. This avoids the cumbersome 5% change-giving on every hand. The commission is collected later; at the end of every shoe, or before the player parts from the game.

With the commission, the average Banker edge over the bettor is only 1.17%, quite low by casino standards. The average house edge over the Player position is only slightly more, 1.36%. These percentages can vary though as cards are removed during the course of play.

BACCARAT AROUND THE WORLD

Let's now look at the differences in the main versions of baccarat as played around the world.

American or Nevada Style Baccarat (Punto Banco)

In this version of play, usually referred to as simply baccarat in the U.S. casinos, the bettor has a choice of betting the Player (Punto), or the Banker (Banco). He plays against the house which books all bets and pays winning hands. There are no third card drawing options for either the Banker (Banco) or Player (Punto) position.

The bettor may wager on a **tie bet** - a poor wager that pays off at 9 *for* 1 (8 to 1) and gives the casino an edge of 14.10%. (This bet is not offered in chemin de fer and baccarat banque.)

In this variation of baccarat, the only decisions a player makes are whether to bet Banker or Player, and how much to bet.

Chemin de Fer

The bettor who plays the Banker position deals the cards and books all bets. The other players oppose the Banker. The Player position has one third card drawing option, and is controlled by the bettor with the highest bet placed. The Banker has two drawing options and plays the hand himself. (See Player and Banker Rules charts.) No tie bet is offered.

The casino acts only in a supervisory capacity and collects its fee as a percentage levy or as an hourly rate charged to the players.

The Banker is decided by either **auction**, where the highest bidder takes the Banker position and puts up his or her bid as the bank, by lot, or by acceptance as the bank moves its way around the table.

A bettor plays Banker until he loses a hand or voluntarily gives it up. The next player, clockwise or counterclockwise, according to the house rules, can play Banker, and set his own limit on the bets he will book. A bettor may refuse the bank and pass it on to the next player.

The total amount of money bet against the Banker in a hand is limited by the amount of money in the bank. Any player who wishes to bet against the entire bank, calls out "**banco**," thus nullifying the other bets.

Baccarat Banque

The casino deals all cards and books all bets. There are two player (punto) positions on this two-sided layout. These spots are manned by bettors who oppose the banker (banco) position which is always taken by the house. Bettors may wager on either Player position or both. The Player has one third card drawing option.

The Banker is not bound by third card drawing restrictions as in other variations and may stand or draw one card. (Some casinos apply restrictions on the banker.)

Baccarat a Tout Va

Everything goes baccarat in the two-sided style of Baccarat banque. No maximum limit on bets.

Mini-Baccarat

The same game as Nevada Style/Punto Banco except that it's played on a miniature blackjack-type table, and that the casino deals the cards.

The following chart shows the positions a bettor may wager in the various versions of baccarat.

PLAYERS BETTING GUIDE		
Game	**Player**	**Banker**
Punto Banco	Yes	Yes
Mini-Baccarat	Yes	Yes
Chemin De Fer	Yes	Only the bettor playing the Banker may bet Banker.
Baccarat Banque	Yes*	No

* Can wager on either or both of the player hands.
Yes - Indicates a player may bet the position.
No - Indicates a player may not bet the position.

The odds vary slightly among the various version of baccarat and the following chart will outline this for you.

HOUSE EDGE AT BACCARAT

Wager	Payoff	House Edge
Nevada Style/Punto Banco		
Player	1 to 1	1.36%
Banker	1 to 1	1.17%
Tie	9 for 1	14.10%
Chemin de Fer		
Player	1 to 1	1.23%
Banker	1 to 1	1.06%
Baccarat Banque		
Average Edge		0.92%

WINNING STRATEGIES

Traditional Betting Strategies

There is very little decision making in baccarat, thus winning strategies were traditionally confined to betting systems and money management techniques. These strategies are based on winning streaks and won/lost trends, going with the positions that are hot and adjusting bets according to whether the last hand won or lost.

There are many interesting approaches available for players who enjoy betting systems. Just keep in mind that these systems don't change the odds of the games they attempt to defeat.

Winning With Card Counting

Card counting techniques, which proved so effective at winning at blackjack, have been attracting a lot of study lately as a winning method at baccarat. Here's how they work.

In baccarat, just like blackjack, the removal of cards from play creates situations where the chances of receiving particular cards or combinations of cards change. The removal of certain types of cards favor the Player while others favor the Banker.

A good count strategy shows you how to recognize situations that favor betting Banker and others where Player is the better bet. By judiciously altering bets with the count, a card counter can improve his or her chances at the table and win money at baccarat.

The basic theory is that low cards favor the Player position, and high cards favor the Banker. Certain cards have little effect and are considered neutral. Counters track the removal of these cards, betting the Player position when there is a higher ratio of low cards in the deck, and the Banker position when there is a higher ratio of the high cards remaining.

For players interested in winning with card counting methods, we recommend the excellent advanced strategy, the Baccarat Master Card Counter, advertised at the end of the book.

Baccarat Summary

Baccarat combines the allure and glamour of European tradition with relatively low house odds for the average player, 1.17% in the Banker's position and 1.36% in the Player's spot.

One advantage of baccarat, especially for high rollers, is that one cannot make mental mistakes which will give the casino an added edge. Compare this to games such as blackjack, craps or poker, where poor decisions in the heat of the game can cause the bettor to make costly errors and you can understand one of the allures of the game.

Despite the exclusive look of the game though, baccarat can be played by anyone. There's no need to bet mini-fortunes to play. It is a leisurely game, and in the version played in the American casinos, an easy one as well. There are no decisions to make save for how much to bet and which position, Player or Banker, to back.

The low casino edge and the exciting winning possibilities available makes baccarat a perfect place to wager in style, surrounded by elegant decor, playing this centuries-old game in the grand tradition.

ROULETTE

INTRODUCTION

Roulette offers players a huge variety of bets, more than any other casino table game, and the constant possibilities of winning and the different payoffs of the wagers, ranging from even-money payoffs to returns of 35 to 1, keeps the game exciting and suspenseful.

The game is set up for systems players, and it is not unusual to find tablefuls of bettors armed with pencil and pad, plying their favorite winning systems. The systems sometimes fail and sometimes win but we'll discuss their virtues and shortcomings, so that you'll be able to approach the game fully prepared to play the best way possible.

The attraction of making fortunes with the spin of the wheel has made roulette the oldest and most famous gambling game in European casinos where roulette is king. Roulette is enormously popular there and is a game favored by royalty and celebrities as well as regular gamblers looking for the thrill of action. Roulette is much less popular in America, and as opposed to the crowded and noisy tables prevalent over on the other side of the Atlantic, tables in the U.S. casinos remain comparatively quiet.

We'll show you how the two styles of play differ, American and European, and why roulette games are so popular in Europe yet play second fiddle to the other table games in American casinos.

We'll also show you how to make all the different bets possible, their designations in French and in English, and the odds involved, so that you'll be ready to play roulette anywhere in the world and be fully prepared to have the best chances of winning!

THE BASICS OF ROULETTE

The Roulette Setting

Roulette is played with a circular wheel containing 36 grooved slots numbered from 1 to 36, half the numbers of which are black and the other half red, a tiny ball which is used in conjunction with the wheel, and a betting layout where players can place their wagers.

In addition to the 36 numbers on the roulette wheel, the American game has a 0 and 00, while the European game has but one 0. The zero slots are neither red nor black as are the other numbers but are green in color.

The wheel is cut into tiny pockets, one for each number - 37 total on a European wheel and 38 on an American - so that the ball, when spun around the wheel, will eventually fall into one of these slots - that number being the winning spin.

The European game generally has the wheel flanked on two sides by a betting layout, so that the busy tables can accommodate players on both sides of the wheel, while the less popular American games typically use but one layout to the side.

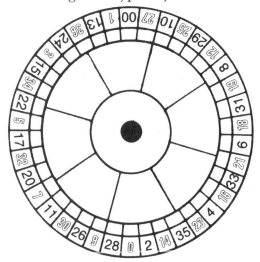

THE AMERICAN WHEEL

THE LAYOUT

		0	00	
1to18	1st 12	1	2	3
		4	5	6
EVEN		7	8	9
		10	11	12
◇	2nd 12	13	14	15
		16	17	18
◆		19	20	21
		22	23	24
ODD	3rd 12	25	26	27
		28	29	30
19to36		31	32	33
		34	35	36
		2-1	2-1	2-1

The Dealer

The American game typically employs just one dealer who handles all of the functions at the table. He changes money into chips, spins the wheel, collects losing bets and pays off the winners. In between he finds time to stack and restack collected chips from the layout into neat, colorful piles, so that payoffs from the next spin will proceed smoothly and rapidly.

If a table is exceptionally busy, the dealer may have an assistant to help run the game.

European style games have one to as many as three or four **croupiers**, the French term for dealers, paying and collecting bets on the two adjacent layouts, and a **tourneur**, whose main responsibility is to spin the wheel and call the result. Often, a supervisor will be present as well.

Thus, when things get rolling and the tables crowded, one might find as many as six casino personnel manning a roulette game - a tourneur, four croupiers and a supervisor.

The Play of the Game

Once players have placed their bets on the layout, choosing from the myriad possibilities available in front of them, the game is officially ready to begin. The roulette wheel will be spun by the dealer or tourneur who immediately afterwards, will throw the ball in the opposite direction from which the wheel is spinning so that both ball and wheel are racing in opposite directions on the wheel itself.

Players must now get in their last minute wagers for when the ball is about to leave the track, the dealer will announce that bets are no longer permitted. The call of *Faites vos jeux*, *messieurs* (Make your bets gentlemen) or *Rien ne va plus* (Nothing more goes) are classic in the French speaking casinos.

Once the ball has stopped, the dealer or tourneur will call out the outcome, and a marker will be placed on the number just spun so that all players and dealers can clearly see the winning number.

The dealers or **croupiers**, as they're called in French, will now settle the wagers. Lost bets are collected first by the dealers, and after this is done, all the winning bets will be paid off.

The Chips

Keeping track of one's bets are easy in American roulette games, for each player is issued special chips applicable only to the roulette game at that casino, and these chips are colored, a different color for each player. Ten different players may be represented by, for example, yellow, red, pink, blue, green, black, white, beige, purple and grey chips.

The colored chips are valid and can be used only at the roulette table which issues them. If the table is crowded and no more colors are available, a player may use regular casino chips for his or her bets.

There is no confusion in ownership of the chips this way. Color coding makes life easy at these tables. When a player approaches the roulette table, he exchanges cash or casino chips for an equivalent value in the colored chips, called in the parlance of the game, **wheel checks**. The value assigned to those colored chips, be it 25¢, $1.00, $5.00 or whatever, is set by the player. Thus, if the player wants to value the chips at 25¢, more chips will be issued from the dealer than if the chips were valued at $1.00.

The dealer will place a coin or **marker button** on top of the colored chips and place these on the stationary outer rim of the wheel, so that the value of that wheel check is clearly marked.

When a player is ready to leave, he converts the wheel checks back into the regular casino checks with the dealer at that table.

Life is a bit more complicated in the European style game where color coding is not used and bettors simply use casino chips or cash to make their bets. Sometimes, in the confusion of a crowded game, vociferous arguments ensue as players lay identical claim to chips on the felt.

The Basic Odds

The primary difference in the popularity of European and American roulette lies in the simple fact that the European game gives the player much better odds of winning, and this is where the 0, 00 difference of the two wheels comes into play.

Let's see how the odds are figured.

There are slots numbered from 1 to 36 on the roulette wheel - a total of 36. There is only one way to win for each number chosen. That leaves 35 other numbers, which if they come up, are losers for the bettor. True odds of 35 to 1 against - 35 ways to lose, one way to win.

And that exactly what the casino will pay on a single number bet.

So where is the casino's profit?

It is the zeros added to the wheel that give casinos their edge, for now there are a total of 37 possibilities on a European wheel (single zero added) and 38 possibilities on an American one (double zero added). The casino's payoff is still 35 to 1, being based on the true odds of a 36 number wheel. However, with the added zeros, the true odds on a single number bet are now 36 to 1 on a single zero wheel (the European game) and 37 to 1 on a double zero wheel (the American game).

Those zeros give the casino its edge on all bets made. Unless the zero (and in American roulette the 00 also) are bet directly, the spin of either on the wheel causes all other wagers to lose.

The sole exceptions are the even-money bets in a European style game (and Atlantic City), for the spin of a zero gives the red-black (rouge-noir), high-low (passe-manque) and odd-even (impair-pair) bettors a second chance, and reduces the house edge on these bets to 1.35% (2.63% in Atlantic City) - the best odds one can receive in roulette.

The zeros represent the house advantage and that is why the 00 in American roulette makes that game a worse gamble for the player than its European counterpart. Atlantic City makes up for this a little by offering surrender on even-money bets, bringing the casino's edge on these wagers down to 2.63%.

Let's sum up the odds for you in chart form so that you can clearly see them in one spot.

CASINO EDGE IN ROULETTE	
	House Edge
American Roulette (Double Zero)	
The 5-Number Bet	7.89%
All Other Bets	5.26%
Atlantic City - Even Money Bets	2.63%
European Roulette (One Zero)	
Even-Money Bets - *En prison* Rule	1.35%
All Other Bets	2.70%

The difference between the 1.35% of European style roulette and 5.26% of the American style is significant, almost a four-fold increase, which calculates directly to a loss rate four times as fast.

Now you can see why roulette with a single zero and *en prison* rule is the rage of Europe, and double zero American roulette is not popular at all.

THE BETS

Roulette offers the player a multitude of possible wagers, more than any other casino table game. All in all, there are over 150 possible combinations to bet. And a player may make as many bets in whatever combinations desired as long as the bets fit within the minimum and maximum limit of the casino.

Let's now examine the bets one by one. (The French names for the bets are listed in parenthesis.)

Combination or Inside Bets

These bets are made within the numbers on the layout, and hence, are termed **inside bets**.

Single Number Bet - (En Plein)

A **single number bet** can be made on any number on the layout including the 0 and 00. To make this wager, place your chip within the lines of the number chosen, being careful not to touch the lines. Otherwise you may have another bet altogether.

The winning payoff is 35 to 1.

The Single Number Bet

Split Bet (A Cheval)

Place the chip on the line adjoining two numbers. If either number comes up, the payoff is 17 to 1.

Split Bet (A Cheval)

Trio Bet (Transversale)

The chip is placed on the outside vertical line alongside any line of numbers. If any of the three are hit, the payoff is 11 to 1.

Trio Bet (Transversale)

13 | 14 | 15

4-Number Bet (Carre)

Also called a square or corner bet. Place the chip on the spot marking the intersection of four numbers. If any of the four come in it is an 8 to 1 payoff.

4-Number Bet (Carre)

Quatre Premiere

Only in European roulette. The bet covering the 0, 1, 2 and 3. An 8 to 1 payoff.

5-Number Bet

Only in American roulette. Place the chip at the end of the intersection where the 0 and 1 overlaps to cover the 0, 00, 1, 2, and 3 five number bet. If any of these five come home, the payoff is 6 to 1. In American roulette, it is the only bet not giving the house an edge of 5.26%. It's worse - 7.89%!

5-Number Bet

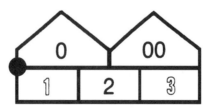

6-Number Bet (Sixaine)

Also called a **block bet**. The chip should be put on the outside line of the layout while intersecting the line separating the sets of numbers chosen. The payoff is 5 to 1.

6-Number Bet (Sixaine)

28	29	30
31	32	33

Outside Bets

The *outside bets* are outside the 36 numbers on the layout. They include the columns, dozens and even money bets - red-black, high-low and odd-even.

Outside Bets

1st 12		2nd 12		3rd 12	
1to18	EVEN	◇	◆	ODD	19to36

Columns Bet (Colonne)

A chip placed at the head of a column, on the far side from the zero or zeros, covers all 12 numbers in the column and has a winning payoff of 2 to 1. The 0 and 00 are not included in this bet and would make this bet a loser if they come up.

Columns Bet (Colonne)

3	6	9	12	15	18	21	24	27	30	33	36	2-1
2	5	8	11	14	17	20	23	26	29	32	35	2-1
1	4	7	10	13	16	19	22	25	28	31	34	2-1

Dozens Bet (Douzaine)

This is another way to bet 12 numbers, either numbers 1 to 12, 13 to 24 or 25 to 36. On the American layout they're called the **first**, **second** and **third dozen** respectively, and on the French layout, they're known as **P12**, **M12** and **D12**. The winning payoff as in the column bet is 2 to 1.

Dozens Bet (Douzaine)

Even-Money Bets

There is one final type of bet, the even money bets: Red-Black (Rouge-Noir), High-Low (Passe-Manque) and Odd-Even (Impair-Pair). Spots for these bets are found outside the numbers, thus these are still classified as outside wagers. These wagers are clearly marked in large boxes.

In Atlantic City and European style roulette, these bets are the best at the roulette table, for they offer the player additional features which are greatly advantageous to the player. In Europe, the features are called *en prison* and *partage*, and in Atlantic City, surrender.

First we'll go over the bets, and after, we'll examine how the *en prison*, *partage* and surrender rules work and how they affect the player.

Even-Money Bets

Red-Black (Rouge-Noir)

There are 18 black and eighteen red numbers. A player may bet either the **red** or the **black** and is paid off at 1 to 1 on a winning spin.

Red-Black (Rouge-Noir)

High-Low (Passe-Manque)

Numbers 1-18 may be bet (**low**) or 19-36 (**high**). Bets are paid off at 1 to 1.

High-Low (Passe-Manque)

Odd-Even (Impair-Pair)

A player may bet on the 18 even numbers, **even**, or **odd**, the 18 odd numbers. Winning bets are paid at 1 to 1.

Odd-Even (Impair-Pair)

En Prison and Partage

En prison - It is on these even number bets (above) where the American and European games really differ. In American roulette, the house automatically wins on these bets when the 0 or 00 is spun (except in Atlantic City).

However, in Europe, if the 0 is spun, the *en prison* rule comes into effect. The player has two choices now.

He or she can either surrender half the bet, called *partage*, or elect to allow the bet to be "imprisoned" one more spin. If the spin is won, the bet stays intact and is "released" for the player to do what he or she will. If the spin is lost, so is the bet.

This rule is greatly advantageous to the player, and brings the odds down on these bets to 1.35% in favor of the casino as opposed to the 2.70% on the rest of the bets in the single zero game.

Surrender

In an attempt to get more gamblers to play roulette, the game in Atlantic City helps make up for the 00 of the American wheel by offering **surrender**, which is really *partage* by another name.

When a 0 or 00 is spun, players with bets on any of the even-money propositions lose only half the bet, "surrendering it," and keep the other half. This brings the house edge down to 2.63% on these bets.

AMERICAN AND EUROPEAN ROULETTE

The European and American game is pretty much the same besides the use of the French terms in Europe, and of course the American terms in the U.S. casinos.

However, there are two significant differences.

1. In addition to the 36 numbers on the roulette wheel, the American game has a 0 and 00, while the European game has but one 0.

2. The European game offers *en prison* and *partage*, rules greatly beneficial to the player. *En prison* and *partage* is not offered in American casinos, with the exception of Atlantic City where surrender (*partage*) is used.

The end result, as we showed earlier, is that the casino edge in the European game is but 1.35% as opposed to American roulette where the player has to overcome a hefty 5.26% house edge (or 2.63% on even-money bets in Atlantic City).

Roulette Payoff Chart

Bets in Roulette

American Name	#	French Name	Payoff
Single Number	1	En Plein	35-1
Split Bet	2	A Cheval	17-1
Trio	3	Transversale	11-1
4-Number (Corner)	4	Carre	8-1
(Not Applicable)	4	Quatre Premiere	8-1
5-Number	5	(Not Applicable)	6-1
6-Number or Block	6	Sixaine	5-1
Columns Bet	12	Colonne	2-1
Dozens Bet	12	Dozaine	2-1
Red or Black	18	Rouge ou Noir	1-1
High or Low	18	Passe ou Manque	1-1
Odd or Even	18	Impair ou Pair	1-1

 # column is the amount of numbers covered by the bet.

THE WINNING STRATEGIES

First it must be stated clearly, that like most other casino games, the casino has the mathematical edge over the player, and that no betting strategy or playing system can overcome those odds unless the wheel is a biased one - which we'll cover.

That edge is 5.26% in American roulette, with the exception of even-money bets in Atlantic City where the edge is 2.63%, and 2.70% in European roulette, unless the even-money wagers are made, where the house edge drops to 1.35%.

Based on the above facts, one must develop a lucid picture on how to approach a winning strategy. The key words here are casino edge or advantage.

First of all, it must be understood that in the long haul, the casino's edge will grind out the player - but that doesn't mean the player can't show a profit in the short run. Fluctuations are normal to gambling, whatever the game, and with a little luck, a player can ride a hot streak into some healthy profits..

There are many betting systems that have been devised to overcome the casino's edge in roulette, but you must keep these in perspective, for they can no more alter or change that fact than one constantly calling a tree a river will change that tree to a river or calling blue red will change that blue to red. One may convince oneself, but irrefutable facts are cemented in reality, and only a distortion or departure from that reality will change the appearance of what one perceives.

This is not to say that some of the betting strategies don't look good - some of them are brilliant in concept so that they "appear" nearly foolproof. (Note the key word, "appear.") However, these systems don't change the short or long term house edge at roulette and the player must view them as no more than a fun approach.

The beauty of these systems is that they entrance the player with such beautiful, though slightly tainted logic, that one actually sees how they can work and how they can beat the odds. And they can work - in the short run - and provide the player with that age-old smokecloud attempt that makes one feel that he's beating the odds. But again, don't be too much entranced with the fun ideas of these systems; the house edge is the house edge.

Man will never give up attempting to overcome the odds, that is one of the beauties of life. And that's why we are so attracted to gambling.

Let's look at one of the most famous systems first, The Martingale.

The Martingale

This dangerous system can dig you into a deep hole quick should you have a long string of losses - if not, like other systems, you'll be sitting pretty.

The system is easy. You attempt to win $1.00 on every sequence of the dice, a sequence being defined as either one spin when you have won, or a number of spins, ending when there is a winner.

Your first bet is $1.00. If the bet is won, you start again, betting $1.00. If you lose, the bet is doubled to $2.00. Should that bet be won, you have won $1.00 on the sequence, a $1.00 loss on the first spin but a $2.00 win on the second. If the second bet is lost, the next bet is again doubled, and is now $4.00. A winner here again brings a $1.00 profit, $1.00 + $2.00 in losers for $3.00, and a $4.00 winner - still $1.00 over the top.

And so the system works. Every won bet is followed by a $1.00 wager, the beginning of a fresh cycle. Every lost bet is followed by a doubling of that bet. And here is the danger of the Martingale. As consecutive losses mount, so does the size of your bet, where the end result is only a $1.00 win!

This is what happens if you lose seven in a row.

MARTINGALE PROGRESSION		
Loss	Initial Bet	Total Loss
1st	$1.00	$1.00
2nd	$2.00	$3.00
3rd	$4.00	$7.00
4th	$8.00	$15.00
5th	$16.00	$31.00
6th	$32.00	$63.00
7th	$64.00	$127.00
8th	$128.00	-

Now suddenly, you're faced with a $128.00 bet with $127.00 worth of losses behind you. That's a lot of sweat and aggravation just to win $1.00 on the sequence. And we all know that seven losses in a row is not that strange of an occurrence.

What happens on the next spin? Surely you're due for a winner now after seven consecutive losses. If you're pregnant or expecting a raise or some such thing, you may be due.

In gambling, you're never due for anything. There are expectations based on the odds, but the fact that seven times the wheel spun black when you've been betting red, has no bearing on the eighth spin. The odds don't change - it's still an 18 out of 37 (European wheel) or 38 (American wheel) shot for your winning red on the next spin.

Remember, it's only a wheel. It has no memory, no brain. It doesn't know who you are, what you're betting, or that seven times in a row, black came up on it.

So back to the game. Heaven forbid that two more spins should go against you, for then you're faced with the following:

MARTINGALE PROGRESSION CONTINUED		
Loss	**Initial Bet**	**Total Loss**
8th	$128.00	$255.00
9th	$256.00	$511.00
10th	$512.00	-

Add up these numbers then get out the Pepto-Bismol. Think twice before using this classic system. Do you really want to risk a situation where you'll need to bet over five hundred dollars just to win $1.00?

The Grand Martingale

If you liked the above example, you'll love this system. The rallying point of the **Grand Martingale** is to attempt to win more than $1.00 on a losing progression by adding $1.00 to the bet after each loss. We'll spare ourselves the anguish of adding up these numbers, but you can see they'll add up even faster than the Martingale, and seriously, who needs that?

The Pyramid System

This system is far more appealing to the player for its winning approach doesn't entail the kind of deep ditch digging that the Martingale and Grand Martingale do.

In this system, also called the **D'Alembert**, we'll look at each bet it terms of units, and to make life easy, we'll use $1.00 as our unit bet. The first bet will be $1.00. If we win, the sequence is ended, and we'll begin a new one.

If the bet is lost, our next bet becomes $2.00. Each subsequent loss adds $1.00 to the bet, so that five consecutive losses would produce a $6.00 bet on the following play. (Compare this to the Martingale, where you'd be watching a $32.00 bet gracing the tables for your $1.00 win, and the first tinges of a headache beginning to pound your skull.)

This system is interesting for after every win, you will decrease your bet by one unit! The end result of this system is that every win (as opposed to every progression) produces a win of $1.00, or if you prefer to think in terms of units, every win produces a one unit gain.

Every won bet is $1.00 more than the previous lost bet.

Let's follow a progression to see how this works.

PYRAMID PROGRESSION		
Bet	**Result**	**Total**
$1.00	Win	+$1.00
$1.00	Loss	$0.00
$2.00	Loss	-$2.00
$3.00	Win	+$1.00
$2.00	Win	+$3.00
$1.00	Loss	+$2.00
$2.00	Loss	+$0.00
$3.00	Loss	-$3.00
$4.00	Loss	-$7.00
$5.00	Loss	-$12.00
$6.00	Win	-$6.00
$5.00	Loss	-$11.00
$6.00	Win	-$5.00
$5.00	Win	$0.00

TOTAL - 14 Plays: 6 Wins, 8 Losses

You can see the attractions of this system, for despite sustaining five straight losses and eight overall as against only six wins, the sequence where we left off showed the player dead even. A win on the next play would forge a profit of $4.00, with the next bet being $3.00, so the bettor's position looks pretty good overall.

This is all well and good on a short run look. However, in the long run, this system like all others trying to fight a game where the house has an edge, will ultimately lose. As the progression continues, there will be more losses than wins and the downward dips will be deeper and more frequent than wins.

As long as this is kept in mind, the immovable house edge, than one might play this system to great enjoyment, and in the short run, maybe some profit!

Biased Wheels

There is a way to beat the casino at roulette, but this involves finding an unbalanced wheel, presumably old and rickety, more likely in a smaller casino, or perhaps at a fair where the mechanics of the wheel are far from state of the art.

It is impossible to make a perfectly balanced wheel, one where each number has exactly the same chance of coming up as any other number. A slight imperfection in the material, normal wear and tear, a warp, a tiny tilt, an unlevel floor, a slightly larger or shorter slot - these possibilities or any of a number of others can cause an imbalance of a wheel and favor some numbers to be spun more than others.

Wheels are made with such tremendous precision nowadays that it is extremely unlikely to find a wheel with a bias significant enough to make this theory interesting.

However, you may find an older wheel in use, one that's been subjected to enough wear and tear of normal usage that a bias is created, or one with faulty mechanics, and until the casino has figured out that you've got something going on and shuts down the wheel, you can make a lot of money - with the odds.

First you must determine if the wheel is biased and how large the bias is. To do this requires a lot of work and patience, but if indeed you're hunch is right and the wheel is significantly biased, you will have made the effort worthwhile. There are many stories of dedicated players patiently clocking wheels, finding a bias, and winning enormous sums of money until the game is shut down on them.

To properly track a wheel, you'll need a partner or an associate or two for every spin of the wheel will need to be recorded for at least 24 hours and ideally two or three times that much to get a fair sampling. A sampling taken for less than 24 hours will only show short run deviations (unless the wheel is incredibly biased) and will not be an accurate look at numbers which may be biased.

The expectation of any single number being spun is 1 in 38 on an American wheel (1 in 37 on a European one).

For a strategy to be effective and show profits, a single number's bias must not only be greater than the 1/38 (1/37 in Europe) expected result, but be sufficient enough to overcome the inherent casino's edge of 5.26% on an American wheel and 2.70% on a European one for single zero betting.

You may find one number or several that stand out on a wheel as being biased and base your winning strategy on those numbers (or number). The superior odds inherent in single zero roulette make those games much better to track for if a bias is found, the smaller house edge is easier to overcome and the profits will be greater.

Winning With Betting Systems

Roulette is a fun way to relax and try your luck at calling and betting the numbers that will come up winners on the wheel. We've presented some basic winning systems for beginning players that you can try at the tables plus the very interesting biased wheel strategy.

There are all sorts of interesting betting systems available - different number parlays, single and multiple number cycle plays, alternate betting systems, jump plays and more. Many of these systems are quite creative, some, in fact are very good.*

With a run of luck, money can be made at roulette if your numbers come up winners and your other wagers ride a streak. However, no matter what bets are made or what system is used, always keep sound money management principles in mind. That is the key to winning at roulette.

Good Luck!

*For serious players, GRI has developed advanced winning systems specially designed for winning at roulette (including advanced multiple number cycle plays and other systems). These are available through our mail order ads in the back.

SLOTS

INTRODUCTION

These ever-popular machines can be found around the world, buzzing, clanging and spitting out rewards to their faithful players. Millions are hooked on the game. Some play for the sheer pleasure, hoping to pass a little time and win a few coins, others play for that elusive thing, the big jackpot, which will set them on easy street.

Charles Fey is credited with being the originator of slot machines in their more or less current format. His original machines, called **Liberty Bells**, were introduced in the late 1800s and first began to appear in the bars and saloons around the San Francisco Bay. There were coin-operated machines before Fey which were based on games of chance such as dice and roulette, but Fey's Liberty Bell was the first to feature a three reel design with automatic payouts to the winners.

These early machines used three reels of ten symbols each, among which were the famous Liberty Bell figures, along with other symbols of the times such as horseshoes. If the 10 possibilities per reel are multiplied by three reels, 10 x 10 x 10, we come up with 1,000 different possible combinations on these early machines.

Fey set the machines to pay back 86% to the players. The other 14%, the profit, he split 50-50 with the bar and saloon owners. The machines really took off and spurred a host of competitors, most notably Herbert Stephen Mills and the Caille Brothers. Slots have come a long way since then and account for important parts of a casino's income.

Nowadays, the average slot machines accept 25¢ and $1.00

coins. However, some of the more plush casino offer their high rollers slot machines that take coins as large as $100 and even $500!

TYPES OF MACHINES

There are basically two types of slot machines. The first type, the **Straight Slots**, pays winning combinations according to the schedule listed on the machine itself. For example, one cherry may pay two coins for each one put in, two cherries may pay five coins and three cherries 10 coins.

The second type of machines are called **Progressive Slots**. These too have a standard set of payoffs listed on the machine itself, but in addition, and what sometimes makes for exciting play, is the big jackpot which progressively gets larger and larger as every coin is put in. The jackpot total is posted above the machine and can grow to enormous sums of money.

THE BASICS OF PLAY

Slots are easy to play. Machines generally take anywhere from 1 to 5 coins, and all one needs to do is insert the coins into the machine, pull the handle and see what Lady Luck brings.

There are many types of slot machine configurations but all work according to the same principles - put the money in the slots and pull the handle!

Often, the number of lines the machine will pay on depends on the amount of coins deposited. One coin only may pay the middle line, a second coin will pay the top line as well, a third coin - the bottom line, so now any of the three horizontals will pay should a paying combination be hit. A fourth coin may pay the diagonal, and a fifth, the other diagonal.

If the proper combination is hit, the machine should make a little noise for you as coins automatically pour into the well at the bottom. And should a really large payoff be hit, a jackpot, the machines will make a bunch of noise, a light may go off atop the machine and you just hang tight, for a casino employee should be there soon to give you the payoff.

More winning rows does not necessarily equate to better odds of winning. It just means more coins per play and therefore more possibilities of a payoff, for each coin gives you another bar or direction that will pay.

The odds are built into the machine and no amount of lines played will change them. The most important factor is how loose or tight the machines are set by the casino - that is what determines the odds facing a slots player.

SAMPLE SLOTS PAYOFF (PER COIN)

Winning Combination	Payoff
7-7-7	100 coins
Bar-Bar-Bar	50 coins
Bell-Bell-Bell	20 coins
Bell-Bell-Bar	18 coins
Bar-Bell-Bell	18 coins
Plum-Plum-Plum	20 coins
Plum-Plum-Bar	14 coins
Bar-Plum-Plum	14 coins
Orange-Orange-Orange	20 coins
Orange-Orange-Bar	10 coins
Bar-Orange-Orange	10 coins
Cherry-Cherry-Cherry	20 coins
Any-Cherry-Cherry	5 coins
Cherry-Cherry-Any	5 coins
Cherry-Any-Cherry	5 coins
Any-Any-Cherry	2 coins
Cherry-Any-Any	2 coins

SLOT PERCENTAGES

The percentage return of slot machines vary from casino to casino, and often within a casino as well. While the Nevada regulatory commission sets no minimum at all, the Atlantic City gaming commission requires a minimum return of 83% back to the players. Within these loose frameworks, a whole range of percentages may apply.

In general, a casino that relies on slots for a good portion of their income will offer players a higher return on their slots money, while those that have the slots as but an incidental income, will pay less on the average.

Some casinos advertise slots with returns as high as 97% to the player, others, even as high as 99%! Obviously, the player stands a much better chance of winning at these places than others where a standard return of only 83% might be the norm. On machines in areas not covered by regulatory minimums, such as Nevada, players may not even get an 83% return.

SLOTS STRATEGY

The most important concept in slots is to locate the machines with the loosest setting, or with progressive machines, to play only the machines with the highest progressive setting.

The first thing to look for are casinos which really push their slot machine business and cater to the players, and also casinos which advertise a higher return. These are places that may offer slot players a better than average return.

In general, the poorer paying machines will be located in areas where the casino or proprietor hopes to grab a few of the bettor's coins as he passes through an area or waits on a line. Airport terminals, restaurant and show lines, bathrooms and the like tend to have smaller returns.

On the other hand, casinos that specialize in slots and look to attract serious players, will set up slots areas within a casino that will have better payoffs, or even, as you can find in Las Vegas, the whole casino will be slots only! These casinos view slots as an important income, and in order to keep regular slots customers, their players must hear those jackpot bells ringing - after all, winning is contagious!

Some machines are set to pay better than others, and these slots will be mixed in with poorer paying ones, so its always a good idea to look for the hot machine. Better yet, ask the change girls. They spend all day near the slots and know which machines tend to return the most money.

Basically, your best strategy is to examine the wide array of machines offered for play, and to find the best one suited to your personal style.

When you hit a good jackpot, make sure you set your stop-loss limit. This guarantees that you walk away a winner!

VIDEO POKER

INTRODUCTION

Video poker is catching on like wildfire and fast becoming one of the most popular casino games. It's really a lot of fun for decision-making and skill are involved and proper play can bring one profits. Even better, the game can be as leisurely or hurried as you want for there is no dealer to hurry you along. You choose your own pace - it's just you against the machine. May the best one win!

The whole setting is really simple. All one needs is some coins to play and an available video poker machine, and you're in business.

This section will show you the basic rules of play, how to work the video poker machine, the different games available, the payoffs at the various machines, and then a winning strategy to arm you with the best odds and hopefully, make you a winner.

THE TYPES OF MACHINES

Video poker offers the player a variety of machines from which to choose. The two basic types of video poker machines are the **Flat-Top** (or **Straight**) machines and the **Progressives**. The Flat-Tops offer set payoffs on all the hands won, with the payoffs proportionately larger for greater amounts of coins played. Thus, a winning payoff on two coins played will be exactly double that for the same winning hand with one coin played.

The one exception is for the royal flush, where a winning payoff will give the player a 4,000 coin return when five coins are played, as opposed to only 200, 400, 600 and 800 coins on a one, two, three and four coin play respectively. All other payoffs are in proportion.

Winning payoffs are posted on the machine, so you can see right off what you're up against.

The Progressive machines differ from the Straight or Flat Tops in that when a royal flush is hit with five coins played, the payoff is not a set amount but is based on a progressive total. This jackpot constantly increases until the royal is hit, when it will start again at a set amount, such as $1,000 on a 25¢ machine.

The Progressives can be exciting for jackpots go higher and higher, and now and again, a quarter machine will soar well into the $2,000+ range or even higher. However, like the Straight machines, the full five coins must be played to reap the full reward when the royal flush is hit.

There are different varieties of the video poker machines within the above classifications. A player may find Jacks or Better, 10s or Better, Deuces Wild and Joker Wild, and these can be played as Straights or Progressives, depending upon what casino players find themselves in and what machines are offered.

We'll talk more about this later when we discuss each game individually.

HOW TO PLAY

Video poker is basically played as draw poker. The machine uses a 52 card deck which is played fresh after each hand. While you won't receive the same card within a play, for the machine will deal cards from the 52 card computer pack, the memory ends there as the deck is "reshuffled" after each deal.

To start, you need to insert anywhere from one to five coins into the machine. The choice is yours - play one or play five at your discretion. We will recommend that serious players insert the full five coins to get the best odds, but we'll go into that later.

If five coins are inserted, the machine will automatically deal a hand to you. However, if less than the maximum amount is inserted, you'll need to press the button marked **DRAW/ DEAL** to receive your cards.

Five cards will show on the screen. These are your cards. You may keep one, some, all or none of the cards. It's your decision. To keep a card, press the button marked "**hold**" underneath the corresponding card you wish to keep. There will be five hold buttons, one for each card, and for each card you want to keep, you must press the hold button.

"**HELD**" will appear on the screen underneath each card or cards so chosen. The other cards, the ones you wish to discard, will not be kept by the machine.

What happens if you press the wrong hold button by accident or change your mind? No problem. Press the corresponding button again. If the card indicated "held," it will no longer do so and will not be held by the computer. If you change your mind again, press the button one more time, and again the "held" sign will come on the screen indicating that the card will be kept on the draw.

Until you press the draw button, it is not too late to change your strategy decision.

A player may keep all five original cards and does so by pushing the hold button under each card or he or she may discard all five original cards if so desired. This is done by pressing the DRAW/DEAL button without having pressed any of the hold buttons.

You now press the DRAW/DEAL button to receive some new cards. The "held" cards will remain and those cards not chosen to be held will be replaced with new ones. This set of cards is the final hand.

If your hand is a winner, the machine will flash "**WINNER**" at the bottom of the screen. Winning hands are automatically paid according to the payoffs shown on the machine.

Credit

There is a useful feature offered on many video poker machines that allows you to play on winnings using a credit function built-in to the machines.

Let's say for example, that you've just hit a win for 20 coins. Two things will happen.

On the machine, you'll see "Credit - 20" appear. To continue playing without cashing out and reinserting coins, you can now press another button that will have lit up and be indicated by the label, **Maximum Bet**, **Bet 5** or some similar name. This allows you to play five of your 20 credits toward a new hand which will appear on the screen along with the information that your credit now stands at 15.

The second thing that will happen after your 20 coin win is that a button called the **Cashout** or **Payout** button will light up. If pressed, the machine will give immediate payment of the winnings registered in the credit area.

The Cashout button can be used after any hand is completed to cash out wins that have accumulated, or if you want to continue playing on credit, keep pressing the Maximum Bet button to get a new hand dealt.

Let's go over the winning hands in video poker and then we'll show the payoffs you'll most likely encounter in the different games available.

Winning Video Poker Hands

- **Jacks or Better** - Two cards of equal value are called a pair. Jacks or better refers to a pairing of Jacks, Queens, Kings or Aces.
- **Two Pair** - Two sets of paired cards, such as 3-3 and 10-10.
- **Three of a Kind** - Three cards of equal value, such as 9-9-9.
- **Straight** - Five cards in numerical sequence, such as 3-4-5-6-7 or 10-J-Q-K-A. The ace can be counted as the highest card or the lowest card in a straight, however, it may not be in the middle of a five card run, such as Q-K-A-2-3, which is not a straight.

- **Flush** - Any five cards of the same suit, such as five hearts.
- **Full House** - Three of a kind and a pair, such as 2-2-2-J-J.
- **Four of a Kind** - Four cards of equal value, such as K-K-K-K.
- **Straight Flush** - A straight all in the same suit, such as 7-8-9-10-J, all in spades.
- **Royal Flush** - 10-J-Q-K-A, all in the same suit.

Jacks or Better: 9-6 Machines

These machines are known as **9-6 machines**, because of the 9 and 6 coin payouts when the Full House and Flush are hit. Note that a pair of 10s will not pay anything back, nor will any lower pair. A hand of jacks or better is needed for a payout.

Payoffs on Jacks or Better · 9-6 Machine					
COINS PLAYED	**1**	**2**	**3**	**4**	**5**
Jacks or Better	1	2	3	4	5
Two Pair	2	4	6	8	10
Three of a Kind	3	6	9	12	15
Straight	4	8	12	16	20
Flush	6	12	18	24	30
Full House	9	18	27	36	45
Four of a Kind	25	50	75	100	125
Straight Flush	50	100	150	200	250
Royal Flush	250	500	750	1000	4000

Progressive Payout

Besides the straight machines discussed above, there are progressive machines, as in slots. All payoffs, like the straight machines are fixed except in the case of a Royal Flush, where this grandaddy pays the accumulated total posted above the machine on the electronic board. This total slowly, but constantly rises, and on a quarter machine in Las Vegas can rise into the thousands of dollars.

The following chart shows typical payoffs for video poker on a Jacks or Better Progressive machine. This machine is known as an **8-5 machine**, so named for the payoffs given on the full house and flush respectively.

Payoffs on Jacks or Better · 8-5 Machine					
Coins Played	**1**	**2**	**3**	**4**	**5**
Jacks or Better	1	2	3	4	5
Two Pair	2	4	6	8	10
Three of a Kind	3	6	9	12	15
Straight	4	8	12	16	20
Flush	5	10	15	20	25
Full House	8	16	24	32	40
Four of a Kind	25	50	75	100	125
Straight Flush	50	100	150	200	250
Royal Flush	250	500	750	1000	*

*When five coins are played and the royal flush is hit, the bettor receives the full amount accumulated for the Progressive jackpot. Note that all five coins must be played to win the jackpot.

10s or Better Video Poker

The 10s or Better machine is only found infrequently. The following is the payout on the non-progressive machines. Note that the Royal Flush is paid at 800-1 only if five coins have been played.

Payoffs on 10s or Better					
Coins Played	**1**	**2**	**3**	**4**	**5**
10s or Better	1	2	3	4	5
Two Pair	2	4	6	8	10
Three of a Kind	3	6	9	12	15
Straight	4	8	12	16	20
Flush	5	10	15	20	25
Full House	6	12	18	24	30
Four of a Kind	25	50	75	100	125
Straight Flush	50	100	150	200	250
Royal Flush	250	500	750	1000	4000

Wild Card Video Poker

Two variations of video poker that have caught on and gained in popularity are the **Deuces Wild** and **Jokers Wild** machines. Wild cards can be given any value or suit and the machine will interpret wild cards in the most advantageous way for the player.

For example, the hand 2 2 5 6 8 in deuces wild would be a straight, for one 2 can be used as a 7 and the other as either a 9 or 4. The deuces could also be used as eights to give three of a kind, but since the straight is more valuable to the player the machine will see it as a straight.

Wild card machines have different payoff schedules than the jacks or better machines, and these machines will start giving credit only on a three of a kind hand or better.

Deuces Wild Video Poker

This variation of video poker is played the same way as the Jacks or Better or 10s or Better machines and uses the same standard 52 card deck, but in this version there is one important difference - the four deuces (2s) are wild, and can be used as any card in the deck, even to make a five of a kind hand.

The video poker machine will recognize the best hand possible using the deuces and will automatically give credit for the maximum hand value that can be made.

Deuces Wild Video Poker Payout					
Coins Played 1	2	3	4	5	
Three of a Kind	1	2	3	4	5
Straight	2	4	6	8	10
Flush	2	4	6	8	10
Full House	3	6	9	12	15
Four of a Kind	5	10	15	20	25
Straight Flush	9	18	27	36	45
Five of a Kind	15	30	45	60	75
Royal Flush (deuces)	25	50	75	100	125
Four Deuces	200	400	600	800	1000
Royal Flush (Natural)	250	500	750	1000	4000

Note that the Royal Flush as a natural hand (without the deuces) will be paid off at 800-1 only if five coins are played at Deuces Wild Video Poker.

Joker Wild Video Poker

There are two version of the joker wild game: **Ace-King** and **Two Pairs**. In the Ace-King version, a minimum hand of a pair of kings must be made for a payoff. In Two Pairs, two pair is the minimum hand needed for a payoff.

Both versions of Joker Wild are played with a 53 card deck, the regular 52 card deck plus the wild card, the **joker**, which can be assigned any value.

Let's look at the payoffs for each game in turn.

Keep in mind that the Royal Flush will only be paid off with the maximum return if five coins are played.

Joker Wild Video Poker Payout · Ace-King					
Coins Played 1	2	3	4	5	
Ace or Kings	1	2	3	4	5
Two Pair	1	2	3	4	5
Three of a Kind	2	4	6	8	10
Straight	3	6	9	12	15
Flush	5	10	15	20	25
Full House	7	14	21	28	35
Four of a Kind	20	40	60	80	100
Straight Flush	50	100	150	200	250
Royal Flush (Joker)	100	200	300	400	500
Five of a Kind	200	400	600	800	1000
Royal Flush (natural)	250	500	750	1000	4000

Note the same payout whether one gets a pair of Aces or Kings, or Two Pair.

Sometimes a machine will be found that pays off only 15 for 1 on the four of a kind instead of the 20 for 1 as listed above. Give these machines a miss.

Joker Wild Video Poker Payout · Two Pair					
Coins Played	1	2	3	4	5
Two Pair	1	2	3	4	5
Three of a Kind	2	4	6	8	10
Straight	5	10	15	20	25
Flush	7	14	21	28	35
Full House	8	16	24	32	40
Four of a Kind	20	40	60	80	100
Straight Flush	50	100	150	200	250
Royal Flush (Joker)	50	100	150	200	250
Five of a Kind	100	200	300	400	500
Royal Flush (natural)	250	500	750	1000	4000*

*Note that five coins must be played, and should always be played to receive the maximum payout for the Royal Flush.

WINNING STRATEGY

The big payoff on video poker machines is for the royal flush. It doesn't matter what variation is played - Jacks or Better, 10s or Better, Deuces Wild or Joker Wild - a whopping 4,000 coins are paid for this big daddy when five coins are played. And on progressive machines, if five coins are played, the total could be a great deal higher, making the game even more interesting.

Of course, the royal doesn't come often. With correct strategy, you'll hit one every 30,000+ hands on the average. This doesn't mean, however, that you won't hit one in your very first hour of play. But meanwhile, you'll be collecting other winners such as straights, full houses and the like, and with proper play, all in all, you can beat the video poker machines - with the odds!

To win, you must play the correct strategies. Like regular poker, there are skillful ways to play your hand. However, unlike regular poker, you're not playing against other players, but against a machine. Strategies that make sense in the Friday night game may not be the proper ones at a video poker machine.

Always Play Five Coins

To achieve the absolute best odds at the video poker machine, five coins must be played. At first glance, this suggestion probably strikes you as being strange. Why not one coin or two? After all, the payoffs on all hands at the video poker machine are proportionately the same whether one, two, three, four or five coins are played.

However, there's one glaring exception - the royal flush.

And though this hand doesn't come often, it does come and much more so than in a regular poker game for we're playing an entirely different strategy in video poker. We're concentrating on the big score, the royal flush. This is different than a regular poker game where your primary goal is simply to win the hand, even if a pair of 7s do the trick. In video poker, of course, 7s don't pay anything.

You'll play hands in video poker that you wouldn't in a regular poker game and vias-versa. The strategies for the two games are entirely different.

Look back at the payoff chart for Jacks or Better and notice what happens on the royal flush payoffs. Interesting, yes? One coin played returns 200 coins, two coins yields 400, three coins 600 and four coins brings home 800 bad boys. Well, the progression for the fifth coin should be 1,000 if you're following along with the addition.

But it's not. The full payoff on a royal flush with five coins played is 4,000 coins!

That's a nice payoff and the reason we're going to play five coins. The royal is not as remote as it seems. You may never see one in a regular poker game, but at the video poker machines, following the strategies we suggest, you've a good chance to land that big fish.

You'll see similar jumps for the Royal Flush payoffs on all the video poker machines. Therefore, to collect the full payoff on a royal flush, proper play dictates that you always play the full five coins for each game. For if you do hit the royal flush, there's a big, big difference between 1,000 coins returned and 4,000 returned.

Find Machines With the Best Payoffs

The payoff schedules we've listed in this section are not the only ones you'll find for the games we've discussed. You may find machines with less generous payouts, so as a general rule, and when possible, always choose machines with the best payouts.

For example, where there's lots of casino competition, as in Las Vegas, some window shopping will definitely be to your advantage.

Winning Strategy for Jacks or Better: 9-6 Flattops

Following is the basic strategy for the 9-6 Flattops. (These strategies are not applicable to the 8-5 Jacks or Better Progressives.)*

1. Whenever you hold **four cards to a royal flush,** discard the fifth card, even if that card gives you a flush or pair.

2. Keep a **jacks or better pair** and any higher hand such as a three of a kind or straight over three to the royal. Play the **three to a royal** over any lesser hand such as a low pair or four flush.

3. With **two cards to a royal**, keep four straights, four flushes, and high pairs or better instead. Otherwise, go for the royal.

4. Never break up a **straight or flush**, unless a one card draw gives you a chance for the royal.

5. Keep **jacks or better** over a four straight or four flush.

6. Never break up a **four of a kind, full house, three of a kind** and **two pair** hands. The *rags*, worthless cards for the latter two hands, should be dropped on the draw.

7. The **jacks or better pair** is always kept, except when you have four cards to the royal, or four to the straight flush.

8. Keep **low pairs** over the four straight, but discard them in favor of the four flushes and three or four to a royal flush.

9. When dealt **unmade hands**, a pre-draw hands with no payable combination of cards, save in order, four to a royal flush and straight flush, three to a royal flush, four flushes, four straights, three to a straight flush, two cards to the royal, two cards jack or higher and one card jack or higher.

10. Lacking any of the above, with no card jack or higher, discard all the cards and draw five fresh ones.

*The full strategy charts for the 9-6 machines and the strategy charts for the 8-5 Progressives are beyond the scope of this book. Serious players looking to have the mathematical advantage and win money at video poker must buy GRI's Professional Video Poker Strategy listed in the back.

Simplified Basic Strategy Chart: Jacks or Better 9-6 Flattop*

The following chart lists hands in order of strength from most powerful first, the Royal Flush, to the least powerful last, the Nothing Hands. Keep the hands listed higher in preference to hands listed lower. For example, keep a High Pair over a three to a royal, but discard it for a four to the royal.

Jacks or Better - Simplified Basic Strategy Chart		
Hand to Be Held	**Cards Held**	**Cards Drawn**
Royal Flush	5	0
Straight Flush	5	0
Four of a Kind	5	0
Full House	5	0
Four to a Royal	4	1
Flush	5	0
Three of a Kind	3	2
Straight	5	0
Four to a Straight Flush	4	1
Two Pair	4	1
High Pair	2	3
Three to a Royal	3	2
Four to a Flush	4	1
Low Pair	2	3
Four to a Straight	4	1
Three to a Straight Flush	3	2
Two to a Royal	2	3
Two High Cards	2	3
One High Card	1	4
Nothing Hand - Draw Five	0	5

Winning Strategy for 10s or Better

10s or Better is played similarly to Jacks or Better, except that a pair of 10s is kept as the high pair. Otherwise, follow the strategy as outlined above in Jacks or Better.

Simplified Winning Strategy for Deuces Wild

Deuces are extremely valuable cards so when you get them, make sure you never discard them by accident. There's no payoff for hands less than three of a kind, so our strategy must be adjusted accordingly.

With four deuces, stand pat with this automatic winner; with three deuces, stand with a royal flush or 5 of a kind, otherwise save the deuces and draw two cards. With two deuces, play 4 and 5 card royal and straight flushes and 4 and 5 of a kinds. On all other hands, keep only the two deuces and draw three.

With one deuce, retain all paying combinations (only breaking up a straight or flush for a 4 to the royal or straight flush). Draw two cards to a 3 card royal and straight flushes, one card if there's 4 to the hand. If none of the above, retain only the wild 2 and draw four. With no deuce, play all hands as in the one deuce strategy plus in order of playing preference; any pair, 4 flushes, 4 straights and 2 to the Royal.

Three card flushes or straights are worthless in this game as are single unmatched high cards so don't be holding onto hands of this nature. You'll also get rid of two pair hands - for they don't pay. Hang onto one of the pairs, and go for three new cards.

You'll find that many of the hands you'll be dealt will contain nothing worth saving and you'll be drawing for five fresh cards. It will take a little while getting used to wild card video poker after playing the non-wild versions, but once you get accustomed you should have a lot of fun at these machines.

Playing to Win Money

Video poker is certainly a fun game, for it is a game of skill, and as we stated in the beginning, with proper play you can have the edge over the casino.

Like blackjack though, you need to study the correct strategies carefully to come out a winner. As all smart gamblers know, preparation can pay off in winnings, so for those players serious about moving forward in the game, the professional video poker strategy advertised in the back is highly recommended.

You'll learn the important differences in strategy between the 8-5 Progressive and 9-6 Jacks or Better machines plus receive complete strategy charts and winning advice for these games, 10s or Better, Deuces Wild, Jokers Wild and others. Most importantly, you'll learn which machines give you an edge over the casino and how best to get that edge.

Meanwhile, use your skill at video poker to good advantage, and make sure you walk away a winner!

BINGO

INTRODUCTION

This immensely popular game has flourished since its 1950s legalization in the United States, and is a popular and fun way for millions and millions of players, primarily women, to let loose with an evening of recreational gambling. It is played in numerous countries around the world, in places as far away as Australia and Africa, and has spurned a life of its own in Indian reservations around the U.S. where the game is very big business.

There are many versions of bingo, from the standard five in a row, column or diagonal group of bingos, to all four corners, to double bingos to combinations as varied as one can imagine.

There's one U.S. county that even runs a cowpie bingo game as a fund raiser. A field is parceled off into squares which are bought by the participants. Where the cow lands its load - bingo! The buyer of the square is the lucky winner.

Bingo is found everywhere in the U.S. and is probably the most popular non-profit fund raiser for organizations around the country. Religious organizations, schools, fire departments and a whole slew of charitable, social and fraternal organizations count on their bingo games as an important source of income.

Funds are often split three ways. One part goes to the organization running the event, a second part to the professional group running the game itself, and the third part being the prizes awarded to the winners.

Let's move on now and see what this fun game is all about!

THE APPARATUS OF PLAY

The Bingo Cards

Bingo is played with **game cards** which have pre-printed numbers on them. The cards can be made of paper or other disposable material, and the player marks numbers called with a crayon or perhaps plastic chips. The game card is no longer valid once the game is finished and can be thrown away.

Other bingo games may use a hard "permanent" board, also with pre-printed numbers, and these game cards, typically made of cardboard or plastic, can be used by the player for multiple games. The player keeps tab of the numbers played by using removable tabs.

The standard bingo card has 25 squares arranged in five columns of five boxes each. Each square is numbered with the exception of the middle square which may be imprinted by **"free"** or **"bingo,"** and which automatically counts as a number called for all players.

The first vertical column is headed by the letter B and contains five numbers in the 1 to 15 range. The second row, under the letter I, has five numbers in the 16 - 30 range, and similarly, the third row, under the letter N, five numbers ranging from 31 - 45, the fourth row, 46 - 60 under the letter G, and finally the last column, the fifth, five numbers in the 61 - 75 range.

The B-I-N-G-O letters above each column serve only as reference points to help the players locate their numbers and otherwise serve no real purpose in the game.

While many cards may contain similarly numbered squares, no numbers will be repeated within the same card.

The Bingo Balls

Bingo is played with 75 ping pong balls which are imprinted with numbers from 1 - 75, one number for each ball, and letters representing the column they fall in. The number 14, for example, will say B14, the number 65 will be O65. This makes it easy for all players to quickly locate the numbers on their card.

(Some bingo variations might use 80 or 90 numbers.)

The 75 balls are randomly mixed in a spherical wire cage or enclosed blower. When the game is ready to ensue, balls are drawn one by one, and announced by the **caller** of the game. As the balls are removed they're placed aside in a **masterboard** or **rack** and generally, flashed onto an electric board so that all players can be aware of the numbers picked.

Bingo Card

B	I	N	G	O
10	25	33	49	71
3	17	42	55	65
11	23	FREE	60	74
2	21	38	50	69
5	20	36	54	73

HOW BINGO IS PLAYED

Each player must be armed with at least one game card to play bingo, though many players, serious bingo fanatics, play multiple cards, as many as 20 or more for one game.

Bingo cards are either purchased individually for each game, included as part of the admission price, or even sold as part of a package covering many games. Whatever the procedure, the player's bingo card or cards contains the numbers which may or may not turn out to be winners.

When the game is ready to begin, the caller announces the type of bingo game to be played. As the numbers are drawn, one by one, the players in the room grow profoundly silent. Players pore over their cards carefully as numbers are drawn, checking off the numbers they hold and checking out the possibilities that can make their bingo card a winner.

The game moves on and numbers fill the cards. A growing buzz electrifies the room and several cards edge just one number away from victory. The tension builds as another number is called, a few players creep forward in their seat, then suddenly, as one more number is called, BINGO! is screamed out across the room, sometimes by more than one player.

BINGO!

And that means there is a winner.

Players claiming bingo get their card verified by an appropriate official of the game and if indeed the call is correct, the game is over and the winner or winners collect the prize.

There can be more than one winner on a call, as there often are. It doesn't matter who calls bingo first or even if a player inadvertently overlooked a bingo the number before. All winning bingos share equally in the prize.

WINNING BINGOS

The standard combination needed to win at bingo is the completion of five winning numbers in a line - horizontally, vertically or diagonally. But in addition to these standard bingos, are a multitude of others limited only by the imagination of the caller.

Some callers, really in tune with the game, have upwards of 100 different bingo games in their arsenal and can really delight the players with names and games that run the gamut of bingo's possibilities.

We'll now show some of the more common winning patterns used in bingo.

HORIZONTAL BINGO

A standard bingo formed by five numbers in a straight horizontal line.

Horizontal Bingo

B	I	N	G	O
10	25	33	49	71
●	●	●	●	●
11	23	FREE	60	74
2	21	38	50	69
5	20	36	54	73

VERTICAL BINGO

A standard bingo formed by five numbers in a straight vertical line.

Vertical Bingo

B	I	N	G	O
10	●	33	49	71
3	●	42	55	65
11	●	FREE	60	74
2	●	38	50	69
5	●	36	54	73

DIAGONAL BINGO

A standard bingo formed by five numbers formed in a straight horizontal line which includes the middle "free" square.

Diagonal Bingo

B	I	N	G	O
●	25	33	49	71
3	●	42	55	65
11	23	●	60	74
2	21	38	●	69
5	20	36	54	●

FOUR CORNER BINGO

Here, the winning bingo tickets have all four corners caught.

Four Corner Bingo

B	I	N	G	O
●	25	33	49	●
3	17	42	55	65
11	23	FREE	60	74
2	21	38	50	69
●	20	36	54	●

COVERALL OR BLACKOUT BINGO

This one takes more work than the others for you need to catch all the numbers on your card to win the blackout or coverall bingo.

Coverall or Blackout Bingo

DOUBLE BINGO

You need two bingo patterns in the game to catch a winner.

Double Bingo

B	I	N	G	O
10	25	●	49	71
3	17	●	55	65
11	23	●	60	74
2	21	●	50	69
●	●	●	●	●

LAYER CAKE

You need to hit all the numbers in the first, third and fifth horizontal rows.

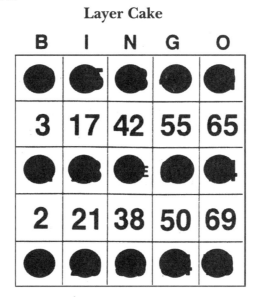

Layer Cake

THE PICTURE FRAME

This is a fun one. You need to fill all the outside numbers, making a picture frame, to win.

The Picture Frame

There are tons of other bingo patterns, with exotic and fun names, but whatever the game called, the caller will make it clear to the players what the winning ticket must resemble.

Progressive Bingo

As bingo becomes a larger and more profitable game, progressive bingos are getting more attractive to players. Prizes nowadays run well into the thousands of dollars at many places and even into the tens of thousands of dollars. Now and then, superjackpots even run into the six figures!

The higher the bingo progressive prize goes, the more fevered the game. Then again, how would you feel if your bingo card looks like it may catch a grand prize of $200,000?

Pretty good, I bet.

To win the progressive jackpot, a player needs to "blackout" his or her ticket and catch all the numbers within a specified period of draws, such as 50 for example.

BINGO ODDS

The odds a player faces at bingo varies from place to place and is a direct function of how much money the bingo parlor pays back to the players in proportion to the amount of money they take in. However, with revenues presumably being split three ways in many bingo games, you can imagine the odds are not very good at all for the player.

Each bingo game has its own set of payback schedules and more often than not, they may not be regulated. The bingo games must return enough money back to keep players coming back for more, but in any case, don't quit your job yet and count on being a professional bingo player.

Without knowing the exact cut of each house and the consequent return to the player, it is impossible to say the odds a player faces at bingo except to say that they're not very favorable.

But in any case, bingo is a great leisure game for many people, providing a place to unwind for some, and for others, a place to get wound up, and as long as good fun is had, bingo serves as good entertainment.

WINNING APPROACH

Basically, you just need to get lucky. You may wish to choose your own numbers or cards if the option is available, carefully combing over the numbers to see which appear most propitious for the moment.

Maybe you want to search out some cards containing your lucky numbers or birthday, maybe something to do with the date, the way the planets are aligned or your clothing sizes.

Or you may simply choose to let fate totally decide the issue and grab your card at random. It comes down to your personal preferences, but however you choose - good luck!

GLOSSARY

BINGO - The winning cry; the name of the game.

BLACKOUT - Bingo combination where all numbers are covered.

BLOWER - The compressed air apparatus used to circulate the ping pong balls used.

CAGE - Hand operated wire enclosure used to manually mix the bingo balls.

CALLER - The bingo official who draws the balls and calls the results.

CARD - The playing card containing the numbers needed to win.

CHECKER - Bingo official whose job it is to verify winning bingo tickets.

COVERALL - See Blackout.

COVERED SQUARE - See Free Space.

EARLY BIRD - Games played before the regular session begins.

FINGERTIP CARD - Plastic or metal bingo card where called numbers can be tracked by closing the shutters.

FREE SPACE - The middle square in the bingo card (in the middle of the N column) which is automatically counted as a hit for the player. Also called Covered Square.

HARD CARD - A reusable, more solid type of bingo card.

INDIAN BINGO - Refers to bingo on the American Indian reservations.

LATE BIRD - Bingo games played after the regular session.

MASTERBOARD - The rack where played bingo balls are placed after   being drawn. Also called Rack.

SLEEPER - Player who suddenly realizes he had a bingo on a previous number called.

SOFT CARD - Disposable paper cards used in bingo.

SUPERJACKPOT - You'll know what this means if you ever hit one.

CHO DAI DI

INTRODUCTION

This exciting card game combines all the elements of a great game - skill, luck and a little of that ever-so-fun backstabbing, with skill being the overriding factor. Cho Dai Di is tremendously popular with the Chinese, and for some reason has not caught on in other cultures yet. This can't last too much longer for the game is not only a lot of fun but is perfectly suited to gamblers as well.

Cho Dai Di is closely related to both poker, in that poker hands and values are used in the play of the game, and to other card game variations where players attempt to rid their hand of all its cards. The game is simple to play, as you'll soon see, but where strategy comes in, there's much to learn.

So, while Cho Dai Di may sound foreign, you'll find this unique game uses element of play you're already familiar with, and thus will be fairly easy to learn.

Take the time to go through this chapter for this great card game is worth knowing. You and your friends will soon be hooked on Cho Dai Di (the Cantonese D is pronounced like a td together) and will find yourself counting the days until the next game begins!

So let's get on with the game!

THE BASICS OF CHO DAI DI

It takes four players to play Cho Dai Di, with each participant playing for themselves against all the others. A standard 52 card pack is used, containing four suits of 13 cards each, the ace through king of diamonds, clubs, hearts and spades.

The Object of the Game

The object of Cho Dai Di is to discard all 13 cards initially received by a player before his opponents do so, or if another player goes out first, to gain points by having fewer cards remaining than the other players.

For all intents and purposes, each card a player is stuck with when the first player goes out counts as one point regardless of the cards' suit or value, and one gains points from any player who is left with more cards than he.

Hand and Card Values

The hands valid in Cho Dai Di are similar to standard poker hands with the main difference being that the 2 is the highest value card in Cho Dai Di and not the ace (which is next in ranking). The other difference is that two pair is not a playable hand in Cho Dai Di.

Order of Suits

Suit values play a role in Cho Dai Di, and are in order of strength, the highest listed first, Spades, Hearts, Clubs and Diamonds. The first order of ranking in a card is its numeric value, thus a four of diamonds is higher than a three of spades.

However, when both cards are of equal numeric value, such as two fours, the suit order determines the higher ranking card. Thus, a four of spades is superior to a four of any other suit, spades being the strongest suit, while a 10 of clubs is higher ranked than a 10 of diamonds.

Cho Dai Di Rankings

For the benefit of players not familiar with poker, we'll list the hands here, beginning with the lowest ranking hands and going on up to the highest ranking. Cards will be abbreviated by the commonly accepted abbreviations such that a three will be 3, a Jack=J, Queen=Q, King=K, Ace=A, two=2 and so on.

You'll see that the rankings pretty much approximate poker rankings with the noticeable exception that the 2 is the highest ranking card and not the ace, and that two pair is not considered a Cho Dai Di hand. Also, though four of a kind is a valid hand, it must be played as a five card hand with any other card thrown in to make the fifth card.

Thus, legitimate Cho Dai Di hands consist of 1,2,3 or 5 cards.

Legitimate Hands by Card

One Card - Any card may be led.
Two Cards - The only valid two card hand is a pair.
Three Cards - Three of a kind is the only valid three card hand. A pair with an odd card is not a valid hand for three of a kind.
Five Cards - In order of strength, lowest to highest, straight, flush, full house, four of a kind with an odd card, straight flush and royal flush are valid five card hands.

HIGH CARD - The high card in Cho Dai Di is the 2, followed by the A, K, Q, J, 10, 9, 8, 7, 6, 5, 4 and then the 3, the weakest card. Equivalent high card hands are decide by suit order.

ONE PAIR - Two cards of identical value, such as 4-4 and K-K from a pair. The highest pair is 2-2, the lowest 3-3. When two pair of equal value, such as 7-7 and 7-7, are in competition, the pair with the spade, the highest ranking suit, is the stronger one.

THREE OF A KIND - Three cards of equal value, such as 9-9-9 from three of a kind. When two players hold a three of a kind, the hand with the higher raking triplets is stronger. 2-2-2- is a higher ranking hand than A-A-A.

STRAIGHT - Five cards in numerical sequence, such as 3-4-5-6-7 or A-2-3-4-5. The ace can be counted as the highest card (A-K-Q-J-10) in a straight, or the lowest card, however, it may not be in the middle of a five card run, such as Q-K-A-2-3, which is not a straight.

When two or more straights are in competition, the highest ranking card determines the stronger hand. K-Q-J-10-9 is higher than J-10-9-8-7. A straight containing a 2 is higher than any other straight. Thus, A-2-3-4-5 is a higher straight than Q-J-10-9-8. However, if the straights are identical in value, such as K-Q-J-10-9 and K-Q-J-10-9, than the strongest suit of the high card, in this example the king, determines the higher ranking hand. A King of hearts straight is higher than a king of clubs one.

FLUSH - Any five cards of the same suit, such as five hearts. When two players have flushes, the highest card in the flush determines the stronger hand, regardless of suit. If both hands have the same high card, than the next highest card determines the stronger hand and so on down to the fifth card. Thus, a 2-A-K-6-4 of clubs is stronger than a 2-K-Q-J-9 of spades. It is only when all five cards are identical that the higher ranking suit makes one flush a higher ranking hand than the other.

FULL HOUSE - Three of a kind and a pair together, such as 2-2-2-J-J. When two players have a full house, the higher ranking full house is the hand with the higher three of a kind.

FOUR OF A KIND - Four cards of equal value, such as K-K-K-K. When two players hold a four of a kind, the higher ranking four of a kind is represented by the higher foursome. J-J-J-J is higher than 3-3-3-3. The four of a kind is played as a five card hand in Cho Dai Di with any other card thrown in to make the fifth card.

STRAIGHT FLUSH - A straight all in the same suit, such as 7-8-9-10-J, all in spades. If two players hold a straight flush, the highest ranking card determines the more powerful straight flush. If the straight flushes are led by an equivalent high card, than the higher ranking suit of the competing straight flushes determines the stronger hand.

ROYAL FLUSH - 10-J-Q-K-A, all in the same suit. In the unlikely event two players hold a royal flush, the higher ranking suit is the dominant hand.

The First Round Deal

The dealer for the first round will be decided by the random drawing of a card from the deck. Beginning with the person picking the card and going counter-clockwise, right to left, one place is counted off for each number value on the card. For this purpose only, the jack equals 11 places, the queen 12 and the king 13. All other cards are at face value.

Thus, if a seven is picked, the person picking the card counts off his place as 1, to his right, 2, opposite will be 3, to his left, 4, back to himself again, 5, to his right, 6, and again opposite, 7.

Now we have the dealer for the first round - the player opposite the one who picked the card.

Thereafter, the dealer will always be the winner of the previous round, but as we'll see in a minute, we still use the traditional draw to determine which player gets dealt to first.

The Traditional Deal

Cards are always dealt counterclockwise in Cho Dai di.

Before the cards are dealt, the traditional draw to determine which player will be dealt the cards occurs first. Though it has no bearing on the game, since the dealer will play first anyway (except for the very first game), this tradition probably arose, like the cut, as a safeguard to the players.

As we did above, the dealer randomly picks a card and counts off one place for each number on the card, starting with himself and proceeding counterclockwise, right to left, around the table.

The cards should now be dealt one at a time, counter-clockwise (right to left), beginning with the player chosen by the traditional draw, and continuing until all players have received 13 face down cards.

Since there are four players in the game, the deck should now be exhausted of all cards.

The Direction of Play

The first round in Cho Dai Di is played in the counterclockwise direction.

Thereafter, each round's play will alternate in direction so that on all odd rounds (first, third, fifth, etc.), play will be from right to left, counterclockwise. And all even rounds (second, fourth, sixth, etc.) will be dealt and played clockwise, left to right.

So if the previous hand was played left to right, than the following one will be played right to left.

The Play of of the Game

The winner of the previous game is always the dealer of the following game and except for the first round in the very first game, which we'll cover after, the dealer will always be the first to lead in a game.

He has a choice of whether to play one, two, three or five cards as his opening hand. If he leads with one card, it can be any card he wants, but if he leads with more than one card, it must be a legitimate Cho Dai Di hand to be a valid discard.

(There is no valid four card lead or hand in Cho Dai Di as two pair is not a valid hand and four of a kind hands are played as five card hands with an extra card thrown in.)

After deciding his move, the dealer lays his hand of 1, 2, 3 or 5 cards face up on the table so that all can see what he has played.

The second player to act, the one to the dealer's right, now has two options: he may either pass by announcing **"Dai,"** the Cantonese equivalent for pass, or simply say **"pass,"** which may also be indicated by rapping one's knuckles on the table, waving one's hand vertically across the table or some such understood expression just as one would do in poker; or the player may lay down cards in response to the dealer's play.

For this next player to be able to play a hand, he must lay down the same number of cards, no more and no less than what the lead player threw, and the card or cards that he plays must not only be a legitimate Cho Dai Di hand but must be of greater value than the previously played hand.

This is true at all times in Cho Dai Di.

For example, if the dealer leads with a pair of fours, the next player, to be able to lay down cards, must play a higher pair than the fours. If he cannot beat the pair of fours by either throwing a higher suited pair of fours or a higher pair, or chooses not to, he may not lay down cards and must pass.

His play must be a two card throw since two cards were led. Thus, a hand of a straight or three fives may not be played for these are not two card hands.

After the second player acts upon his hand, play then moves to the next player in turn who faces the same options; either discarding a higher hand of the same number of cards, or passing.

If, for example, the second player played a pair of nines, which he places face up in the middle, on top of the fours, the third player must throw a higher suited pair of nines or higher pair to lay down cards.

Any time a hand is played within a round, the following player must lay down a higher valued hand of the same number of cards to be able to play.

The action in any round, like poker, does not end until three passes in a row are called and the last player to throw cards has had his play unanswered by his three opponents.

When a player's throw goes unanswered by three succeeding players, he now has the advantage, for he or she gets to lead the next round and may lay off any legitimate hand of 1, 2, 3 or 5 cards.

And so the game goes, with one player leading 1, 2, 3 or 5 cards, and the other players answering his lead until three passes in a row have occurred. The last to throw, gets to lead now, and another round ensues.

The game is over when any player gets rid of his last card. And then its time to tally the score.

The First Game Only

In the first round of the first game only, the player holding the three of diamonds goes first and must lead that card. The card may be led by itself, or as part of a 2, 3 or 5 card Cho Dai Di hand.

Thereafter, the winner of each game leads first in the following game, as we showed previous (and is also the dealer).

Scoring

Every card that a player has remaining when an opponent goes out counts as one point against him. Players gain points from any other player who is left with more cards than they. Thus, strictly speaking, there's usually more than one winner in a round.

However, should a player get stuck with 10 cards or more when an opponent goes out, he must pay double the points to the other players. Even worse, should a player be unable to get rid of any cards at all, and be stuck with the original 13 cards, the penalty is triple points to every player, even those stuck with more than 10 cards themselves.

Should two players have more than 10 points, let's say 10 and 11 points, than they would both pay the double penalty to the other players, though the one having 11 cards pays just one point to the player having 10 cards.

There is one other scoring rule and that is the four deuce bonus. If any player is dealt four deuces, he should immediately turn over his hand. The four deuce bonus nets the lucky player 39 points from each player - the triple penalty times the 13 cards each player holds. Then a new game is dealt.

Keeping Score

Cho Dai Di, like poker, can be played with chips, coins or cash. After each game is played out, players settle with each other. The Chinese generally prefer this method, for like poker, the instant gratification of touching the winnings is more fun.

If, on the other hand, you're playing just for the challenge of the game or simply prefer using a scorepad to keep track of accounts, Cho Dai Di is best played to a set amount of points - say

150, though you can play for less or more points as you find appropriate. Once any player goes over 150 points or whatever amount is set, the game is over, and for those playing for more than the points, accounts can be settled.

Of course, the idea of the game is not to get points, so the player over the point total first will obviously be the big loser and will have to pay off the difference in the scores to the other three players.

Likewise, the second highest score pays off the two lower scores and the second lowest score pays off only the low point total while collecting from the two players with more points. The player with the low point total, the one who went out first and has no cards remaining, is in the money, for all three of his opponents owe him the difference in their scores.

However, either way, keeping score or settling after each game, works equally well and is just as valid as the other.

SAMPLE GAME OF CHO DAI DI

Let's go through a sample game so you can get a feel of how the game is played.

We'll pick up our example earlier where the dealer led a pair of 4s to start the game and was followed by the next player who threw 9s. Let's put some names on the players to make the game easy to follow. Going counter-clockwise, the direction of play for this round, we have Phil, the dealer, who played the 4s, then Quilo, who threw the 9s, Marta and finally Chang.

Marta now plays a pair of 10s; Chang passes. Play comes back to the dealer, Phil, who also passes and then on to Quilo who plays two queens. Marta calls "Dai," pass, as does Chang and Phil, neither of whom have a higher pair or at least don't want to play one if they do.

Since his pair of queens went unanswered by three passes, Quilo wins the round and gets to lead the play for the following round.

Quilo looks around at his opponents: Phil, looking like a preacher needing his prayer to get answered; Marta wearing a thinly-veiled smile ready to burst into flower should the cards prove fertile; and Chang cool as night, unreadable, but wearing some strange green socks.

Quilo now leads with a four of clubs and places it atop the other cards in the center of the table. In Cho Dai Di, cards are played out in the center of the table, and there is no need to collect them until the game is over and the cards are ready to be shuffled.

Quilo looks again and notices that Chang's socks don't match, the left one close in color, but more blue in it. Stoneface notices and lets loose with an uncharacteristic golden grin, but he's looking somewhere else, and Quilo can't figure if it's this world he sees.

Proceeding counterclockwise, the direction of the game, it is Marta's turn, and since one card is led, she may only play one card as well. She throws a four of spades, which is a higher suited four. "Your play Chang."

Play continues as before, with each player, in turn, laying down higher ranking hands or passing.

Chang, very softly and very quietly, plays a 5. Phil throws a 9, then Quilo a higher suited nine, followed by Marta's king and Chang's ace of diamonds. Phil passes and Quilo, still bothered by something about Chang's socks, puts down the 2 of spades.

He has no need to wait for his opponents response, for the 2 is the highest ranking card and no card can outrank that deuce.

Now, that the 2 of spades is out of play, the highest ranking unplayed card is the 2 of hearts. Continuing on, Quilo leads with a five card diamond flush and promptly announces **"Bo Do,"** the Cantonese expression signifying that he has one card left.

Whenever a player is down to one card, he must announce that fact to the other players.

It is Marta's turn and she must have a higher five card hand than the flush to play, and if she does have it she better play it, for Quilo is one card away from going out. Marta doesn't and passes, but Chang does and plays a full house. Nobody answers that play, and after three consecutive passes, Chang, as the winner of this round, gets the lead.

Chang sees that the Quilo has but one card left and would like to feed him that one card and let him go out. For if Quilo does go out, they will both collect points from Phil, stuck with 10 cards and Marta, loaded with 9.

The problem is that Phil plays first, and if he plays a controlling card, or at least one higher than Quilo holds, Quilo won't be able to go out and Phil will take control of the lead and maybe turn the game to his own advantage.

In any case, the play is clear-cut for Chang has a pair and plays them, sevens. All three opponents rap their knuckles on the table, pass. Nobody has a higher pair, and in Quilo's case, he can't play against two cards with a one card hand anyway. Chang leads with another pair, eights this time, and again takes the round.

Chang leads again, and more softly than before, leans forward, plays a 10, and announces in a whisper, "Bo Do." Chang also has but one card left. He looks over at Quilo, then coolly at the money in front of his place, and dreamily, awaits the next play.

Phil, holding the 2 of hearts, the highest ranking card now that the spade two is gone, immediately plays it and takes the round. With 10 cards in his hand, he can't play games, not with two players one card away from going out.

He leads a small straight which no player can answer, then leads again with the 2 of clubs which also takes the round without response. It is the highest ranking card remaining, and with its removal, the ace of spades is king. (The diamond two had been played earlier in a flush).

Normally, the correct strategy is to save a **controlling card**, the highest ranking card remaining, to win a round and gain the lead, but if a smaller card is led, Phil will never see the chance, not with two players one card away.

Phil is down to three cards, and having little other choice plays a queen of hearts. Continuing around, right to left, Quilo can't go out with his 10 and passes. Marta plays the queen of spades, a higher ranked queen.

Chang hesitates for a few seconds and bowing his head ever so slightly, plays the king of hearts and goes out.

Scoring of the Sample Round

After Chang went out, players were left with the following cards.

Chang	0 Cards
Quilo	1 Card
Phil	2 Cards
Marta	8 Cards

For Chang, who went out first, it's a good win, for the three other players owe him points, one for each card they have remaining. Thus, he wins 8 points from Marta, 2 from Phil and 1 from Quilo.

Quilo doesn't fare so bad at all, for while he loses 1 point to Chang, the winner of the round, he collects points from the other two players, 1 from Phil and 7 from Marta, an overall gain of 8 points.

Phil loses 2 points to Chang and 1 point to Quilo but gains 6 from Marta. Despite paying off two opponents, Phil wins enough from Marta for an overall win of 3 points.

Marta, on the other hand, uncharacteristically quiet, didn't have the best luck this round, and winds up paying 8 points to Chang, 7 to Quilo and 6 to Phil for a total loss this round of 21 points. (The next round however, the rest of the players will pay their dues, for Marta will steam in with a big victory and a big gloating smile.)

In the round above, we saw three winners, of varying degrees, and one loser. Let's see how it works when a player gets caught with penalty points.

In this round, Marta goes out first, and with a flourish of knowing looks, particularly at Phil, who mutters about her luck in return.

Marta	0 Cards
Quilo	4 Cards
Chang	4 Cards
Phil	11 Cards

In this game, Marta collects 4 points from both Quilo and Chang, plus a big 22 (2 x 11) from Phil. A pretty good round, she wins 30 points.

Quilo loses four points to Marta, is dead even with Chang, but gains a hefty 14 points (7 point difference x 2) from Phil thanks to the double penalty Phil is paying, and comes out ahead 10 points for the round.

Having the same number of cards remaining, Chang and Quilo neither win or lose from each other, and Chang's total is also +10 points for the round.

Phil bites the big one this round. After losing 10 points to both Chang and Quilo and 22 to Marta, who was screeching with delight at the victory, he finds himself with a 42 point loss for the round.

If you're keeping score on paper, this is how the first two games would look.

Quilo	Chang	Marta	Phil
1	0	8	2
4	4	0	22
5	4	8	24

Advantage by Position

The dealer enjoys a distinct advantage over the others for he gets to play the first hand, and thus, controls the initial tempo of the game. And since the goal is to get rid of cards, the player who acts first certainly has that head start as well.

The worst position in a round is the fourth to act, for sometimes, by the time play comes around to his or her position, the cards already played may be stronger than what is held, and this player will be forced to pass without getting to play any cards at all.

Other Styles of Play

There are different styles of play in Cho Dai Di, however, whatever the style, it is still basically the same game. For example, some players play that when there is only one card left, opponents must play their highest cards, and may not "feed" a small card to the "Bo Do" player and let him go out.

Some games use a different bonus schedule as well. They may penalize a player double penalties when he's stuck with but 8 cards (as opposed to 10) and triple penalties for any point total above 10 (as opposed to 13). They may also disallow the four deuce instant 39 point bonus from each player, and instead, the game will be played out according to the normal conventions.

You may find games where play always goes in the counterclockwise direction, instead of alternating as we have shown, but whatever the particular rules, you can see that Cho Dai Di, for all intents and purposes, is the same game, and once you know how to play, the nuances of a different style of play are no trouble at all to adjust to.

STRATEGY

Laying Cards

Generally speaking, a player will lay down cards whenever possible. However, there are times when a player may find it advisable not to put down playable cards, either because it may break up a bigger hand for example, or because of future positioning.

Control

Making the first discards in a playing round is advantageous, for the player laying down cards first not only controls the number of cards to be played in the round but also dictates the initial strength of the cards that must be beat for others to lay down cards as well. This player controls the tempo of the round and may play into his own strengths in an attempt to rid himself of all cards.

The name of the game in Cho Dai Di is *control* and a lot of your strategy is worked around that. For, if you can control a round by playing the final cards, then you get to lead the next round and that's a big advantage. For example, if you hold the 2 of spades, the most powerful card in the deck, and the lead is a single card, you know you can control that round because nobody has a higher ranking card.

Playing First

The player going first in the game will usually, though not always, want to play a five card hand, especially if it's a low ranking one such as a 10 high straight. The straight is unlikely to control the round, but it does quickly get rid of five cards and prevents the player from being blocked out of playing the straight later on because another player plays a higher five card hand.

Gaining Points

In Cho Dai Di the strategy is not so much to be the first one to go out in a round, but to gain points overall against the other players. This could be done by having the next fewest number of cards or even sometimes, as we saw in the sample game, having the third largest number of cards with only one player having more.

Thus, if the player to go next has one card remaining and it's your lead, you might not mind throwing a small one card lead if a third player will get caught with 10 cards or more and you'll win double. Of course, you would rather be the player going out first, for the wins are larger, but that is not always possible, and as we have just shown, not always necessary.

Let's outline some other important winning concepts.

• **Try to lead with smaller cards first**. Generally speaking, you want to play your low cards first, and get rid of these weaker cards. The weaker the card, the less playable that card is. For example, if a player has two cards remaining, a four and a three, he'll have great difficulty in going out. For one thing, he will have difficulty in gaining the lead with a small card, if he can even play it at all, and even if he is lucky enough to get rid of one of them, it is doubtful that it will be enough to control a round and permit the unloading of the second small fry.

On the other hand, if one of two remaining cards is high, one may be able to maneuver that card into a controlling position and win the round. The small card can now be led, and since that's the last card, the game is over.

•**Don't Get Caught With 10 or More Cards.** If the game progresses and a player comes within striking distance of going out, the wise move is to break up a good hand so that you don't get caught with a double penalty. It's better to be stuck with eight cards and have to pay three players their dues, than to risk being caught with 10 or more cards and a double penalty to all three opponents.

If you can't control the game, don't take chances if a player gets close to going out - break up your hand and play the game safe.

• **Keep Track of the High Cards**. It's extremely important to know what twos and aces have been played. When it gets near the end, you need to know if the single lead you play can be followed later by a card you hold and know to be the highest, thereby giving you control over the next rounds start. You always need to know what the current controlling card is at all times.

(Remember, the 2 of spades is the initial controlling card, and when it's played, the 2 of hearts becomes the controlling card, then the 2 of clubs, the 2 of diamonds, the ace of spades and so on.)

Knowing how many aces and deuces played also clues you in to the highest possible pairs that can be made. If you know that three aces and all four deuces have already been used, your pair of kings rules as the largest pair left. Or if you hold the remaining ace, you've got the highest card left and can control with it.

• **Defensive Play**. If an opposing player has but one card left, do not lead with one card unless you lead with the highest single card remaining, which means that player cannot go out in his turn and also that you'll control the round, or that, by his going out, you'll benefit, for you have few cards remaining and the other players have many cards to go.

This strategy also applies when opposing players have two, three, four or five cards remaining before they go out. If you're stuck with a lot of cards and one player has but two to go, a two card lead is dangerous, for a pair gives that player an opportunity to go out.

SUMMARY

We hope you enjoy this exciting game. There's a lot of strategy in Cho Dai Di and therefore lots of challenges. Write in to us here and let us know if you enjoyed Cho Dai Di.

Until then, "Jhoy King" - see you later.

Cjok Lay Ho Wan
(Good Fortune)

HORSERACING

INTRODUCTION

Horseracing is the largest spectator sport in the United States, drawing countless fans every year at tracks across the country. It is also quite popular in numerous other countries around the world. The thrill of competition and the challenge of analyzing all the relevant data to pick a winner, continues to enthrall fans everywhere.

The tracks are fervid with the excitement, color and anticipation of the race. Men and women, buried deep into their racing forms, analyze and handicap the races, figuring which horse going off at what odds presents them the best bet. They look at various factors, discuss the possibilities and watch the tote board to see how the odds are moving.

Others, out to the track for the first time, or simply less handicapping-minded, may choose the horse with a name that strikes their fancy - perhaps its similar to the name of a person they know, a place they've been or it just sounds good to them. Or maybe they like the color associated with that horse.

This section will show the language of the track, the various wagers available to the bettor, the different philosophies and strategies of winning, the odds you face every time you wager on a horse and 11 suggestions for winning at the track!

THE BETS

Straight Betting

The win, place and show bets, called **straight bets**, are the most popular wagers at the horsetrack, and we'll discuss them first.

The **win** bet, is a wager that a horse will finish first in the race. Any other finish, second, third or whatever is irrelevant. It is only the first place finish that counts with a win bet.

The **place** bet is a wager that the horse will come in first or second - either way the bet is a winner.

A bet to **show** allows the bettor even more leeway, for the horse may come in first, second or third for the bet to be a winner.

Finishing either first, second or third is called **being in the money**, a classic term used outside the track as well.

Of the straight bets, win tickets will pay the best, for they are hardest to pick. Place and show bets pay less than win bets for more horses share the betting pool, two in the case of place bets and three in the case of show bets.

Exacta Bets

The **exacta** is a bet that the two horses chosen in a race come in first and second, in exact order. Many bettors like this type of wager for if the exacta is a winner, the payoffs can be pretty good.

Quinella Bets

On this wager you're betting on the top two finishers in a race, like the exacta, only with the **quinella**, you don't care about the order of finish - you only care that your two horses are the first and second place finishers.

The quinella bet is easier to win than the exacta, and consequently pays less.

Daily Double

This popular bet is a wager on the winners of the first two races. If you picked the winner of one race only, it counts for nothing. To win a daily double, both the first and second races must be picked correctly.

Triples

This bet is similar to the Daily Double except that with the **triple**, you must choose the winner of the three consecutive races designated by the track.

Pick Six

You can make a fortune correctly picking this ticket but it's not easy - you must pick the winner of six races! Good luck on this one. Usually there is a smaller payoff if five winners are chosen as well.

Other Exotic Bets

There are other exotic bets offered at some tracks but these should be clearly explained on their programs. You may find bets like a **Pick Nine**, where you have to choose the winners of nine races! Win that one and all your money troubles are over.

SOME TRACK BASICS

The Tote Board

The big computerized board at the track, called the **Totalizer** or **Tote Board**, displays the amount of money bet on each horse to win, place and show, and the resultant odds that constantly change as wagers come in on particular horses.

The lines listed on the tote board, reflect the betting at the track - the more money bet on a horse, the lower its odds will be. Thus, if many people favor a particular horse to win and back that horse with more bets than any other horse, that horse will be the **favorite**, and will have the smallest payoff of any horse in the race.

Horses that get little action, are considered **longshots**, and will go off at high odds, 10 -1 or 17-1 for example.

The tote board is important to watch for it shows the odds of each horse and lets you know which horse is the current favorite and which horse is the **longest shot** (the horse with the least amount of money bet on it and consequently, the highest odds).

The odds continually change as more betting money comes in and this will be reflected on the tote board for all to see. Sometimes a favorite will become a bigger favorite or even become supplanted by another horse as the favorite as late money comes in.

When the race is ready to begin, no more bets will be accepted and the posted odds become the actual odds of the race on which all payoffs are based. If you were lucky enough to pick the winner, it will be the final odds at post time that determines your payoff, not the odds at the time you placed your bet.

The Morning Line

The initial line at which the odds on competing horses are quoted is set by the track handicapper and is his estimation of how the horses might be bet by the public. This line is called the **morning line** and has no final bearing on the actual payoff on a horse if it wins.

Once bets start coming on, the odds on the tote board will change to reflect the amounts bet on each horse.

Many bettors use the morning line as a rough guide to the comparative strengths of the horses. Horses listed at low odds, say 2 to 1, probably have a good chance of winning the race, while those going off at 25 to 1, considered high odds, probably have little chance of finishing in the money.

Bets and Payoffs

The minimum bet in horseracing is generally $2.00. The amount of money a bettor receives back will reflect the winning odds as listed on the tote board plus the original $2.00 bet. For example, if your horse goes off at 5 to 2 odds and is a winner, you'll receive $5.00 for the win plus the original $2.00 bet for a total of $7.00.

The results posted are always based on the $2.00 bet so if you have a larger bet, say $10.00, you simply multiply the $2.00 results by 5 ($10.00 is five $2.00 wagers) to come out with the total won. In the above example, a $10.00 bet would pay off $25.00 in winnings plus the original bet of $10.00 for a total $35.00 return.

The tote board will read $7.00 on the 5-2 win anyway, already reflecting the $2.00 bet placed.

Let's say that in a particular race, horse #2, **Liberty Charles** wins the race at 3 to 1 odds, horse #5, Skidmore Jones comes in second, and horse # 1 **Begboke Vindaloo** comes in third. This is how it may be listed:

Order of Finish	Win	Place	Show
2 Winning Horse	8.00	4.80	4.00
5 Second Horse		11.60	4.80
1 Third Horse			2.60

Only those who bet horse #2 (**Liberty Charles**) to win collect the $8.00 - $6.00 in winnings for the 3-1 odds plus the $2.00 bet. Players who bet **Liberty Charles** to place collect only $4.80 and ones who bet to show get back $4.00.

Players who bet either the #5 or #1 horse to win are losers, for those horses didn't win, though place and show bets on #5 and show bets on #1, in this example, will pay as shown on the chart.

How to Bet

Horses are identified by post position in the racing program as well as on the tote board and the tickets you will buy at the betting windows. Thus, a horse sporting a 1 in the program, will be running out from the first post position, and a horse identified by a 7 will be exiting from the seventh post position.

The tote board uses the post position numbers as well to identify horses. To follow the betting line as it progresses, simply track your horse by the number.

Let's say that you've added up the pros and cons of each horse and are now ready to place your bet. The horses on your program are listed as follows:

Squarebacks	1
Bongo Player	2
Rubics	3
Ted the T.	4
Chess	5
Octogon	6
Woodstock	7
Bird in the Cage	8

If you want to bet on **Bongo Player** to show and **Octogon** to win, you would identify #2 as the place and #6 as your win bet. Similarly, if you want to pick **Octagon** (post position 6) and **Bird in the Cage** (post position 8) as your 1-2 horses in an exacta, you'll identify the ticket as a 6-8 exacta.

The Pari-Mutuel Pool

The total amount of money on a race is collected into what is called the **Pari-Mutuel pool**, and after the government and track take are pulled from the total, the rest is proportionately divided among the winners.

The higher the odds of a winning horse, the greater the payoff will be should the horse win or come into the money, and likewise, the lower the odds, meaning more bettors wagered on the horse, the smaller the winning payoff will be.

(Keep in mind that historically, the higher the odds against a horse, the less chance this horse has of winning.)

Let's see just how big a cut is taken from the Pari-Mutuel pool before the bettors get their share.

The Percentages

Betting is as embedded in horseracing as the horses themselves, but it is one of the tougher gambling pursuits to beat. The racing fan faces a stiff tax at the mutuels in America, and he must overcome this albatross to come ahead a winner. Few do.

Here is why.

Most U.S. states levy at least a 17% tax on every dollar bet at the horsetrack, a gargantuan percentage to try and beat. Additionally, fans who make such exotic bets as the Pick Six and Triple, get taxed at an even greater rate - 25%!

There is one additional price the horse bettor must pay, and that is called **breakage**. The track pays out winnings to the dime only, and keeps whatever odd pennies left over. For example, if the mutuel payoff figures to be $5.78, the bettor would receive only $5.70 back, or a $3.56 win would pay off at $3.50.

Some tracks pay out only to the 20¢, and on the above $5.78 mutuel would return only $5.60, at even greater cost to the winner.

So what's the big deal, a few pennies here or there? Plenty. On average, this costs the bettor about another 2% per dollar wagered - more straws on the camels back.

And may the betting gods help you if you happen to be a New York OTB bettor, for their commission runs you another 5%.

Where this leaves the serious horseracing fan is in a big ditch if he's got profits on his mind. You have to be a very good handicapper to overcome these percentages.

It's a lot of fun to watch the horses and jockeys compete, to be part of the colorful track atmosphere, and to study the racing form and figure the winning horses. However, keep the races and the heavy odds in perspective when you hit the mutuels for a little action.

THE CLASS OF RACES

There are five basic classes of horseracing, and while there is some overlap between the groupings, these classifications will give you a good idea about the relative strength of horses in one group as compared to another.

Claiming Races

Out of the nine or so races you'll see featured in a racing program, the **claiming race** will be the type of race most frequently encountered. The purses for winning horses are the smallest of any of the races, and consequently the horses entered are the lowest in quality.

The concept of the claiming race is really quite interesting. Any horse entered in a claiming race can be bought, in the jargon of the track, **claimed**, by anyone for the **claiming price** listed in the program. Generally, another stable or horseman will be the buyer, but now and then, an amateur out of the stands might pick one up.

A horse must be claimed prior to a race, in writing, and once claimed, is fully the property of the new owner. The purse for that race, however, will still belong to the previous owner.

It is more difficult to handicap these types of races for the horses entered, being of the lowest quality, are more inconsistent, and therefore more difficult to predict.

There are varying claiming prices on these horses, and you can figure that a higher claiming price generally indicates a better class of horse. Sometimes you'll see a horse **going down in class**, being entered at a lower claiming price than previous.

This might indicate that the horse was unable to successfully compete at the higher level, and has therefore dropped down, the owner perhaps hoping to catch some purses against lesser class horses, or maybe hoping to unload the horse with the cheaper price. Horses cost a lot of money to maintain, and the owners, being businessmen or businesswomen, need to keep the ship afloat.

The claiming system is clever and is a deterrent against higher class horses, clearly superior, from entering the race and stealing the purse, for once the horse is entered, it is open market for another buyer who feels the horse is worth the price.

Some trainers and owners are real good evaluators of talent, and make a good little business out of claiming horses. They are referred to as **claiming trainers** or **claiming owners**.

Maiden Races

These races are clearly a cut above the claiming races, and sometimes the best of horses start out at this level. Horses are entered in these races who have not yet won a race and are too valuable to the owner to run in a claimer.

Within this category is the **Maiden Special Weight** race, for two year old horses who also, have not won a race.

Allowance Races

In these races a variety of elements are factored in, such as amount of races run and money won previously, and the horse is assigned a **weight allowance** to help offset the differences between it and the other contestants in a race.

For example, a seemingly superior horse may be assigned five extra pounds on the theory that those extra pounds will equalize its talents with lesser horses in the race.

There are all sorts of allowance races, run for different ages of horses and run for different size purses. There are class levels within the allowance category. You can figure a horse running a $25,000 allowance to be superior to a horse running a $15,000 one.

Handicap Races

These races are for near top level horses, offering high purses and game horses going for the winners spot. The track handicapper examines each horses credentials carefully and assigns weights to each one, in an attempt to equalize the speeds and skills, so that each horse has a fair shot at winning the race.

Stakes Races

These races feature the cream of the talent, the top thoroughbreds competing for the top prizes. Races such as **The Preakness**, **The Kentucky Derby** and **The Belmont Stakes**, the events of horseracing's famous **Triple Crown**, are all stakes races.

Here is where famous horses such as Secretariat and Seattle Slew cement their fame in horseracing's hall of fame.

These races create the most excitement of all the thoroughbred events for it is the top contenders in the world competing horse to horse in a thrilling spectacle that is discussed long before the race is ever run, and glorified long after.

A Word on Horserace Betting

Keep in mind that you're bucking big odds when you take on the track, so we heartily recommend that one pursue betting on the horses as strictly recreational.

If you decide you want to play the track on a more serious level, than you should first test your skills on a small scale and be sure to win at that level before putting out the big bucks.

Don't jump up in bet size until you've proven your skills for the difference between betting small dollars and betting big dollars, might only be that the losses will be bigger. Bigger bets won't necessarily change your luck.

HANDICAPPING PHILOSOPHIES

Form Handicapping

A horse's current form, how it has fared in the last few races, is what racetrackers call **form handicapping**. The proponents of this type of handicapping argue that horses, like humans, are conditioned athletes - they reach peaks of high performance at times, and other times, are just not as good.

If a horse has not run well lately, form handicapping says that all the other handicapping factors just don't make sense. Plainly, the horse is not in good enough form to win the race.

Form handicappers attempt to back the horse that, according to recent past performance charts, is in the peak of its form, and on that basis, has the best chances of winning the race.

Trip Handicapping

Trip handicappers are looking for inconsistency in a horse caused by a track mishap which caused an otherwise strong contender to perhaps finish out of the money. The final result may show that the horse didn't fare so well, but the trip handicapper, noting that the horse started fast, suddenly lost a bunch of lengths, but then finished strong, may conclude that the horse got tripped-up, and is really a better horse than the order of finish in the past race might indicate.

Class Handicapping

This form of handicapping proposes that there is no more important factor than a horse's class. Horseplayers define **class** as a comparison of the quality of a race a horse has competed in as judged by the level or claiming price of the race, the importance of the race or the stakes involved.

A better horse will compete at better levels they feel, and will look for opportunities where a superior horse, judged on class, will race against inferior horses.

There are many formulas used to judge class. One of the more popular ones is to judge the amount of money earned by a horse over a specified period of time, divide the earnings amount of the horse by the number of races run, and come up with a figure that could be used for comparison.

For example, when a horse attempts to move up in class, the class handicappers will look carefully at the horses credentials, and if they conclude it's racing out of class, they would consider this horse a poor bet. But on the other hand, a horse moving down in class enjoys a marked advantage over the lesser horses, and given the right odds, may indeed be a very good bet.

Speed Handicapping

This method specifies that the speed with which the horse has run its races is the most important variable in picking winners. A general rule of thumb at the track is to assign one second to every five lengths at the track. Thus if a horse finished 10 lengths behind the winner's time of 1.11 in a six furlong race, you would call the speed 1.13.

Horses run races under different conditions and speed handicappers would adjust times or give weighting to these factors so that horses with different racing backgrounds can be compared to each other. Some tracks are faster than others, some horses carried different weights, some may have run on an off track (not a fast track), some may have ran at different track lengths.

Once these variable have been adjusted, the speed handicapper finds the horse which shows the greatest speed and would back that horse for the race.

Pace Handicapping

Pace handicappers believe that it's not so important how fast a horse can run per se, but how well the horse paces itself during a race that is the crucial element in winning route races.

A pure speed horse can have the edge in a sprint race, but when the race is a route, other elements such as pace come into play.

On the theory that a horse cannot run a route at absolute full speed for the length of the track, but must pace itself against the others and save its maximum energy for the stretch run, the pace handicappers spot the horses they feel can run the distance at the best pace. Fast sprint horses may be avoided by the pace handicappers, instead opting for horses that have a proven record in routes.

Other Handicapping Elements

There are numerous other ways that horseplayers figure an angle on the race, not the least on which is to judge a jockey's abilities and a trainer's abilities. Some jockeys and trainers are proven winners with records far exceeding their peers and this is an element bettors may factor into their analysis.

And that is what makes horseracing so interesting, all the various theories of why a horse should be better than another, the tangibles and intangibles that when added up, make the analysis of a horserace so mysterious and elusive. There are people who spend their lives figuring the horses and constantly refining and updating their techniques to get a better edge.

There are many theories on beating the track, and we'll leave that up to you to figure the best way to approach the horses to fit your style of thinking.

However, let's present some standard percentages that have held true over many years and then give you some winning techniques to get you started on the road.

STANDARD WINNING PERCENTAGES

It is interesting to note that over the long run, a horse's winning percentage is in direct correlation to its **send-off position**, the relative listing of odds on the horse at race time.

Over the years, horses going off as favorites will win approximately 33% of the time, while **second choices**, horses with the next lowest odds after the favorite, will win about 20% of the time, and **third choices**, the next down in send-off position, will win the race about 15% of the time.

Similarly, **fourth choices**, **fifth choices** and lesser will win a smaller proportion of the races in order of send-off position.

Altogether, the top three choices account for just below 70% of all wins.

Favorites will place a bit over 50% of the time, while second choices place around 40% and third choices 30%.

Keep in mind that these figures have stayed fairly constant over the years, but that doesn't mean that they'll hold true over a limited period of time at a particular track. Short run anomalies are normal in horseracing as in all forms of gambling but certainly, these figures are good guideposts to go by when formulating your winning approach at the track.

WINNING STRATEGIES

Following are some general guidelines followed by many pros which will give you a leg up on many other horse bettors.

1. When betting straight, restrict your bets to win and show only.

2. As a general rule, bet horses you like with odds of 5-1 or greater to win and odds of 5-1 or less, to place.

3. Pay close attention to a horses recent performances. Form handicapping has a lot of merit, and you face your best chances with a horse in top condition.

4. Horses backed heavily by touting services and computer handicappers may win more, but so many bettors are placing their dollars on them, they give poor value for the money. Try to find the **"dark horse,"** one that has a good shot at the tape but is not overly backed.

5. Be wary of the "smart money," bets placed at the last minute by supposedly, those in the know. There isn't much smart money at the tracks.

6. Go with you gut feelings. If there's a horse you like, by all means bet that horse. There's no worse feeling than not doing what you felt you should have done, and it working out - without

you. And if it doesn't work out, no big deal.

7. Pay special attention to fast starters on off tracks. It's more difficult to maneuver on a muddy or slow track, and these conditions will favor the horse that takes the early lead.

8. Avoid horses moving up in class. They may have looked good against lesser horses, but now the move to better competition may reveal some different colors.

9. Avoid horses that have not raced in the past four weeks. They may be recuperating from illness and the owners are using the race as a tune-up. The winning percentages of long-idled horse are way below the average.

10. Bet only winners. If you see a horse that has been around but has never won a race, why figure that today's race will be a reversal of past performance? Instead, choose a horse that has some background of winning.

11. Bet only horses you feel have a good chance of winning. If you had eliminated all the horses you've bet in the past but have not really believed in, you would be sitting with a much higher winning percentage. If you don't like a horse, don't bet it.

KENO

INTRODUCTION

The origins of this fun game go back some 2,000 years to the Han Dynasty in China - quite a long history, and quite a long distance to travel to make it to casinos as far away as Nevada, halfway across the globe.

Keno is quite popular and one of the attractions of the game is that it's easy to play. The only decisions a player need be concerned with are which numbers he or she will play, and how much to bet. Once the bet is placed, the fun begins as number upon number appear on the board, and the player waits to see if indeed, enough lucky numbers were hit to bring in the big fish.

And there's always that attraction of the giant win - that a 70¢ or $1.00 or $1.40 wager, whatever is played, may catch the right numbers and land the lucky bettor a $50,000 bonanza.

Keno has that lure, the big win, the myriad possibilities of numbers that can land, the almost wins, the "if I had played those numbers," and bettors keep coming back for more.

Let's move on now, see how the game is played, and how best to make yourself a winner.

THE BASICS OF KENO

How to Play

All bets in keno are made and recorded on a **keno ticket**, a pre-printed form where a player indicates the choices he or she will make. The tickets are readily available in the keno lounge and are kept in generous supply on the counters and next to every seat in the keno area.

Situated near the tickets will be the thick, black crayons which are used to mark keno tickets, and the casinos **rate card**, showing the exact payoffs for tickets played and won.

There are 80 numbered squares on a keno ticket which correspond exactly to the 80 numbered balls in the keno cage. A player may choose anywhere from one to fifteen numbers to play, and does so by marking an **"x"** on the keno ticket for each number or numbers he or she so chooses.

You'll notice on the keno ticket, "KENO LIMIT $50,000, To aggregate players each game." This means that if you do hit the big $50,000 prize in the same game as another player, that you'll have to split the jackpot. However, the likelihood of this occurring stretches the imagination into far off places - in other words - don't worry about it.

Twenty balls will be drawn each game, and will appear as lighted numbers on the keno screens. As the game progresses, each number will be lit as it is drawn, so that the player can easily keep track of the numbers drawn and see how his or her ticket is faring.

Winnings are determined by consulting the payoff chart each casino provides. If enough numbers have been correctly picked, you have a winner, and the chart will show the payoff. The more numbers that come up, the greater the winnings.

Betting

Bets are usually made in 70¢ or $1.00 multiples, though other standard bets may apply. A player may bet as many multiples of this bet as he desires. For example, a player may bet $5.00 on a $1.00 ticket, giving him or her in fact, five games with the same combinations.

How to Mark the Ticket

The amount being wagered on a game should be placed in the box marked **Mark Price Here** in the upper right hand corner of the ticket. Leave out dollar or cents signs though. $1 would be indicated by simply placing **"1-"** and 70 cents by **".70-"**. Of course, any amount up to the house limit can be wagered.

Underneath this box is a column of white space. The number of spots selected for the game is put here. If six spots were selected on the ticket, mark the number "**6**", if fifteen numbers, mark "**15**".

Let's show a five spot ticket that we've marked for a $1 game.

This type of ticket, which is the most common one bet, is called a **straight ticket**, or more precisely, in this example, a **five-spot straight ticket**. Similarly, if 11 numbers were chosen, it would be called an **11 spot straight ticket**.

Payoff Charts

Let's look at typical Las Vegas payoff charts for $1.00 and $1.40 games. You'll notice that there are payoff schedules for any amount of numbers picked, 1 through 15, and that each one has its own minimum set of numbers needed to win.

For example, if you play a 9 spot game with a $1.00 bet, you'll need to "**catch**" a minimum of five numbers for a payoff. In this case, $4.00 would be returned - your original $1.00 bet plus the

$3.00 in winnings. If all nine numbers are caught, however, a cool $25,000 perfumes your senses.

Rate Card: 1 - 15 Spots · $1.00, $3.00, $5.00, $1.40 Wagers

MARK 1 SPOT

Winning Spots	$1.00 Ticket Pays	$3.00 Ticket Pays	$5.00 Ticket Pays	$1.40 Ticket Pays
1	3.00	9.00	15.00	4.20

MARK 2 SPOTS

Winning Spots	$1.00 Ticket Pays	$3.00 Ticket Pays	$5.00 Ticket Pays	$1.40 Ticket Pays
2	12.00	36.00	60.00	17.00

MARK 3 SPOTS

Winning Spots	$1.00 Ticket Pays	$3.00 Ticket Pays	$5.00 Ticket Pays	$1.40 Ticket Pays
2	1.00	3.00	5.00	1.40
3	42.00	126.00	210.00	60.00

MARK 4 SPOTS

Winning Spots	$1.00 Ticket Pays	$3.00 Ticket Pays	$5.00 Ticket Pays	$1.40 Ticket Pays
2	1.00	3.00	5.00	1.40
3	4.00	12.00	20.00	5.40
4	112.00	336.00	560.00	160.00

MARK 5 SPOTS

Winning Spots	$1.00 Ticket Pays	$3.00 Ticket Pays	$5.00 Ticket Pays	$1.40 Ticket Pays
3	1.00	3.00	5.00	2.40
4	14.00	42.00	70.00	30.00
5	720.00	2,160.00	3,600.00	680.00

MARK 6 SPOTS

Winning Spots	$1.00 Ticket Pays	$3.00 Ticket Pays	$5.00 Ticket Pays	$1.40 Ticket Pays
3	1.00	3.00	5.00	1.20
4	4.00	12.00	20.00	6.60
5	88.00	264.00	440.00	120.00
6	1,480.00	4,440.00	7,400.00	2,200.00

MARK 7 SPOTS

Winning Spots	$1.00 Ticket Pays	$3.00 Ticket Pays	$5.00 Ticket Pays	$1.40 Ticket Pays
3				60
4	1.00	3.00	5.00	2.40
5	20.00	60.00	100.00	30.00
6	380.00	1,140.00	1,900.00	460.00
7	8,000.00	24,000.00	40,000.00	7,000.00

MARK 8 SPOTS

Winning Spots	$1.00 Ticket Pays	$3.00 Ticket Pays	$5.00 Ticket Pays	$1.40 Ticket Pays
5	9.00	27.00	45.00	12.00
6	80.00	240.00	400.00	120.00
7	1,480.00	4,440.00	7,400.00	2,300.00
8	25,000.00	50,000.00	50,000.00	25,000.00

MARK 9 SPOTS

Winning Spots	$1.00 Ticket Pays	$3.00 Ticket Pays	$5.00 Ticket Pays	$1.40 Ticket Pays
4				60
5	4.00	12.00	20.00	4.60
6	44.00	132.00	220.00	60.00
7	300.00	900.00	1,500.00	400.00
8	4,000.00	12,000.00	20,000.00	5,600.00
9	25,000.00	50,000.00	50,000.00	25,000.00

MARK 10 SPOTS

Winning Spots	$1.00 Ticket Pays	$3.00 Ticket Pays	$5.00 Ticket Pays	$1.40 Ticket Pays
5	2.00	6.00	10.00	2.80
6	20.00	60.00	100.00	28.00
7	136.00	408.00	680.00	196.00
8	960.00	2,880.00	4,800.00	1,400.00
9	4,000.00	12,000.00	20,000.00	5,320.00
10	25,000.00	50,000.00	50,000.00	25,000.00

MARK 11 SPOTS

Winning Spots	$1.00 Ticket Pays	$3.00 Ticket Pays	$5.00 Ticket Pays	$1.40 Ticket Pays
5	1.00	3.00	5.00	1.20
6	8.00	24.00	40.00	12.00
7	72.00	216.00	360.00	100.00
8	360.00	1,080.00	1,800.00	500.00
9	1,800.00	5,400.00	9,000.00	2,400.00
10	12,000.00	36,000.00	50,000.00	15,000.00
11	28,000.00	50,000.00	50,000.00	40,000.00

MARK 12 SPOTS

Winning Spots	$1.00 Ticket Pays	$3.00 Ticket Pays	$5.00 Ticket Pays	$1.40 Ticket Pays
5				1.20
6	5.00	15.00	25.00	6.00
7	32.00	96.00	160.00	40.00
8	240.00	720.00	1,200.00	300.00
9	600.00	1,800.00	3,000.00	800.00
10	1,480.00	4,440.00	7,400.00	2,000.00
11	12,000.00	36,000.00	50,000.00	10,000.00
12	36,000.00	50,000.00	50,000.00	50,000.00

MARK 13 SPOTS

Winning Spots	$1.00 Ticket Pays	$3.00 Ticket Pays	$5.00 Ticket Pays	$1.40 Ticket Pays
6	1.00	3.00	5.00	2.40
7	16.00	48.00	80.00	24.00
8	80.00	240.00	400.00	100.00
9	720.00	2,160.00	3,600.00	950.00
10	4,000.00	12,000.00	20,000.00	5,000.00
11	8,000.00	24,000.00	40,000.00	9,000.00
12	25,000.00	50,000.00	50,000.00	20,000.00
13	36,000.00	50,000.00	50,000.00	50,000.00

MARK 14 SPOTS

Winning Spots	$1.00 Ticket Pays	$3.00 Ticket Pays	$5.00 Ticket Pays	$1.40 Ticket Pays
6	1.00	3.00	5.00	4.40
7	10.00	30.00	50.00	11.00
8	40.00	120.00	200.00	44.00
9	320.00	960.00	1,600.00	350.00
10	1,000.00	3,000.00	5,000.00	1,000.00
11	3,200.00	9,600.00	16,000.00	4,000.00
12	16,000.00	48,000.00	50,000.00	15,000.00
13	25,000.00	50,000.00	50,000.00	30,000.00
14	40,000.00	50,000.00	50,000.00	50,000.00

MARK 15 SPOTS

Winning Spots	$1.00 Ticket Pays	$3.00 Ticket Pays	$5.00 Ticket Pays	$1.40 Ticket Pays
6				2.00
7	8.00	24.00	40.00	10.00
8	28.00	84.00	140.00	30.00
9	132.00	396.00	660.00	150.00
10	300.00	900.00	1,500.00	400.00
11	2,600.00	7,800.00	13,000.00	3,000.00
12	8,000.00	24,000.00	40,000.00	10,000.00
13	25,000.00	50,000.00	50,000.00	30,000.00
14	32,000.00	50,000.00	50,000.00	40,000.00
15	40,000.00	50,000.00	50,000.00	50,000.00

Keno runners are available for your convenience. Since they must transport your tickets to the main counter for validation, please have the tickets ready as early as possible. We cannot accept responsibility if tickets are too late for the current game.

The Duplicate Ticket

Now you have your ticket filled in and are ready to play the game. You take this **original** or **master ticket** to the keno writer at the window and hand it in with the $ amount for which you'll be playing.

The writer will retain your original ticket and hand back a **duplicate ticket**. This ticket will show the same numbers you have chosen, which are generally marked in thick black strokes from the brush they use, the dollar amount of the game and the total numbers played, just like your ticket did.

It will also show some things that were not on your original. The duplicate will have printed on it, the date and time of the game, the game's number, and a particular code number used by the casino. You'll also see the printing, "Winning tickets must be paid immediately after each keno game," or some such writing.

Take this piece of writing very seriously.

If you have a winning ticket, you must present your duplicate before the next game resumes, or you will forfeit that payoff. There is a quirk in the legal structure of the game which differentiates keno from a lottery in that the immediate payoff prevents the keno game from being called a lottery.

Remember, if you have a winning ticket, cash it in immediately.

The Keno Runner

Many casinos offer players the luxury of playing keno from virtually anywhere in the casino. One can play the game while at the slots or while luxuriating over a meal in the restaurant.

This is done through the services of a keno runner, casino employees, usually women, whose sole job is to take keno bets from patrons in various parts of the casino, return to them a duplicate ticket and collect their payoff should the ticket be a winner.

Ah, the easy life! If you do win, it is customary to tip a little something to the runner (the bearer of good tidings).

The Punch-Out Ticket

To make life easy, the casinos employ what is called a **punch-out ticket or draw**, to verify if a player's ticket is a winner. The 20 called numbers are "punched-out" of a ticket, and by placing this ticket over a player's, it allows one to see the amount of winning numbers at a glance.

Since the tickets are identical in size and alignment, only marked off numbers will appear in the spaces. This clever method clears up any doubts about the number of winning spots hit.

When in doubt about whether you've won, request that a punch-out ticket be placed over your duplicate, and the result will clearly show through.

Replaying A Ticket

You may have a lucky set of numbers you like to play, or a particular set that either just won for you, or which you've just played, and feel that the same numbers are ripe to score.

In any case, the casino allows you to replay the same numbers again, and to save you the trouble of rewriting your ticket, you simply need to hand in your duplicate, which now becomes your original ticket, and the keno writer will issue you a new duplicate.

Easy as that. You can do this all day long if you like, exchanging duplicate as original for a new duplicate.

OTHER TICKETS

Split Tickets

Players are not limited to just straight tickets but may also play as many combinations as they choose. A **split ticket** allows a player to bet two or more combinations in one game.

This is done by marking two sets (or more) of 1-15 numbers on a ticket and separating them by either a line, or by circling the separate groups. Numbers may not be duplicated between the two sets.

On split tickets, in which several games are being played in one, the keno ticket should be marked as follows. In addition to the x's indicating the numbers, and the lines or circles showing the groups, the ticket should clearly indicate the amount of games being played.

For example, a split ticket playing two groups of six spots each would be marked 2/6 in the column of white space. The 2 shows that two combinations are being played, and the 6 shows that six numbers are being chosen per game.

If $1 is being bet per combination, we would put a **"1-"** and circle it underneath the slashed numbers to show this, and of course, in the Mark Price Here box, we would enter **"2"**, to show $2 is being bet - $1 on each combination.

We'll show two examples of a split ticket, one separated by a line, and the other, separated by circles.

Split Ticket · Line Separated

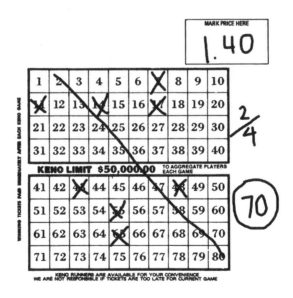

Split Ticket · Circle Separated

A player could theoretically play 80 one spots on one split ticket, or 40 two spots or 10 five spots - as long as numbers aren't duplicated.

Remember that on split tickets, each split game, for all intents and purposes, is played separately and counts as a separate game. Numbers cannot be combined among different groups to create a winner, the winning numbers must be among one group.

Any odd combination of split groups is allowed on a split ticket. If a player desires, for example, he or she could play two groups of five spots, one seven spot, one four spot and one three spot on the same ticket. Different amounts of money can be wagered on each group. In the above example, $1.00 could be bet on the five, seven and four spot groups, while $2.00 could be wagered on the three spot.

The only restriction to the different dollar amounts allowed to be bet on one split ticket is that equal groupings of numbers, in the above example, the two five spots, must be bet with the same amount of money. Otherwise, bet what you will on each grouping as long as it conforms to the minimum and maximum amounts permitted by the casino.

Combination Tickets

Combination tickets allow the player to combine groups of numbers in all sorts of ways with the player betting one unit for each combination possible.

For example, a player can indicate groups of two, three and four numbers on a ticket. Using all possible combinations, he can play the game as a 2-spot, 3-spot, 4-spot, 5-spot (2 + 3), 6-spot (2-spot + 4 spot), 7-spot (3-spot + 4 spot) and 9-spot (2-spot, 3-spot and 4-spot) for a total of a seven unit bet.

Whew - lots of combinations!

The groups bet on combination tickets should all be clearly marked in the white space on the right of the keno ticket. In the above example of a combination ticket, we would mark 1/2, 1/3, 1/4, 1/5, 1/6, 1/7 and 1/9, showing that one combination is being played on each of these groupings.

If $1 was bet per grouping, we would circle a **1-** underneath, just like on the way ticket. Seven combinations by $1 per group, and we have a total bet of $7. This gets marked as 7- in the Mark Price Here area.

Let's show one more example, this time a simpler combination ticket. This time the player circles two groups of five. At $1.00 per game, $3.00 total is bet, $1.00 each on two groups of five, and $1.00 on one grouping of ten.

Combination Ticket

Way Ticket

The fun of this ticket, unlike split tickets, is that you can have several winners at once on the way ticket, for groups are combined and not separated as on the split. This way you can get your favorite numbers playing in more than one combination.

Way tickets combine at least three groups of equal numbers which can be combined in several ways as straight ticket combinations. The groupings must be equal and the dollar amount bet must be the same for all groups.

For example, three group of five can be chosen. In the first group, the odd numbers 1, 3, 5, 7 and 9 are chosen; in the second group, the even numbers 28, 38, 48, 58 and 68; and in the third group, the doubles 11, 22, 33, 44 and 55.

The way ticket combines these groupings into three groups of ten-spots and this ticket would be bet on as three games. Thus, the odd numbers would combine with the evens for one ten spot, with the doubles for a second, and the even numbers and the doubles would combine for the third group.

In this example, the ticket would have 3/10 marked on the side to show that three groups of 10 are being played.

This is how the ticket would be marked:

Way Ticket

King Tickets

Finally, there is the **king ticket** in which one number is circled by itself, called the **king**, and used in combination with other circled groups on the ticket.

For example, along with the "king," a player circles a group of two numbers and three numbers. The game can now be played as a 3-spot (king + 2-spot), 4-spot (king + 3-spot), 5-spot (2-spot + 3-spot) and a 6-spot (king + 2-spot + 3-spot) for a total of 4 ways. If each group cost $1, than this ticket would cost $4 to play.

You can make king tickets complicated by combining the king in all sorts of variations and giving yourself a myriad of possibilities to appease your gods of chance - but in any case, when's the last time you had a chance to play with the king?

King tickets are marked similarly to the way and split tickets, showing the combinations played, the amount bet per grouping and the total bet.

Let's show the above example of a king ticket, using the number 69 as the king.

King Ticket

MARK PRICE HERE

4 —

1	2	3	4	5	6	7	8	9	10
11	12	✕	14	✕	✕	17	18	19	20
21	22	23	24	25	26	27	28	29	30
31	32	33	34	35	36	37	38	39	40

KENO LIMIT $50,000.00   TO AGGREGATE PLAYERS EACH GAME

41	42	43	44	45	46	47	48	49	50
51	✕	✕	✕	55	56	57	58	59	60
61	62	63	64	65	66	67	68	✕	70
71	72	73	74	75	76	77	78	79	80

KENO RUNNERS ARE AVAILABLE FOR YOUR CONVENIENCE. WE ARE NOT RESPONSIBLE IF TICKETS ARE TOO LATE FOR CURRENT GAME

Special Tickets

Casinos often promote their keno games in various ways, perhaps through a coupon or special incentive, and in many of these instances they'll present the player with a **special ticket** - a keno ticket that must be played a certain way and that will pay according to a different payoff structure - marked on the special payoff chart you will receive.

These tickets generally offer the player a little better deal than the regular ticket and are an incentive to get him or her to play a game, for generally speaking, it's difficult to play just one game. However, do check the payoff rate to make sure that indeed the payoff is more attractive than the regular card.

When playing a special card, make sure you indicate this on your ticket by marking **"SP"** for special on your original ticket, or otherwise following the instructions on the special ticket sheet.

WINNING STRATEGY

Keno is a game that should not be played seriously for the odds are prohibitively against the player. The house edge is typically well over 20% and can be as high as 35% - daunting odds if one wants to win in the long run.

However, keno can be a fun game - its certainly been fun enough to last 2,000 years - and the attraction of a big payoff for only a small bet keeps many players entranced.

One thing to look out for is that some casinos offer better payoffs on the big win than others so a little shopping might get you closer to a bigger payoff. For example, downtown Las Vegas casinos generally have a better payoff per dollar bet than the strip casinos.

And if you find a casino offering $50,000 on a big win as opposed to $25,000 or whatever for the same number of spots hit, by all means, play for the bigger total.

Keno is a great game to test out your lucky numbers. Picking birth dates, anniversaries, license plate numbers and the like offer a big pool of possibilities to see which ones will really pay off.

Perhaps you like the evens, odds and doubles as used in one of our examples, or a progression using every fourth number, or numbers having either a 3 or a 5 in it.

Do you play the same numbers and combinations every game or switch around when one set fails? And what if the original set then wins, or if you didn't switch and the numbers you would have played won? Oh, the heartaches!

If you know your lucky numbers, you may just give them a whirl and see if you can't walk away with a $50,000 bonanza!

POKER

INTRODUCTION

Poker is the greatest and most exciting gambling game, an American tradition where rich and poor, and men and women of all classes gather around a table and vie for stakes ranging from mere pennies to thousands of dollars. No other game provides the challenges of skill, luck and psychology - and the drama of the bluff - in such a fascinating wave. In this chapter, we'll show you how to conquer these challenges and be a winner at poker!

We cover the major poker variations - draw poker: jacks or better and anything opens, seven card high stud, high-low stud, hold'em, lowball: draw poker and seven card low stud (Razz) - and show the basics of play for each of these games. We discuss the differences between casino and private games and go into all the fundamentals of poker: the jargon, the rules of the games, the player's options, the ranks of hands for high, low and wild card poker, how to bet and how to play and everything else needed to make you an informed player.

We'll show you how to apply the five winning strategies to get an edge on your opponents and to turn that edge into winnings. You'll learn how to recognize lock, strong, marginal and weak hands and how to play these cards; how to play position at the table; how to use pot odds to determine the soundness of a bet; how to read opponent's playing styles and cash in on that information; how to play against opponents who bluff a lot or rarely bluff or are loose or tight players, and much, much more, so that by adjusting your play accordingly, you'll have a big edge on your opponents.

It's all here in this section - now let's go out there and win!

HISTORY

Poker is as American as apple pie, a truly great gambling game whose popularity seems to grow with time. It flourishes in private homes and clubs throughout the United States and has devotees around the world as well. For many players, the Friday night poker game has been an uninterrupted ritual for years.

The first seeds of poker drifted across the oceans from the European and Asian continents and found cultivation around the burgeoning Mississippi River port of New Orleans in the early 1800's. The Louisiana Purchase of 1803 opened up this wild and new frontier, and soon thereafter, poker began to capture the gambling spirits and imagination of the new settlers.

The original American poker game used only a 20 card deck of four suits: spades, diamonds, clubs and hearts. The deck contained four each of aces, kings, queens, jacks and 10s, one ordinal per suit. This early form did not yet recognize straights and flushes. Card games from Persia (As Nas or As), France (Poque) and Germany (Pochen or Poch) are credited with being the forerunners of poker.

By the 1840's, the full 52 card deck had been adopted, with the four suits now represented in card values of aces (high) through deuces (low). Straights and flushes made their way into the game by the late 1850's, establishing poker in its more or less modern day form.

Poker is currently played in many styles, from the standard draw poker variations familiar to almost all players, amateur or pro, to the popular casino games we cover in this section, to the many weird, wild and wacky home variations that are being played in private games by enthusiasts.

THE BASICS OF POKER

Object of the Game

The player's object in poker is to win the money in the **pot**, the accumulation of bets and antes gathered in the center of the table.

This can be done two ways. The first way is to have the highest ranking hand at the **showdown**, the final act in poker, where all active player's hands are revealed to see who's got the best. The second way is when all other players drop out of play. In these instances, there is no showdown and the remaining player automatically wins the pot.

Participants

Poker can be played with two players to as many as the 52 card deck can support, usually around eight or nine players. One version of poker, hold 'em, can theoretically support as many as 20 players, though more than 11 players is rarely seen in any poker variation.

In a private game, one of the players is designated as the **dealer**, the person who shuffles and deals the cards to the players. The deal changes with each hand, rotating around the table in a clockwise direction, with each player having a chance to deal. The dealer is still an active player in a private game and enjoys no advantage other than any positional edge he may have for the particular game played.

In casino poker, the dealer is a house employee and non-player. In addition to shuffling and dealing the cards, the house dealer is responsible for the supervision and general running of the game, making sure that all betting is in order and that the proper procedures of play are followed.

In poker variations where the dealer enjoys a positional advantage, such as hold'em, lowball and draw poker, a **button** is utilized to designate the imaginary dealer's position. The button rotates around the table, one spot at a time, in clockwise fashion, so that like the private game, each player in turn has a chance to enjoy the advantages of acting last.

Each player in poker plays by himself and for himself alone against all other players. Collusion or partnership play are illegal and are considered cheating.

The Deck of Cards

Poker is played with a standard 52 card deck containing four suits of thirteen cards each: clubs, diamonds, spades and hearts. The cards are valued in descending order with the ace being the most powerful and followed respectively by the king, queen, jack, ten, nine, eight, seven, six, five, four, three and, finally, the **deuce** or two, that being the lowest ranked card.

The Four Suits

The king, queen and the jack are known as **picture cards** or **face cards**.

The four suits in poker have no basic value in the determination of winning hands, and, as we shall see, it is not the value of the individual cards that reign supreme in poker, but the combination of cards which determine the value of a player's hand.

Card Abbreviations

We will refer to the cards by the following commonly used symbols: ace (A), king (K), queen (Q), jack (J), and all others directly by their numerical value. Thus, the three will be indicated by (3), the nine by (9) and the ten by (10).

Rank of Hands: High Poker

Poker is generally played as high poker, and listed here are the relative rankings of hands in descending order, from best to worst. Later, in the lowball: draw poker section, we'll discuss that poker variation and the ranking of low poker hands.

Note that all poker hands eventually consist of five cards, regardless of the variation played.

Royal Flush

An A K Q J 10, all of the same suit is called a **royal flush**. For example, the A K Q J 10, all in spades, is a royal flush. The odds of being dealt a royal flush in a five card poker game is one in 649,740.

The royal flush is the most powerful hand in poker and one a player may never see in a lifetime of play. In the unlikely event that two players hold a royal flush, the hand is a tie and the pot split.

Royal Flush

Straight Flush

Five cards of the same suit in numerical sequence, such as the Q J 10 9 8 of diamonds, is called a **straight flush**. This particular example is called a queen high straight flush since the queen is the highest ranking card.

Straight Flush

When two straight flushes are in competition for the pot, the straight flush with the highest ranking card wins. Thus, a queen high straight flush beats out a 10 high straight flush. If two players hold equivalently ranked straight flushes, such as 9 8 7 6 5 of clubs and 9 8 7 6 5 of hearts, then the hand is a tie and the pot is split. Suits have no predominance over one another in poker.

The ace must be used as either the highest card in the straight flush (an ace high one being a royal flush) or the lowest card, as in A 2 3 4 5 of diamonds, to be valid. The hand of Q K A 2 3 of clubs is not a straight flush, simply a flush only.

Four of a Kind

Four cards of identical rank, such as the hand J J J J 3, is called a four of a kind, and is almost a sure win in straight poker (poker without a wild card). The odd card in the above example, the 3, is irrelevant and has no bearing on the rank of the hand. When two players hold a four of a kind, the higher ranking four of a kind will win the hand. For example, J J J J 3 beats out 7 7 7 7A.

Four-of-a-Kind

Full House

A **full house** consists of three cards of identical rank along with two cards of an identical but different rank. The hands 3 3 3 A A and 5 5 5 7 7 are two examples of a full house.

Full House

When two players hold full houses, it is the hand holding the higher ranking three of a kind that wins the pot. In the above example, the latter hand, 5 5 5 7 7 is the higher ranking full house.

Flush

Any five cards of the same suit constitutes a **flush** in poker. An A K 7 3 2 of spades is called an ace high flush in spades and Q 10 7 5 3 of hearts is a queen high flush in hearts. When two or more players hold flushes, the flush with the highest ranking card wins the pot. In the above example, the ace high flush holds the higher ranking card, the ace, and is therefore the stronger hand.

Flush

If the highest ranking cards in competing flushes are of equivalent rank, then the next highest cards decide the winner, and if they too are tied, then the next cards and so on down to the fifth card if necessary. For example, in the two flushes, K Q 9 7 6 of diamonds, and K Q J 5 2 of hearts, the heart flush is the stronger flush for its third highest ranking card, the jack, is higher ranking than the 9, the diamond flush's third highest ranking card.

When all five cards of competing flushes are identical, the hand is a tie, and the drawn winners split the pot. Suits are of no relevance in determining a higher ranking flush.

Straight

Five non-suited cards in sequential order, such as 10 9 8 7 6, are called a **straight**. When straights contain an ace, the ace must serve as either the highest card in the run, such as the ace high straight hand A K Q J 10, or the lowest card, as in the five high straight hand, 5 4 3 2 A. The cards Q K A 2 3, is not a straight and is merely an ace high hand, and is beaten by even a lowly pair.

Straight

When two or more straights are in competition, the straight with the highest ranking card takes the pot. A 9 high straight beats out a 7 high straight. When two straights are of equal value, the hand is a tie and the pot is split.

Three of a Kind

Three matched cards of identical value along with two odd cards (unmatched) are called a **three of a kind**. 7 7 7 Q 2 is called "three sevens" or "trip sevens". When two players hold a three of a kind, the player with the higher ranking triplets takes the pot. Three jacks, J J J 3 4, beats out the trip eight hand of 8 8 8 Q 5.

Three-of-a-Kind

Two Pair

Two sets of equivalently valued or "paired" cards along with an unmatched card, are called **two pairs**. 10 10 8 8 5 is a two pair hand and is called "tens up" or "tens over eights," since the tens are the higher ranking pair. Similarly, A A 3 3 J is called "aces up" or "aces over threes."

Two Pair

If more than one player holds a two pair hand, the winner would be the player holding the higher ranked of the two paired hand. J J 7 7 K beats out 10 10 9 9 A. When the higher ranking pairs are identical, the next paired cards determine the winner. 8 8 4 4 10 loses to 8 8 5 5 9. When both pairs are evenly matched, the higher ranking fifth card, the odd card, determines the victor. If all cards are equally ranked, such as 5 5 3 3 2 and 5 5 3 3 2, then the hand is a tie and the pot is split.

One Pair

One set of identically valued cards along with three unmatched cards are called a pair. The hand 2 2 8 4 A is referred to as "a pair of twos". Pairs are ranked in order of value from aces, the highest, down to the deuces, the lowest. Thus, a pair of aces beats out a pair of kings, and a pair of nines wins over a pair of sixes.

One Pair

When two players hold equally paired hands, the highest odd card held decides the winner. 8 8 Q 7 3 triumphs over 8 8 J 9 7. If the highest unmatched cards are also equivalently valued, then the next highest cards are compared and then the last cards if necessary. J J 10 9 8 beats out J J 10 9 7. If all cards are identical, then the hand is a tie and the pot is split.

High Card

A hand containing five unmatched cards, that is, lacking any of the above combinations - a pair, two pairs, three of a kind, straights, flushes, full houses, four of a kind, straight flushes or royal flushes - is determined by its highest ranking card. The hand A 10 9 8 7 is considered an "ace high" hand and beats out the lesser "king high" hand of K Q J 4 3.

When the highest ranking cards are identical, the hand with the next highest card wins, and if they too are equivalent, then the next two highest are paired and so on to the fifth card. The hand K Q 7 5 2 beats out K Q 7 4 3. If all cards are identical, the hand is a draw and the pot is split.

King-High Hand

There are a total of 2,598,960 five-card combinations possible with a 52-card deck. The following chart illustrates the chances of being dealt each type of hand.

Probabilities of Five-Card Poker Hands

	Number	Approximate Odds
Royal Flush	4	649,740 to 1
Straight Flush	36	72,192 to 1
Four of a Kind*	624	4,164 to 1
Full House	3,744	693 to 1
Flush	5,108	508 to 1
Straight	10,200	254 to 1
Three of a Kind	54,912	46 to 1
Two Pair	123,552	20 to 1
One Pair	1,098,240	1.37 to 1
No Hand	1,302,540	1 to 1

*Though there are only 13 four of a kind combinations, this calculation takes into account the total of possibilities when the fifth card is figured in to make a five-card hand.

Wild Cards

In some poker games, players will designate certain cards as **wild cards**, cards which can take on any value and suit at the holder's discretion - even as a duplicate of a card already held. Sometimes the "53rd" and "54th" cards of the deck, the jokers, are used, or players might designate the deuces or the one-eyed jacks as wild cards. Any card can be considered wild at the common consent of the players.

For example, if the deuces were used as wild cards, the hand 6 5 3 2 2 could be a straight by designating one deuce as a 7 and the other as a 4. At the showdown, the holder of this hand would represent a 7 high straight as his best total.

Rank of Hands: Wild Card Poker

The only difference in the ranking of hands in wild card poker from high poker is that five of a kind in wild poker is the highest ranking hand. Otherwise, all other rankings from the royal flush down to the high card follow the same relative rankings.

Here are the relative rankings of hands, from highest to lowest, in wild card poker.

Ranks of Hands · Wild Card Poker
Five of a Kind
Royal Flush
Straight Flush
Four of a Kind
Full House
Flush
Straight
Three of a Kind
Two Pairs
One Pair
High Card Wins

Rank of Hands: Low Poker

In low poker, the ranking of hands are the opposite to that of high poker, with the lowest hand being the most powerful. The ace is considered the lowest and therefore most powerful card, with the hand 5 4 3 2 A being the best low total possible. (See the lowball: draw poker section for further discussion of low poker rankings.)

Money and Chips

Chips are the standard and accepted currency for casino and private poker games, though cash is sometimes used as well. Players prefer the use of chips for betting purposes as the handling of money at the tables is cumbersome and can slow a game down. Chips are easily handled and stacked at a table, and let a game of poker flow more smoothly than one played with cash.

In casino poker, the standard denominations of chips are $1, $5, $25, $100, and for big money games, $5000 and $1,000 chips can sometimes be found. In games with 25¢ and 50¢ antes, regular quarters and half dollars are also used. Though some casinos use their own color code, the usual color scheme of the chips are : $1 - Silver, $5 - red, $25 - green and $100 - black.

To receive chips in a casino game, give the dealer cash, and you'll receive the equivalent value back in chips. This exchange of cash for chips is called a **buy-in**. Dealers will only accept cash or chips, so if you have traveler's checks, credit cards or other forms of money, you need to exchange these for cash at the area marked **Casino Cashier**. Then, with cash in hand, you can buy chips at the poker table.

In private games, players generally use chips, though often, the game will be cash only. When chips are used, one player acts as the **bank** or **banker**, and converts player's cash buy-ins to an equivalent value in chips. The most common denominations of chips used in private games are one unit, five units, ten units and twenty-five units. A unit can equal a penny, a dollar or whatever value is agreed upon and set by the players. One unit chips are generally white; five units - red; ten units - blue; and twenty-five units - yellow, though any equivalencies or colors may be used.

Preliminaries of Play

The dealer is responsible for shuffling the cards after each round of play so that the cards are mixed well and are in random order. The deck is then offered to a player, usually on the dealer's right, for the cut. This player initiates the cut by removing the top part of the deck and placing it to one side, face down. The dealer completes the cut by placing the former lower portion of the deck on top of the former upper section, thereby effecting the cut, and making the deck of cards whole again.

To be valid, a cut must go deeper than the top five cards of the deck and may not go further in than the last five. This helps prevent players who had inadvertently or otherwise seen the top or bottom cards from using the cut to undue advantage. The cut of any number of cards between these two extremes is valid and perfectly acceptable.

The game is ready to begin.

Antes

An **ante**, also known as a **sweetener**, is a uniform bet placed by players into the pot before the cards are dealt. The size of the ante is prearranged by the players, or in a casino is set by the house, and is required of all players.

The ante is used in a majority of private poker games and virtually all casino games, and is a way to "sweeten the pie," and create more action in the game. The ante creates an immediate pot, which sharp players, under the right circumstances, may go after right from the start. Called **stealing the pot**, a player will bet forcefully in first round play hoping to force opposing players out of the pot, thereby winning the pot and the antes in it by the process of elimination.

The Play of the Game

After the dealer shuffles the cards and offers the cut, the deal is ready to begin. If the game requires an ante, the dealer may announce ante-up, a call for all players to place their antes into the pot. The center of the table is used as the area for the pot and that is where all antes and bets should be placed.

The dealer begins dealing to the player on his immediate left, and deals cards one at a time in a clockwise rotation, until each player has received the requisite number of cards for the variation being played. In casino games, where a rotating button is used to mark the dealer's position, the deal begins with the player to the left of the button and continues around in the same fashion as in the private game.

Like the dealing of the cards, play always proceeds in clockwise fashion, beginning in the first round, with either the player sitting to the immediate left of the dealer, or in some of the stud games, with either the high or low card opening play, as the case may be, and continues around the table until each player in turn has acted.

In later rounds though, the first player to act will vary depending on the variation being played. In the stud games, the strongest ranking open cards will open betting, and in the draw games, either the first active player to the left of the dealer will open betting or the last player to have raised or opened betting in the previous round will initiate play.

However, we'll cover the particulars of play under the games themselves and see how the betting works for the different variations.

The Player's Options

Except for the times when a bet is mandatory, as is usually the case in the initial round of play, the first player to act in a betting round has three options: He can place a **bet**, money wagered and placed into the pot; he can **check**, make no bet at all and pass play on to the next player while remaining an active player; or he can **fold** or **go out**, throw away his cards and forfeit the hand for the current deal.

However, once a bet is placed, a player no longer has the option of checking his turn. To remain an active player, he must either **call the bet** or **see the bet**, place an amount of money into the pot equal to the bet; or he can **raise (call and raise)**, call the bet and make an additional bet on top of the bet called. If a player doesn't want to bet, then he must fold and go out of play. Each succeeding player, in turn, is faced with the same options: calling, folding or raising.

To continue playing for the pot, a player must call the original bet and any raises that were made, or he may fold his cards if he doesn't want to call the bets and raises that preceded him.

When play swings around again to the original bettor, he or she must call any previous raises to continue as an active player as must any subsequent players who have raises due, or he must fold. A player may also raise again if the raise limit hasn't been reached.

The number of raises permitted vary from game to game, but generally, casino games are limited to either three or five total raises in one round, except in instances where just two players remain, called **head to head** play, when unlimited raising is allowed. Most private games allow unlimited raising at all times.

However, a player may not raise his own bet. He may only raise another player's bet or raise.

Play continues until the last bet or raise is called by all active players, and no more bets or raises are due any player. The betting round is now completed and over.

One important rule of poker etiquette is that player's check, bet, raise or fold in their proper turn only. This rule must always be respected by all players.

Some games use a **blind**, a mandatory bet that is made by the first player to act in the opening round of play. This player, called the **blind bettor**, must make the blind bet regardless of the hand he or she holds. The blind is a set bet and forces immediate action in a poker game. Players cannot check after a blind bet is made and must either call the blind, raise or fold. Otherwise, play proceeds the same as in games which don't use a blind. The amount of a blind bet varies, but is usually less than or equal to the minimum bet.

Check and raise, a player's raising of a bet after already checking in a round, is usually not allowed in private games, though many casino games permit its use. Before sitting down to play in a game, ask if check and raise is allowed.

Betting Limits (Limit Poker)

Betting in poker is generally structured in a two-tiered level, with the lower level of betting occurring before the draw in the draw poker variations or in the early rounds of the stud games, and the upper level occurring after the draw in the draw poker games and in the later rounds in the stud variations. Some commonly used betting structures are $1-$2, $1-$3, $5-$10 and $10-$20, though other limits are found as well.

In a $5-$10 limit game, when the lower limit of betting is in effect, all bets and raises must be in $5 increments, and when the upper range is in effect, all bets and raises must be in $10 increments.

In the discussions covering the individual poker variations, we'll discuss when the lower and upper ranges of betting are in play for each of the games.

The betting limits of casino games are generally posted above the table, or can be found out by asking the dealer or one of the players. The betting limits of private games are prearranged and agreed upon by the players before play.

Table Stakes

Table stakes is the rule in casino poker and almost all private games, and states that a player's bet or call of a bet may not exceed the amount of money he has on the table in front of him. For example, if the bet due a player is $25, and he only has $10 remaining on the table, this player is considered **tapped-out**, and may only call the bet to the tune of $10. He is not allowed to withdraw money from his wallet, borrow from others or receive credit during a deal. That is permissible only before the cards are dealt.

In the above example, the remaining $15 and all future monies bet during this hand would be segregated into a separate pot. The tapped-out player can still receive cards until the showdown and play for the original pot, but he can no longer take part in the betting, and has no interest in the side pot. The other players however, can continue to bet and wager against each other for the side pot as well.

Should the tapped-out player have the best hand at the showdown, he receives only the money in the original pot, before he tapped-out. The side pot is won by the player having the best hand among the remaining players. Should one of the other players hold the overall best hand, that player wins both the original and the side pot.

If only one other bettor remains when a player taps out, then the betting stops and cards are played out until the showdown. In the above example, the opposing player would have $15 of his $25 bet returned to him, since only $10 of his bet can be called. At the showdown, the best hand would win the existing pot.

Pot Limit and No Limit

Poker is sometimes played as pot limit or no limit, betting structures often used in high stakes poker games. **Pot limit** games allow players to bet any amount up to the current size of the pot, but no more. For example, if the pot holds $75, the largest allowable bet is $75. If a player then bets pot limit and places $75 more into the pot, the pot would now contain $150. The betting limit is now set at a maximum of $150.

No limit poker is even a wilder version and states that a player's maximum bet is limited only by the table stakes rule. The World Series of Poker played at the Horseshoe Casino in Las Vegas every year plays no limit style of hold'em poker with a $10,000 buy-in.

Pot limit and no limit poker are too vicious for the average player (unless comfortable maximum betting ranges are set by the players) and should not be considered by anyone but top level players with big purses. In this book, we'll assume just the limit variety of poker, the game almost universally played by most players in private and casino games.

Sample Round of Betting

For illustrative purposes, let's follow the play in the first betting round of a private draw poker: anything opens game. This game is played without a blind (as is jacks or better), and the first player to act may check or bet as desired. In the other games we discuss - hold'em, lowball: draw poker and the seven card stud variations - the opening player has no such luxury and must either make a mandatory opening bet or fold (when allowed). In these games, checking is not allowed in first round play.

(We'll look at the particular rules of play for each game in the individual games sections, and show which player is the first to act in a betting round and whether that player must make a mandatory opening bet.)

Let's pick up the action now and see how the betting works. The eight players have agreed to play with a $1 ante, so the pot holds $8 before any of the cards are dealt. The participants are, in order, clockwise from the dealer, Julian, Eddie-boy, Vicenzo, Fay,

Donto, Flavian, Uncle J. and Big Phil (the current dealer).

They are playing **dealer's choice**, a rule which allows each successive dealer to choose the variation played during his deal. In casino poker games, dealer's choice is not played, and players are limited to playing the variations designated for their table. If a player wishes to play a different variation, he or she must switch to a table offering the game desired.

Big Phil is the current dealer and has chosen draw poker: anything opens as the game he wants to deal. The player sitting to the immediate left of the dealer goes first in draw poker, and after the cards are dealt all players await Julian's decision.

Julian raps on the table with his knuckles, a nonverbal signal used in poker to indicate that a player is checking. He may also indicate checking by saying "Check" or some such communication. Eddie-boy and Vicenzo, in turn, check as well, and pass play on to Fay, the next player.

Fay announces, "I'll bet $5", and throws a $5 chip into the pot. Now that a bet is placed, no player can check and remain in the game.

Donto, sitting at Fay's left, decides his hand isn't worth $5 and flips his cards face down toward the dealer. Donto is no longer a participant in the pot and forfeits his $1 ante. He must wait until the next deal to resume play.

Flavian draws a big puff out of his cigar, "Cuban," he claims, and throws $10 into the pot, calling Fay's $5 bet and raising it $5 more. He announces, "$10 to you, Uncle J."

Raises, like bets, are made by the physical placement of chips in the pot area and, as is often the custom in a private game, they may be announced as well. Raising may be indicated by saying, "I'll raise you" or "I'll call that bet and raise," or any such communication that clearly indicates that a raise is being made.

Uncle J. is either daunted by the $10 due him or the cigar, for he folds. Big Phil, the dealer for this round of play, calls the $5 bet and the $5 raise, and re-raises $5 more. He places $15 into the pot.

Flavians' cigar whirls across his mouth like a brigate cannon searching out new targets, and sends the long overdue ashes crashing against the dizzying colors of his Hawaiian short-sleeved shirt. One ash, still hot, works its way into a palm tree, and then fades away in lasting glory.

Play now returns to Julian, who had checked earlier. To play, he must call $15 worth of bets, one $5 bet plus two $5 raises. He throws his cards in without hesitation, and is followed by Eddie-boy who does the same. Vicenzo, who had also checked, bets the $15. He may not raise, for this private games disallows check and raise. However, if check and raise was permitted, he would be allowed to raise $5 more.

Since this is the first round of betting, all bets and raises are in $5 increments. $10 bets and raises are not allowed this round.

Fay plays next, and she must call the two $5 raises of her original bet to remain playing. She may have called just one raise, but with two raises facing her and Flavian's cigar bent at a mean angle, she decides her hand is not worth $10 more, and decides to fold. She's out her earlier $5 bet and $1 ante - that money belongs to the pot.

Play passes by Donto, for he had folded earlier, and proceeds to Flavian and his cigar, the first raiser. Since his raise had been upped $5 by Big Phil, he must call that re-raise to play. The cigar rotates slowly as it weighs the possibility of raising again and then pointedly stops, aimed dead ahead at the middle of Big Phil's forehead. Another second passes, drawn out by a long puff, and then Flavian flips a $5 chip into the pot, calling Big Phil's raise.

The only active players remaining are, in order from here, Big Phil, Vicenzo and Flavian. Big Phil cannot raise again, for he was the last player to raise, and a player cannot raise his own bet. Therefore, since all bets and raises have been called by the remaining players, the betting round is over.

The Showdown

Following the conclusion of all betting in the final betting round, if two or more players remain, then the **showdown** occurs. It is the final act in a poker game where remaining players reveal their hands to determine the winner of the pot.

The player whose last bet or raise was called is the first to turn over his cards and reveal his hand. If his hand proves to be the best, he wins the pot and collects all the money in it. However, any player who claims a superior hand must show his. Players holding losing hands at the showdown may concede the pot without showing their cards.

The player with the best hand at the showdown wins all the money in the pot. In the event of a tie, or when there are two winners as may be the case in high-low, then the pot is split evenly among the winners.

If only one player remains after the final betting round, or at any point during the game, then there is no showdown, and the remaining player automatically wins the pot.

The Rake

The biggest difference between casino poker and private poker games is that in the casino games the house gets a cut of the action, called a **rake**, for their services. The rake varies from casino to casino, and is usually proportionately higher in lower limit games.

Do not play in a game where the rake is greater than five percent of the total bet made. It is too much of an overhead. Find a more reasonable game where your winnings won't get dwindled to nothing by weighty house cuts. Always ask how much the house rake is before sitting down to play.

Understanding the Rules of the Table

Though poker is basically the same game played anywhere, at home or in the casino, rules can vary from game to game. Make sure that you're clear about the particulars of play before sitting down at a new poker game.

The Most Important Questions to Ask Are:
· What are the betting limits?
· Is "check and raise" allowed?
· Are antes or blinds used, and if so, how much?
· What are the maximum number of raises allowed?

When playing a casino game, most of the above information is generally posted on a sign above the table, but if not ask the dealer or a player and find out. The additional question, "How much is the rake?" should be asked in casino games.

DRAW POKER - JACKS OR BETTER ANYTHING OPENS

Jacks or Better

Also called **jackpots**, draw poker - **jacks or better** is a **closed poker** variation, where all cards are dealt face down (closed) and known only by the holder of that hand. It is played with two betting rounds. The first betting round occurs before the **draw**, with players having an opportunity to exchange up to three unwanted cards for new ones. (In some games, players are allowed to draw four cards if their remaining card is an ace, and in casino draw poker, players may exchange up to five unwanted cards for new ones.) The second round of betting occurs after the draw.

At the showdown, the highest hand wins the pot, or if all other players have folded, the last remaining player is the winner.

The Play of the Game

Both the casino and private versions of jacks or better require antes and these must be placed into the pot before the cards are dealt. Antes usually range from 10% of the maximum bet (normal size) to 20% (considered a high ante). In a $5-$10 game, a $1 or $2 ante would be the most common found.

Each player is dealt five face down cards. The deal begins with the player to the immediate left of the dealer receiving the first card and continues clockwise, one card at a time, until all players have received their five cards. The first round of betting begins at this point, with the first player to have received cards, the one on the dealer's left, making the first play.

To open betting in jacks or better, a player must have a hand with a minimum ranking of a pair of jacks. For example, a pair of queens, three deuces or a straight are hands that could open betting, while a pair of sevens or an ace-high hand could not. However, a player holding jacks or better does not have to open betting and may check his turn.

The first player to act must check if he cannot open betting (or holds jacks or better and elects not to). The next player, in turn, must also check if he doesn't hold the requisite opening cards. Players continue checking until an **opener**, the opening bet of jacks or better, is made.

Once an opening bet is placed, subsequent players, in order, may call, fold or raise the opener. Checking is no longer permitted. A bet has been made and players must call that bet to play for the pot. Play continues around the table in clockwise fashion until all bets and raises have been called.

If all players check on the opening round of play, the hand is said to be **passed out**. The cards will be collected and shuffled and the next player in turn will have the dealer's position. New antes will be required of all players and these are added to the antes already in the pot.

The draw occurs after the first betting round is completed. Each remaining player, beginning with the first active player to the dealer's left, can discard up to three cards (or five when allowed). The cards should be tossed face down toward the dealer who will issue an equivalent number of new cards from the unused portion of the deck. Players should draw in turn, waiting for the previous player to receive his new cards before making their own discards. The dealer draws last, if he is still in the pot.

Discards should be announced so that all players are aware of the number of cards drawn. Players who do not draw any cards are said to **stand pat**. This can be indicated verbally or by knocking on the table with the hand.

The second round of betting follows the draw and is begun by either the opener or the last raiser if there were any raises during the round. If no raises had occurred, and the opener has folded, the first active player to the dealer's left opens the betting. This player may check or bet as desired. Each succeeding player has the option of checking or betting, but once a bet is placed, active players must call that bet, if not raise; or go out.

The showdown, occurs after this betting round is completed. At this time, the player whose last bet or raise had been called (as opposed to players calling those bets) turns over his cards first. Any opponent who claims a superior hand must turn over his cards for verification. Players holding inferior hands may go out without revealing their cards.

The best hand wins the pot and gets to rake in the chips.

Let's return to our original crew and see how the betting works in a $5-$10 limit game of jacks or better. They're playing with a $2 ante, a high ante for this type of betting, and one which encourages aggressive early betting to "steal the antes." The pot holds $16 to start (8 players times $2).

These are the cards held after the deal:

Julian	K	10	7	3	2
Eddie-boy	8	8	10	4	2
Vicenzo	A	A	J	10	8
Fay	6	6	A	4	3
Donto	A	J	7	6	3
Flavian	K	10	9	8	7
Uncle J	J	J	5	4	2
Big Phil	5	5	5	8	7

Julian is on the dealer's immediate left and opens play.

Not having a hand of jacks or better, Julian checks, as does Eddie-boy, who holds only a pair of eights. Vicenzo can open and does so, flipping a $5 chip into the pot. Fay has nothing worth betting on and folds.

Donto is excited enough by his ace-high hand to call the bet, but it's a poor play. He's a big underdog with those cards and has little chances of winning.

Flavian's cigar is blowing smoke like a train coming down the tracks. With two players in the action and a large ante, the $25 in the pot gives him good pot odds to go for his straight (26-5, greater than the approximately 4-1 odds he needs to make the play justifiable) and he calls the $5 bet as well.

Uncle J. figures that the opener, Vicenzo, holds the jacks or better and probably at least kings or aces to have opened in such early position, and with two other players in the game, folds his pair of jacks knowing they're of little value. Big Phil tosses $10 into the pot, calling the $5 opener and bumping that bet $5 more. His three fives are strong cards, but if too many players are allowed to draw out against them, they could get beat.

Julian and Eddie-boy see that their free ride is over and fold in turn. Neither sees their cards being worth a $5 bet let alone a $5 raise on top. Vicenzo calls the raise and flips his $5 into the pot. Donto finally folds, poorer by his earlier $5 call. Flavian is playing for the draw and calls the $5 raise.

The raise has now been called by all active players and the first betting round is over. On this first round of betting, before the draw, all bets and raises are in the lower tier of the $5-$10 game, and are therefore in $5 increments. After the draw, all bets will be in the upper tier or in $10 increments.

Three players remain for the draw: Vicenzo, Flavian and Big Phil. Vicenzo throws his discards toward the dealer and draws three cards to his aces. Flavian calls for one card and after he receives his draw, Big Phil takes one card as well. Though Big Phil theoretically has better chances of improving his hand with a two card draw, his one card draw is a clever play, for opponents must figure him for two pair. Meanwhile, he's sitting pretty with his three fives, a favorite against his two opponents.

Here's how the hands look after the draw:

Vicenzo	A	A	9	9	2
Flavian	10	9	8	7	4
Big Phil	5	5	5	K	6

The opener, Vicenzo, acts first and bets $10. His aces over nines is a strong hand, and he figures it's a stronger hand than Big Phil's probable two pair. Flavian's train has slowed down and he folds. The four that he drew fell a little short of his needs and there's not much he can do with a 10-high hand.

Big Phil raises the bet to $20 (a $10 raise) and Vicenzo calls the bet. Since Vicenzo called Big Phil's raise, Big Phil must show his cards first and he turns over his trip fives. Vicenzo sees that he is beat, and mumbling something about his boss, throws his cards face down and concedes the pot.

Big Phil is the winner and collects all the chips in the pot, giving them a new home in his private stack. A new deal is ready to begin.

Strategy at Jacks or Better

As with all the other poker variations, the single most important strategy in jacks or better is to start out with cards which have good winning possibilities. The opening requirement of jacks or better tells us right off that any pair held which is less than the minimum opening hand of jacks is automatically a big underdog. For example, if a player opens the betting, what chances do a pair of eights have against this opener? We know that jacks or better are held.

Position is also an important consideration in jackpots. The relative position a player has in the order of betting affects the types of hands that should be played and how those hands should be bet. For example, if a player opens betting with a pair of jacks or queens in an early position, he's in a bad situation should his opener get raised by several players. You have to figure the raisers for at least kings or aces, possibly better, and with a lowly pair of jacks nobody is scared. The jacks are underdogs and must be folded.

Let's examine the minimum requirements for correct play in jacks or better.

Jacks or Better - Minimum Opening Cards

First Four Positions (Early): Kings or Better
Second Two Positions (Middle): Queens or Better
Last Two Positions (Late): Jacks or Better

In late position, with no openers yet made, the pair of jacks becomes a stronger hand. The jacks are in a good leveraged position, and an opening bet may be able to force other players out of the pot, effectively stealing the antes. If only one or two players call the opener, the jacks are in a decent enough position going into the draw to improve to a winner.

Once betting is opened, players holding jacks or queens should call only if two players or less are in the pot and no raises have been made. Otherwise, jacks and queens should be folded. Their winning chances rapidly diminish as the number of active players increase.

Four card straights and flushes have good potential and should be played to the draw, but only if the pot odds justify calling the bet. (See "How to Use Pot Odds.") However, do not raise with these hands, for at this stage they're speculative and hold no value. But should the draw fill these cards into a straight or flush, then you've got the goods to be raising and building up the pot.

Players holding kings, aces and low three-of-a-kind hands should not only call the opener but raise as well. These are strong cards. If weaker and speculative hands are not forced out, these inferior hands may bury our favorites with a lucky draw. Against fewer opponents, there are less chances of this occurring. The more players that stay in for the draw, the higher the average winning hand will be, and the greater the opportunity that the kings, aces and small trips will get beat out by an inferior hand that improves. Raise with these strong cards. Don't make the game cheap for speculators.

On the other hand, with a high three-of-a-kind, such as trip 10s or higher, don't raise - call! We have a powerful hand which can win without improvement and want to keep as many players in as possible.

Do not play three card straights or flushes, or inside straights. An **inside straight** is a four card straight that has only one way of improving, such as 4 5 7 8. They are nothing hands, and the chances of improving are too steep for the money.

Playing a Small Two Pair

Smaller two pair hands, such as nines over threes, are deceptive hands in draw poker and must be played carefully. At first glance, two small pairs appear to be strong hands with good winning possibilities, but in reality, these cards spell trouble.

While a small two pair may stand tall before the draw, against three players trying to improve as well, they in fact become underdogs. If you're facing bets and raises before the draw and more bets after, your small two pair (with 11-1 odds against improving) starts looking even smaller.

Fold two small pairs in early position if the pot is opened ahead of you, or if you're in late position and three or more players are in the pot. In last position, against just one or two players, raise, and try to force them out.

The Draw

When drawing to a pair, the best odds of improving is to take a three card draw. Sometimes, however, holding a **kicker**, an extra card to a pair, can be a powerful bluffing tool. Players have to suspect your two card draw for three-of-a-king. Occasionally, use of the kicker in this fashion can really work to your advantage.

Drawing one card to a three-of-kind is a good bluffing strategy as well. Let's say you're playing a $5-$10 game. The first two players check and the third player opens betting with a $5 bet. The next player folds. You're in the next seat holding three eights and raise the opener $5. Players fold in turn around the table with only the opener calling the bet. He goes first and draws one card. You take one card as well.

After the draw, the opener bets $10, probably holding kings or aces up and figuring us for a lower two pair. We raise $10, banking on the 11-1 odds against him improving. He calls and then quietly folds his cards after we turn over our three eights.

Fold four flushes and four straights if they don't improve at the draw.

The dealer has a decisive advantage in draw poker, for he acts last. With marginal hands, he can come in the pot cheaply, or fold if the action is too stiff. He's in a great position to bluff, and being the last to draw can make use of his drawing strategy to a powerful edge. Due to the dealer's big positional advantage, draw poker is an excellent choice in dealer's choice games.

Play alertly and apply the winning strategies of poker to gain an advantage over your opposition and be a winner at draw poker.

Odds Against Improving Draw Poker Hands

Cards Held	Cards Drawn	Improved Hand	Approximate Odds Against
One Pair	3	Two Pair	5.3-1
		Three of a Kind	7.8-1
		Full House	97-1
		Four of a Kind	360-1
		Any Improvement	2.5-1
One Pair plus kicker	2	Two Pairs	4.8-1
		Three of a Kind	12-1
		Full House	120-1
		Four of a Kind	1080-1
		Any Improvement	2.8-1
Three of a kind	2	Full House	15.3-1
		Four of a Kind	22.5-1
		Any Improvement	8.7-1
Four Card Straight (Open Both Ways)	1	Straight	5-1
Inside Straight	1	Straight	10.8-1
Four Card Flush	1	Flush	4.2-1
Four Card Straight Flush (Open Ended)	1	Straight Flush	22.5-1
	1	Straight or Better	2-1
Four Card Straight Flush (Inside)	1	Straight Flush	46-1
		Straight or Better	3-1

Draw Poker: Anything Opens

Draw poker: anything opens is played the same as jacks or better except that any hand regardless of strength may open the betting. Thus, for example, a pair of sevens could open betting in anything opens, or even a queen-high hand. Otherwise, the rules and methods of play are identical to jacks or better.

Strategy at Draw Poker: Anything Opens

The strategies in draw poker: anything opens are virtually the same as in jacks or better. Though any cards can open the betting, don't be fooled into opening or calling bets with anything less than you would do in jackpots. Whether the game requires jacks or better or requires nothing to open betting doesn't change the fact that you'll be dealt just as many good and bad hands in one game as in the other, and, therefore, the same minimum starting hands apply in strategy.

LOWBALL: DRAW POKER

This interesting variation presents a different twist on poker in that the lowest hand is the strongest in **lowball**, or "loball" as it is sometimes spelled, as opposed to the standard high poker game where the highest hand is the best. The ace is the best card in lowball, but, unlike high poker where the ace counts as the highest card held, in this game the ace is counted as the lowest card of a hand. The two is the next lowest card, and therefore the next best lowball card, and is followed in order by the three, four, five and so on up to the king, which is the worst card in lowball.

In lowball, the high card counts in determining the value of a hand: the lower the high card, the better the hand. Hands are announced by the two highest cards held. For example, the hand 7 6 4 2 A is announced as a "7 6" or "7 high", and the hand 8 4 3 2 A is announced as an "8 4" or "8 high". Of the two above-mentioned hands, the "7 6" is the more powerful lowball total since its highest card, the seven, is lower than the eight, the high card of the "8 4" hand.

In instances where the highest values of two hands are equivalent, the next highest cards of the hands are matched up, and the lowest value of these matched cards determines the winner. Thus, the hand 8 6 4 3 2 is a stronger total than 8 7 3 2 A, and 9 6 5 2 A beats out the hand 9 6 5 4 A. When the competing hands are equivalent, such as 8 5 4 3 A versus 8 5 4 3 A, the hand is considered a tie and the pot is split.

The **wheel or bicycle**, 5 4 3 2 A, is the perfect lowball hand, and can never be beat. At best, it can only be tied by another wheel. 6 4 3 2 A is the next strongest lowball total, followed in order by 6 5 3 2 A, 6 5 4 2 A and 6 5 4 3 A. And so on.

In lowball, straights and flushes are not relevant and do not count. The wheel, 5 4 3 2 A, is not considered a straight, but a perfect "5 4" while an 8 4 3 2 A, all of hearts is simply an "8 4" hand, not a flush as it would be considered in high poker.

Any five card best containing a pair is a weak hand and can be beat by any five unmatched cards. For example, K Q 7 6 5 is a winner over 2 2 3 4 5. Two pair, three of a kind, full houses and four of a kind are respectively worse holdings, and the odds of these hands winning are very slim indeed.

The term **smooth** in lowball refers to a relatively good back four cards, such as the hand 9 5 4 3 A, a *smooth nine*. **Rough** suggests a relatively weak back four cards, such as the hand 9 7 6 5 2, a *rough nine*.

Lowball is a draw poker variation, and, as such, is played similarly to high draw poker, featuring two betting rounds, one before the draw and one after.

The Play of the Game

Lowball is often played with an ante, and that bet should be placed into the pot before the cards are dealt. When no ante is required, a blind bettor is used, though sometimes both a blind bettor and an ante are part of the structure.

After the shuffle and cut, cards are dealt clockwise, one at a time, until all players have received five face down cards. The first player to receive the cards, the one at the immediate left of the button or dealer, is also the first player to act. For purposes of illustration, let's assume a $5-$10 lowball game using a blind. This first player, being the blind, is required to make a $5 blind bet and he promptly does so, flipping a $5 chip into the pot.

All bets before the draw in draw poker, high or low, are in the lower tier of the betting limit. In this example, all bets and raises are in $5 increments.

The next player to act sits at the blind's left, for play in all poker variations proceeds in a clockwise direction. He has three choices. He can call the $5 blind bet and remain an active player; he can raise that bet $5 more and place $10 into the pot; or he can fold his cards.

Play proceeds around the table until all players have made their decisions, either calling the blind and any raises that have been made, or folding and waiting for the next cycle of poker life to begin.

Now the draw occurs, and in the same order of the betting and dealing of the cards. The blind, if he is still in the pot, goes first, and can exchange up to five cards for new ones. Each active player, in turn, can exchange as many of his original cards as he likes, and should do so only after the preceding player has received his or her cards. Discards should be announced so that all players are aware of the number of cards drawn.

Players who elect to stand pat, not draw any cards, can indicate this verbally or by knocking on the table with their fist.

After the draw is completed, the second and last betting round occurs, and is begun by the blind, or, if he has folded, by the first active player closest to the dealer's left. All bets and raises in this round are in the upper tier of the $5-$10 limit, and are therefore in $10 increments. If the game was a $1-$3 games, all bets after the draw would be in $3 increments.

After the betting round is completed, we have the showdown, where the lowest hand collects the fruits of his or her labors, the pot, and all the money in it. If, at any point in the game, all opponents drop out of play, the remaining player would be the automatic winner, and he claims the pot.

The deal now moves to the left. In the case of a casino game, the former blind is now the button, and can enjoy all the advantages of playing the dealer's position.

Strategy at Lowball: Draw Poker

Lowball gives the knowledgeable player a tremendous advantage over uninitiated opponents, for the strategic thinking is different in this poker variation. Players are shooting for different types of hands, and it takes the high poker player a while to become accustomed to the peculiarities of the game.

The first rule in lowball is never to play a hand which needs more than one card drawn to improve to a winner. Unlike high poker, draws of two or even three cards are terrible draws and immediately single out a player as a weak opponent. A two card draw is a shot in the dark and is equivalent to trying to fill a three card straight in high poker.

To win at lowball, you must start out with cards that can win. If the cards you're dealt are weak, throw them away unless you can get a free ride. For example, if you're the blind, and there are no raises following the forced bet, it costs nothing more to play and you should stay in for the draw. Always play further if there is no cost, no matter the cards. But if you're faced with a bet, fold, unless you've got the goods.

Position is important in lowball and must be considered in the opening strategies.

Here's our minimum opening cards in lowball:

Lowball: Draw Poker - Minimum Starting Cards

First Four Positions: (Early)	8 high pat hand 7 high - one card draw
Second Two Positions: (Middle)	9 high pat hand 8 high - one card draw
Third Two Positions: (Late)	10 high pat hand 9 high - one card draw

---

Unless we hold an 8 high pat hand or have a four card seven high in early position, we can't call the blind's bet or make an opener ourselves, as the case may be, and must fold. We're too vulnerable to raises behind our position to call with these hands in the first four spots. There is a strong possibility that players will up the stakes in the middle and late positions. It is foolish to call hands in middle and early position if we will be forced to fold on a raise.

Do not call bets with anything less than the minimum openers in early and middle positions.

In late position, if a bet and a raise have preceded our play, call with a minimum holding of an 8 high pat hand or a four card 7 high draw.

With a 7 high pat hand, we hold a strong hand and should play aggressively. Raise the opener from any position at the table, or, if a raiser precedes you, re-raise.

When dealt a 6 high pat hand, you're *in like Flint,* and have almost a sure winner. Don't raise in early position, for you want to keep as many players as possible in the game. If, however, a player raises behind you, and it's just you and him plus maybe one other player, re-raise and build up the pot. There's something pleasurable about winning big pots.

SEVEN CARD STUD - HIGH, LOW (RAZZ) AND HIGH-LOW

Seven card stud's three main variations - **high, low** (which is also called **Razz**) and **high-low** - all pack five exciting betting rounds into play. In each variation, players form their best five card combination out of the seven dealt to produce their final hand. In seven card high stud, the highest ranking hand remaining wins the pot. In seven card low, the lowest hand claims the gold. And in high-low stud, players vie for either the highest ranking or lowest ranking hands, with the best of each claiming half the pot; or players can go for the high-low pot and risk all to win all.

Players also can win the pot by being the last remaining player in the pot, either as a result of skillful bluffing or by attrition of opponents because of stiff betting.

In each variation, players receive seven cards. After the first three cards are dealt, two face down (closed) and one face up (open), the first betting round commences. The following three cards are dealt open, one at a time, with a betting round accompanying each card. The last card, the seventh, comes "down and dirty," and is the third closed card received by the players.

All remaining players now hold three hole cards and four open cards. These are the final cards they will hold. One more round of betting follows the seventh card. Then the showdown occurs, where the best hand, or hands (as may be the case in high-low), claims the pot.

The Play of the Game

Following the shuffle and the cut, the cards are dealt in a clockwise direction beginning with the player to the dealer's left and continuing around the table, in order, until all players have received two closed cards and one open card. The two face down cards are called **hole cards**, as is the seventh card, also closed, that the player receives last.

All antes, if required, should be placed into the pot before the cards are dealt. Once an ante reaches the pot, it is like any other bet. It is the property of the pot and will belong to the eventual winner of the hand.

In the private high and high-low seven card stud games, it is the player with the highest ranking open card that starts the betting, or, if two or more players hold equivalent values, the high card player closest to the dealer's left begins play first. The high card player must bet to open play on **third street**, the name for this betting round, the first in seven card stud. It is a required wager. There is no checking on this round. Subsequent players must either call the bet, raise or fold.

On all following rounds, the highest ranking open hand, in high and high-low seven card stud private games, opens the play. Also, from **fourth street** on (the name for the second betting round in seven card stud), the high hand may check to open betting. It is only on the first betting round that a mandatory opening bet is required.

In casino versions of seven card high stud, unlike the private game, the player holding the lowest open card must open betting, or when two players have identically valued low cards, the player with the lower ranked suit plays first. For this purpose only, the suits are ranked in order of strength, beginning with spades, the highest, and followed in descending order by hearts, diamonds and clubs. For example, if the lowest cards showing are a three of clubs and a three of hearts, the player with the three of clubs opens betting since he holds the lower three. Like the private game, in the first round of play the player who goes first must make a required opening bet, and all following players, in turn, must call, raise or fold.

In all subsequent rounds of casino seven card high stud, the player holding the highest ranking open hand acts first, and also like the private game, he may check to begin play.

In casino high-low seven card stud, the lowest card opens the betting in the first round of play, a mandatory bet, but thereafter, in all future rounds, the high hand acts first, and may begin play by checking or betting as desired.

In private seven card low stud games, the player holding the lowest open card (the ace counts as the lowest card in low poker) acts first and must make the mandatory opening bet. Conversely, in the casino games of seven card low stud, the highest ranking open card makes the required opening bet. There is no first round checking in these games either - players must call the opener, raise or fold.

In all subsequent rounds, in the private and casino versions of seven card low stud, the lowest ranking open hand acts first and may check or bet as desired. For example, a player showing 8 6 2 A on board, an 8 6 hand, opens against a player showing a pair of sixes, 6 6 32, while a 6 4 2 A hand would open against a 7 3 2 A.

Let's see how the betting works in seven card poker using a $5-$10 high stud game as an example. In the private game, the high card player must make a set bet, in this case $5. If the game was $1-$2, the opener would be $1, or in a $10-$20 games, $10 would be the opener. Subsequent players must either call that $5 bet, fold, or, if they want, raise that bet by $5 to make it $10 to the next player.

All bets and raises in this first betting round, called **third street**, are in $5 increments, the lower limit of the $5-$10 betting tier.

The casino $5-$10 game varies slightly in that the forced opening bet, the blind, is a $1 bet, and that the first raise is $3 only. (These numbers may vary depending upon the casino.) Thereafter, all bets and raises this round are in $5 increments. For example, if the opening $1 bet was raised $3 by the second player to act, the third player needs to call the $1 blind and the $3 raise, a total of $4 to stay in the pot. If the third player raises as well, the next player would need to call $9 worth of bets and raises to play.

When play returns to the opener in either the casino or private game, the opener must call all raises that succeeded his opener to stay in the game, as would any player who also had a raise follow his or her position. In the above example, the opener needs to call the $3 and $5 raises to play, while the second player, the first raiser, must call just the $5 raise.

The next round, **fourth street**, follows the conclusion of third street betting. Each active player receives a face up card and now holds a total of four cards, two open and two closed. Play in this round, as in all future rounds, is the same in both the casino and private versions, and begins with the player holding the highest ranking hand on board (or, in low poker, with the lowest ranking cards acting first), and continues around the table in clockwise fashion. When two or more players hold identically ranked cards, the player closest to the dealer's left will play first.

All bets and raises this round are in $5 increments unless an open pair shows on board, in which case players can open with a $10 bet. However, from fourth street on, the opening player is not forced to make a bet and may open betting by just checking. It is only on third street that a forced opening bet is required.

Once fourth street betting is concluded, another open card is dealt, giving players a total of three face up cards in addition to their two down cards. This round is called **fifth street**, and all bets and raises on this round and the following two rounds, sixth and seventh streets, are in $10 increments, the upper tier of the $5-$10 betting limit. (In a $1-$2 game, bets would be in $2 increments, and in a $10-$20 games, $20 increments.)

After fifth street betting closes, **sixth street** occurs with players receiving their fourth open card, giving all remaining players a total of six cards. Another round of betting follows.

Seventh street arrives, and each remaining player receives his last card face down. This is the final betting round in seven card stud and is followed by the showdown. Each player chooses five cards out of the seven total he holds to form his best hand. In seven card high stud, the best high hand wins, and in the lower stud version, the five best low cards will claim the pot.

Let's examine the showdown in seven card high-low stud to see how it differs from the high and low stud variations.

The Showdown - Seven Card High-Low Stud

Seven card high-low stud is played similarly to the high or low seven card stud games with the major difference being that players are actually playing for two halves of the pot: half the pot going to the player with the best high hand and the other half going to the player holding the strongest low hand. If a player holds the best high and low hand, he will take the entire pot.

High-low seven card stud is played as either **declaration** or **cards speak**. In declaration, which is predominantly played in private poker games, players declare at the showdown whether they're going for the high, the low, or the high-low end of the pot. Declaration is accomplished by each player hiding a colored chip in his fist and extending his closed fist over the table. At a given signal, players simultaneously open their hands and reveal their declarations: white chips are usually used for a low declaration, blue chips for high and red chips for high-low though using coins or different color assignments will work just as well for the declaration.

Of the players who declared "high," the best high hand wins that half of the pot, while the best low hand of players who declared "low" takes the other half. If just one player calls "high" and the rest "low", the player declaring high automatically wins half the pot and need not show his hand, while the low callers must compete for their respective half with the best low total winning. And vice versa. If all players declare the same way, for example, all declare high, then the best high hand wins the entire pot. If all players declared low, then the best low hand claims the entire pot.

Players that declare "high-low" risk all, and must win both the best high hand *and* the best low hand or they forfeit the entire pot. It's an all or nothing proposition - they either win it all or lose it all. If a high-low declarer wins only one way, then he's out of the pot, and the best high hand and the best low hand split the monies.

Let's follow an illustrative showdown. Five players remain: Donto, Fay, Julian, Eddie-boy and Big Phil. The first three declare "high," the fourth "low", and the fifth, Big Phil, goes all out and declares "high-low," (Flavian has already folded and both he and his cigar watch passively from the sidelines.)

Here's the hands they hold:

Donto (Declared high)   Jack high straight
Fay (Declared high)   Three Kings
Julian (Declared high)   Ace high flush
Eddie-boy (Declared low)   Seven-six hand
Big Phil (Declared high-low)   Best High: King high flush,
                                     Best Low: Seven-five hand

Big Phil's seven-five hand is a stronger low than Eddie-boy's seven-six, but his king high flush is weaker than Julian's ace high flush, and therefore Big Phil, unable to win both ways, loses his high-low declaration and wins nothing. Julian and Eddie-boy hold the best high and low hands respectively, and split the pot. Had Big Phil declared "low" only, he would have won that half of the pot.

In cards speak, also called high-low split, the seven card high-low stud game played in the Nevada casinos, there is no declaration at the showdown. Players simply reveal their cards and the best high hand and the best low hand split the pot, or, if one player is fortunate enough to have the best high and low, he claims it all.

Strategy at Seven Card Stud: High Poker

The first three cards received in seven card stud lay the groundwork for the future possibilities of a hand. Therefore, to build winners we will only stay in with cards that have the right winning ingredients. Starting and staying with promising cards is especially important in seven card stud, for the five betting rounds of this game add up to a lot of bets and raises, and we want to give ourselves every chance of winning.

These are the minimum starting cards needed to enter the betting in seven card high stud:

Seven Card High Stud - Minimum Starting Cards
Three of a kind
Three card straight flush
Three card flush
Three card straight
Pair of 10s or higher
Low or middle pair with ace or king kicker
Concealed pair with face card kicker
Three high cards with two straight or flush

Starting cards of three-of-a-kind are powerful cards and are heavily favored to win. With these cards, you want to keep as many players in the pot as possible. Play low key on third and fourth street, calling bets but not raising, and later, on fifth street, if opponents start showing threatening signs of flushes or straights, bet heavy. You should either force them out or make them pay for the privilege of trying to buy their hands. However, if your trips turn into a full house, you have nothing to fear from straights or flushes and want them filling their straights and flushes. And how!

With three card flushes and straights, call third street betting, but do not raise. It's too early to force the action to higher stakes with these hands when at least two more card must be drawn to make the hand into a force that can win at the showdown. As a matter of fact, if our three card straight or flush doesn't improve by fourth street, it's time to say goodbye. Fold the hand. The odds against filling are getting too steep for the cost of calling bets and chasing cards for three more betting rounds.

Medium pairs that haven't improved by fourth street must be folded if either a higher pair shows on board or if raises precede our turn.

A key element in winning at seven card stud, or any poker game for that matter, is to lose as little as possible in the deals we don't win. Hands which have not panned out or have become big underdogs must be folded. Avoid the temptation of playing "just one more card." That one more card costs money, and if it's not a sound call it's a bet out of our overall winnings.

To be a winner, we must wager with the odds, not against them. And those odds are defined by the cards held vis-a-vis our opponents, not based on the hopes of what might happen "if." Again, when a hand's possibilities fade and it becomes second best, bury it.

One indicator of how powerful hands may be going into the showdown is the intensity of the betting. If betting is heavy, with raises and re-raises, there's probably a reason - expect to see strong cards at the show down. If betting is light, with just a few players left, the average winning hand will probably be less powerful than otherwise.

It is important to play alertly and be aware of all cards that are dealt open in seven card stud. These cards give lots of information on the possibilities of improving a hand or on the chances of an opponent improving his hand or having certain cards in the hole. For example, if an opponent holds an open pair of kings and earlier you saw two kings folded, you know that no matter what kind of luck that player has, there's no way he can buy a third king. On the other hand, you'll be more hesitant playing for a flush if you realize that six of the clubs you need have already been played.

Heads up play is important in seven card stud and will make a big difference toward more profitable winning sessions.

Strategy for Seven Card Low Stud (Razz)

In seven card low stud, players use their best five cards out of the seven dealt to form the lowest hand possible, as opposed to high stud, where players look to form their highest totals. (See lowball: draw poker for ranking hands in low poker.) Strategic thinking in razz is different than high poker, for good lowball hands always start out as **drawing hands**, hands which need advantageous draws to develop into winners.

A player's first four cards may be A 2 3 4, a golden start, but if the following three cards received are a pair of jacks and a king, then that hands melts into nothing. On the other hand, seven card high stud presents situations where players are dealt powerful hands for starters, such as the starting cards K K K. Regardless of future draws, these trip kings are heavily favored to win. Subsequent draws cannot diminish the inherent strength of those cards, while lowball hands which don't pan out die on the vine and become worthless.

However, to be competitive in seven card lowball, a player must enter the betting with strong starting cards, ones that can go all the way. Following are the minimum opening or calling hands that should be played in Razz.

Seven Card Low Stud - Minimum Starting Cards

Three card seven high or better (lower)
Three card eight high with two cards valued five or lower
Three card nine high, with the other cards being an
ace, two or three
Ace plus five or lower card, and an odd card.

If none of the above combinations are held, the hand must be folded. You don't want to play underdog cards and contribute to other players' pots. If you can get a free ride into fourth street, take it, but hands less than the above-mentioned caliber cannot call a blind or opening bet. However, if you're the blind, and no raises occur behind your position, you're already in - take the free card on fourth street.

Relatively low supporting cards in low poker are called **smooth** hands, such as the trey and deuce in the starting hand of 7 3 2, or the four, three, two and ace in the hand 8 4 3 2 A, a *smooth eight*. Hands where the supporting cards are relatively high are called **rough**, such as the six and four in the starting cards 7 6 4, called a *rough seven*, or the seven, five, four and three in the hand 8 7 5 4 3, a rough eight. Smooth hands have greater possibilities than their rough counterparts and should be played more aggressively.

If an eight high hand or a smooth nine is made on fifth street, you're in a strong position and can play forcefully against players still holding drawing hands. You should raise their drawing hands. We're the favorite and want to either force them out of the pot or make them pay for every card they try to buy

Play aggressively against weak players for they'll stay in too long with inferior hands and when you've got the goods, why not make your winning pot that much larger?

Strategy for Seven Card High-Low Stud

The splitting of the pot into two halves, one for the best high hand and one for the best low, makes seven card stud an action-packed and exciting game, and one where an astute player can win healthy sums against loose opponents.

And though there are more ways to win at high-low stud, players must not let the increased opportunities of winning pots tempt them into looser playing habits. The same winning principles apply - players must enter the betting only with good starting cards, ones which hold possibilities of winning either the high or low end of the pot.

Straddling the middle with hands that hold both high and low possibilities but are mediocre in both directions is costly and weak strategy. You can only work with the cards that you're dealt, and if the hand is not strong as either a high or low hand, then the hand is not strong - and the cards should be folded. We'll save our bets and play only with cards that can make us winners.

We'll enter the betting with the same starting cards we would play in either high seven card stud for the high pot or in Razz for the low pot. If our cards develop into potential two way winners, even better - but, for now, we'll concentrate on winning at least one way.

Here are the minimum starting cards needed to play for the low pot:

Seven Card High-Low Stud- Minimum Low End Starting Cards

Three card 7 high or lower
Three card 8 high containing two cards 5 or less
Three card 9 high, with the two back up cards being
an ace, two or three

Now let's look at our minimum starting high hands.

Seven Card High-Low Stud- Minimum High End Starting Cards

Three of a kind
Three card straight flush
Three card flush
Three card straight
Pair of 10s or higher
Low middle pair with ace or king kicker
Concealed pair with face card kicker
Three high cards with two straight or flush

We can also play a concealed low pair, sevens or less, with a low open card, six or less, until fourth street. If the hand doesn't improve there, that hand should be folded.

Though we'll go in with a lot of hands, we'll also be quick to fold many of them if there is no immediate improvement on fourth street.

Three card flushes and straights should be ditched if the fourth card isn't bought unless fourth street position leaves us with a combination three flush or straight and three card seven high low. In that case, we'll take the hand to fifth street, and stay there only if we improve to a four card low or four card flush or straight. Otherwise, the hand should be folded.

Low or medium pairs that don't improve should be thrown away. With only half a pot to be taken, the odds don't justify playing these marginal cards. Similarly, the three high card hand, two straight and two flush hands should be returned to their makers if they don't improve.

On the lowball side of the coin, a fourth low card must be bought to make the original three low cards worth playing. Three more betting rounds have to be faced, and with heavy betting and raising, trying to catch two more low cards is an expensive proposition, especially with only half a pot as the prize. However, if other low hand possibilities haven't improved either and it seems our hand is still a competitor for the low pot, fifth street could be worth a play.

Low hands with flush or straight possibilities, such as the 7 5 2 of hearts or 5 4 3 of mixed suits are ideal high-low hands. They provide the double threat of taking the high and the low pot, and, if the cards pan out, of winning the high-low pot outright.

The nature of high-low stud calls for more aggressive play. When you have a lock on either the high or low end of the pot, bet forcefully. You want to create big pots and make the winnings that much sweeter.

HOLD'EM

Hold'em, or **Texas hold'em** as the game is sometimes called, is steadily growing in popularity, and is perhaps best associated with freewheeling high action poker. Players received two face down cards and combine these with the five face-up community cards shared by all the players to form their best five card hand. Altogether, hold'em has four betting rounds. At the showdown, the highest ranking hand wins the pot, or, if heavy betting has forced out all opponents, the last remaining player is the winner.

The Play of the Game

The dealer deals cards one at a time, beginning with the player at the button or dealer's left, and proceeding clockwise, until all players have received two face down cards. The player to the left of the dealer goes first in this round and he is known as the **blind bettor**, since he must bet the blind, a mandatory opening bet.

The blind bet is normally smaller than the lower range bet in limit poker. For example, in a $10-$20 limit game, the blind might be a $5 bet. The required blind bet can vary from game to game so you should ascertain the particulars before sitting down to play. The blind bet creates immediate action in hold'em since it forces succeeding players to call the blind to remain an active player. Some hold'em games play without a blind, but in these instances players must either bet or fold. Blind or no blind, checking is not allowed on the first round of hold'em.

In casino games, a button is used to simulate the dealers position, since a house employee actually deals the game. The button is moved clockwise around the table after each deal so that every player in turn gets to be the imaginary dealer and can benefit from that advantageous position.

Let's examine a $3-$6 limit game to see how the betting works. The first player to act sits at the dealer's left and must open betting by placing a $1 blind into the pot. This is a forced bet and must be made regardless of how the player feels about his cards. The player sitting at the blind's left must either call the $1 blind, raise the blind $2, or fold. If this player folds, each succeeding player is faced with the same options: calling, raising or folding.

If the blind gets raised $2, the next player must either call the $3 ($1 blind plus $2 raise); raise $3 to make the total bet $6 to the following player; or fold. After the $1 blind and initial $2 raise, all further raises during this round must be in $3 increments. The maximum number of raises permitted during a round is generally limited to three or five raises.

If no player has called the $1 blind bet, the blind wins the antes. The deal passes on clockwise to the next player for the next deal.

Once the initial betting round is over, three cards are turned face up in the center of the table. Known as the **flop**, these cards are used collectively by all the players. Each player now has five cards to form a hand - his two hole cards and three community cards.

The next round of betting begins, starting with the blind, or, if he has dropped, the player in the next active position to his left. Bets and raises during this round are in $3 increments only. In a $5-$10 game, bets and raises would be limited to $5 increments, and in a $10-$20 game, $10 increments.

On the following round, **fourth street**, a fourth community card is dealt face up on the table. Players now have a total of six cards possible to form their best five. Betting in this round and on the following round, **fifth street**, begins with the blind, or, if he has folded, the next active player to his left, and is in the upper limit. In the $3-$6 game, all bets and raises are in $6 increments.

In the $5-$10 game, bets and raises would be in $10 increments, and in a $10-$20 game, $20 increments.

There is no forced opening bet on fourth street (or fifth street, which follows), and the first player to act may check to open play. Subsequent players may check as well. If all players check, then the betting round is over and fifth street play will follow. However, should a player open betting on fourth street all active players must call that bet to remain in the pot. On fourth street and fifth street, all bets are in the upper tier of the betting range. In a $3-$6 game, the opening bet and all future raises must be in $6 increments.

After fourth street betting, the fifth and final community card will be turned over in the center of the table. Players now combine their two hole cards with five of the community cards to form their best and final five card hand.

At **fifth street**, which this round is called, there is one final betting round, followed by the showdown. The highest ranking hand wins at the showdown, or, if all opponents have folded, the last remaining player wins the pot by default, and collects all the antes, bets and raises that had been made.

Strategy at Hold'em

The first two cards in hold'em, the player's down cards, along with a player's position at the table, are the most important considerations in strategy. Like all poker variations, players must start out with solid cards to give themselves the best chances of winning.

We'll divide the starting hands into four different categories: strongest, strong, marginal and weak.

Strongest Starting Hold 'Em Hands
These hands are listed in descending order, best hand first:

AA
KK
AK (suited)
QQ
AQ (suited)
AK

The above six starting card combinations are the best in hold'em. They are strong enough to call from any position at the table and should be played aggressively. Excellent starting cards in hold'em, more than in any other poker variation, will hold up and finish as winners, so with these cards we'll be raising at the first opportunity.

We're the favorites in this game and want to build up the pot, but, at the same time, want to force out players with strong or marginal hands. If the cost to play is too cheap, more players will take a shot at the flop. The more players who stay in the pot, the greater the risks are that a weaker hand will draw out and beat our favorite.

Strong Starting Hold 'Em Hands
These hands are listed in descending order, best hand first:

AQ
AJ (suited)
A10 (suited)
KQ (suited)

Hands holding an ace plus a high card are powerful combinations in hold'em. If the flop, on fourth or fifth street, shows an ace, these paired aces tower over any kings, queens or lesser pairs that other players may hold. It's tough to play picture pairs against an ace flop - you've got to figure at least one opponent for a hidden ace.

Since only the best hand wins, lesser pairs must be folded against an open ace.

Suited high cards give a player the twin chance of forming a high pair or suiting up to a possible flush.

The hands in the **strong** category can be played in any position, and, though not as strong as the hands in the "strongest" group, should still be played aggressively.

Let's now move on and see which hands fit into the next lowest tier of rankings, the marginal hands.

Marginal Starting Hands in Hold 'Em
These hands are listed in descending order, best hand first:

JJ
AJ
KQ
A10
KJ (suited)
1010
QJ (suited)
K10 (suited)
KJ
Q10 (suited)
99

We'll play our marginal hands in hold'em as we would play marginal hands in the other poker variations - we'll stay in only if the cost is cheap. Our hands have possibilities, but are not worth the price of a stiff bet. The viability of entering the betting with marginal hands must take into account a player's position at the table.

The last position is the best for it permits a player to see what prior bets were made before committing his hand. Facing heavy bets and raises, marginal hands must be folded. However, if only a call is necessary we'll give these cards a chance at the flop. A good flop can turn these cards into favorites.

In early or middle position, players holding marginal hands can call the opening bet, but if there's been a raise the cards must be folded. If there is a raise after the initial bet has been called, this raise can be seen also, but we must fold in the face of a double raise, or in situations where yet another raise can follow.

Weak Hands

All other hands, ones not shown in the above three categories, should be folded. They are heavy underdogs with little chances of winning. If you're playing in a hold'em game requiring a blind or opening bet, by all means take the flop for free. But if it costs you to see the flop, fold immediately. It's much cheaper watching this round as a bystander.

THE FIVE WINNING STRATEGIES

The knowledgeable poker player can win big money playing poker, and in this chapter we'll show you how to use the five winning strategies to get an edge on your opponents and be a winner at poker. You'll learn how to analyze situations and determine whether the relative strength of your hand is strong enough to call a bet or even raise, or whether, because of the bet size, the amount of money in the pot, our position at the table or our knowledge of our opponents playing styles, we're better off folding the hand and conceding the pot.

A poker session is an accumulation of hands won and lost, and to come out an overall winner we must maximize our gains when we win and minimize our losses when we lose so that our winnings overshadow our losses and leave us a profit to show. Of course, we never really know until the showdown whether we're holding winners, but we can approximate our relative standing and adjust our play accordingly. Thus, when we're the favorite to win we'll get as much mileage out of our hand as we can.

However, minimizing losses at poker is perhaps the more crucial factor in the winning formula. Players who stay in pots too long trying to make every hand a winner will lose steadily and heavily. The extra pots these players capture by playing longshots will rarely offset the steady beatings taken in their losing efforts.

It is important for a player not to fall in love with his cards. There are no prizes for second best at poker. Only the winner takes the pot. If we have kings over sixes on Fifth Street in seven card stud, and an opponent gets dealt an open pair of aces, the dirge has begun. If those aces are paired with a second pair, we're chasing with a dead hand. Aces up beat kings up in poker, and even though we may improve, those aces have an equal chance of improving. The romantic interlude is over - time to fold.

Sometimes strong hands must be folded in the face of heavy betting even though an opponent is suspected of bluffing. There's nothing wrong with being bluffed out of pots. That's part of the game. If a player is never bluffed out of a pot, that means he's calling too often, and opponents are reaping showdown harvest with this loose play. Good players respect cards and can be bluffed. Weak players will never give up the ship until it sinks, and these are the type of players we like to play against.

The above example illustrates a crucial aspect of winnings:

> **It's just as important to make good folds in poker as it is to make good bets.**

Never lose sight of that concept when playing. Do not play with cards that cannot win. This principle holds true at all points of the game in poker. When you lose, you should lose on hands you thought were good enough to be winners or gave you good pot odds to justify the bets made. Don't lose on hands you didn't think could win the pot, because you shouldn't even be playing them.

Let's now look at the five winning strategies of poker.

1. How to Play the Four Types of Hands

Play only with starting cards that can win. This is the single most important strategic consideration in poker, and a theme we constantly refer to in the strategy sections of the individual games.

The object in poker is to have the best hand at the showdown, which means that to win you must enter into the betting with hands that have reasonable chances of winning.

The biggest mistake weak players make is playing too many hands. They're hypnotized by the action and don't want to miss any opportunities of catching a card that can make a winner out of their hands. Weak players will call bets and raises with inferior hands, incessantly waiting for a golden card that will take them down the yellow brick road. Now and again, underdog hands will draw out to win pots, but the wizard won't always be there and that type of play will ultimately result in heavy losses. We're playing to win, and that means we must be selective in the cards we play.

Poker hands can be classified into four different categories: lock, strong, marginal and weak. Let's discuss the strategic principles for each in turn. We discuss their concrete applications under the strategy sections for the individual games.

a. Lock Hands. Hands that are heavily favored to win, even without improvements, are called "locks." For example, the hand J J J 3 3, a jacks-up full house, would be played as a lock in high draw poker. This powerful hand is a big favorite to win.

Our strategy with lock hands is to keep as many players in the pot as long as possible. We've got a hand strong enough to weather almost any storm, and are in for big winnings, especially if opponents draw out strong but less powerful totals.

With lock hands, we'll concentrate on building big pots for ourselves and then exercising our famous arm sweep to collect the winnings.

b. Strong Hands. This category represents cards which have excellent possibilities of improving into winners, and in fact are favorites or near-favorites, but can in no way be considered lock hands. For example, the starting cards A K in hold'em is a strong hand with excellent winning potential, but it still has a flop to go through with all sorts of possibilities for opponents as well.

With strong hands we want to play aggressively. These types of hands have a good head start, but if we don't raise and force some players out, we take the risk of allowing mediocre hands to draw out on us. The more players in the pot, the higher the average winning hand will be and the higher the chance that our strong hand will turn into second best.

Our strategy with strong hands is to raise right from the start and either force out the marginal and weak hands or to build up a pot which we're favored to win. When we have a strong but non-lock hand, we will never allow marginal or weak hands to play cheaply. If they want to see the show, they'll have to buy the tickets - at our price.

If our strong hand appears to be second best to a stronger hand, the correct play is to fold unless we can play for another card at little or no cost. For example, if we think that our strong hands has become a relatively marginal hand in the situation at hand, then we will only play further if the round is checked by all players or we face only a nominal bet. However, if our second best total has excellent chances of improving to be a winner, and a cheap call is warranted by the pot odds (later), it may be worth it for us to go another round.

It's important to adjust strategies to the situation at hand, for poker is not a game of rigid corrects and incorrects. We must be able to think on our feet, and use our skills and instincts in the context of smart poker play.

c. Marginal Hands. Marginal hands have some possibilities of winning or improving to be a winner, but are not strong enough to be considered favorites. If marginal hands can get into a pot cheaply or even grab a **free card** - the concept whereby a player can proceed to the next round without cost (receive a free card) for all players have checked during a betting round - then these hands are worth playing longer. However, at the cost of a stiff bet, marginal hands must be folded and thrown to the wind. The winning possibilities of borderline hands aren't strong enough to warrant heavy investments into a pot.

For example, a pair of jacks is a marginal starting hand at hold'em and holds some possibilities of becoming a strong hand with a favorable flop, but at the cost of weighty betting, or the threat of having to meet raises behind its position, this hand isn't worth a call. If an ace, king or queen appears on the flop, the jacks begin to pall under the bright lights. A pair of jacks are heavy underdogs to the probable queens, kings or aces of opponents, and this hand must be thrown away.

Position also plays an important role in calling decisions when holding marginal hands. Sometimes with just one or two players left in the betting, it is advantageous to play a little longer with a marginal hand. However, we'll discuss positional considerations further in the next section and also under the individual games themselves.

To sum up, marginal hands are worth a play when price is right, but if the cost is at a premium, they're rarely worth betting on - we'll save our sweet dreams for the late night, after the poker game. And we'll save our money as well.

d. Weak Hands. Weak hands should be junked at the first opportunity. When we're heavy underdogs with little hopes of winning, we have no business investing our money in the pot, and must fold the cards immediately. At any point in the game that our cards become weak, regardless of how promising their career may have started, the fact is the cards are losers and must be folded.

Every bet saved is that much richer our bankroll will be.

2. How to Play Position

Your position at the poker table is an important determinant in strategy decisions, for you must always consider how many players will act after your calls, bets or raises, and how they might respond to these plays.

Players acting **under the gun**, that is, first, are in the weakest position, for they have the least amount of information about how the opposing players are playing their hands, and therefore must play a more conservative and cautious game. On the other hand, the player who acts last is in the best position for he gets a read of the entire table before acting on his hand, and can adjust his strategy accordingly.

Playing the last position allows a player more leverage and flexibility, and allows him to play a more aggressive game. With the appropriate hands, he's in an excellent position to raise or bluff opponents out of the pot. He can steal more antes in this position than any other spot at the table. Player's holding marginal hands get extra life in last position for there is no fear of a raise behind this position, unless, of course, a raise has preceded the play - but, then again, a marginal hand wouldn't play a call and a raise anyway.

On the other hand, players holding marginal hands in earlier positions have no such choice. They cannot call bets for fear of raises being made behind their position. Marginal hands are only worth a play at a marginal cost. We don't want to get caught between two players betting and raising each other. That would be costly.

In borderline situations, go out with bad positioning and stay in with good positioning. That's a good rule to follow.

In dealer's choice games, the most advantageous games for the dealer to play are hold'em and draw poker because of the special positional advantages the dealer holds in these games.

3. How to Use Pot Odds

Pot odds examines the risks against the rewards of making a bet; the risks being the cost of a bet, and the rewards being the amount of money to be won from the pot. For example, if the pot holds $100 and the bet to be called is $20, then the pot odds are $100 to $20, or 5 to 1.

You use pot odds to help determine if the cost of going for the pot is justified by the perceived chances of winning. Let's look at an illustrative situation to see how this works.

We're playing $10-$20 seven card stud and two opponents are left. We hold aces over threes and $40 is due our position. The first opponent, whom we figure for a probable three of a king, has opened on sixth street with a $20 bet, and was raised by the second player $20 more. The second player sits with four hearts and has straight possibilities as well, good scare cards against our two pair. With the $40 worth of bets, the pot now holds $240. According to the pot odds, should we call?

Of course, we don't know for sure what cards our opponents hold in the hole, but we figure our hand to be second best without improvement, and must draw an ace or three to fill the two pair into a full house, the only way we can win. However, the hearts hand has one of our threes, and we noticed another three pass out of play earlier, leaving us, in fact, only two live cards, the remaining aces.

We've seen a total of 28 cards: the eight open cards of our opponents, our six cards and the 14 cards folded earlier by the other players. That leaves 24 unknown cards, and only two of those cards, the aces, can help us. The odds of our hand improving to be a winner are 2 in 24 (1 in 12) or 11 to 1 against. The pot offers us only 6 to 1, poor odds against an 11 to 1 chance of improvement. Aces up is normally a powerful hand, but in this situation the correct play is to fold.

The above hand worked well as an illustration, for only one card was yet to be played. Estimating pot odds value with more than one card to play becomes more difficult for more unknowns come into play. How fast will the pot grow? What future bets will have to be called? What new cards dealt will change our projected strength vis-a-vis our opponents? However, though more variables may come into play, and pot odds analysis may become less exact, a rough cost of playing versus money-to-be-won analysis is always helpful in determining whether a hand is worth playing.

Let's look at a pot odds application for draw poker.

A look at the pot odds involved indicate that four card straights and flushes should be folded before the draw if two other players or less are in the pot, unless the game is being played with a large ante. The chances of improving these four card totals to a straight or flush are approximately 4 to 1 against. With less than three players in contention, the money in the pot is generally not large enough to justify a call.

For example, in a $5-$10 poker game with eight participants and a $1 ante, the pot initially holds $8 worth of antes. If the opener is called by only one player, these two $5 bets boost the pot up to $17 in bets and antes. With only $17 to win and costing $5 to call, the pot offers less than the 4 to 1 odds needed to make the call a good play. The smart move here is to fold.

On the other hand, if the above game was played with a high ante, say $2 per player, calling in the above situation would be an excellent play. The $10 in bets added to $16 in antes ($2 ante per player times eight players), fills the pot with $26 in bets and antes, 26 to 5 odds on the bet, better than the 4 to 1 odds needed to justify the call. Playing to the draw in this situation is an excellent move.

Pot odds evaluations are not an exact science, for there are always unknowns. However, pot odds is a useful and important evaluation tool, and used in the context of other skills presented in this book will make you a winning player.

4. How to Read an Opponent

Alertness is an important trait in a winning poker player, for opposing players inadvertently give away information and clues on the cards they hold - and if you pay attention carefully, you may be able to read the signals and use them to advantage.

There are two main ways of gathering this information. The first is by observing the way a player bets and plays his or her hands. Poker players, like people in any pursuit, are creatures of habit, and you will be able to discern patterns in their play. For example, you may observe the types of hands a player tends to open his or her betting with or notice the types of cards they like to hold before raising. You can gain an edge on these players by adjusting your play accordingly. The more you understand your opponent, the better you'll be able to read his or her playing style and take advantage of it.

The second way of gathering useful information about an opponent's cards is by the observation of **tells**, the mannerisms and idiosyncrasies of a player which give away the contents of his or her hand. There are a million and one tells to be observed. For example, some beginning players are so over-anxious to bet when they're holding big cards that they're like a radar station broadcasting signals that nobody can miss - somehow, their opponents always seem to fold rapidly when the player's been dealt the goods.

Learn to develop a **poker face**, an expressionless demeanor that gives away no poker secrets, for just as we can take advantage of a player's tells, so they can take advantage of ours if we're not careful. It is important to be aware of your own habits during poker games and make sure none of them are telegraphing the news.

5. How to Gain an Edge Against an Opponent's Playing Style

In this section, we'll discuss a few types of playing styles commonly encountered at the poker tables and show you how to gain an edge by adjusting your strategies accordingly.

a. How to Play Against a Loose Player. Loose players love action. They will play too many hands, call too many bets and stay in games too long. By playing more hands, they will win more pots, but at the expense of giving away too many bets when they finish out of the money.

We'll play a tight, fundamental game in the early and middle rounds against a loose player. Since they love betting, we'll let them contribute to our pots. We'll avoid bluffing for it is difficult to bluff a loose player. In the late rounds, at the showdown, we'll call more often, for loose players tend to go in with weaker hands.

b. How to Play Against Players Who Bluff A Lot. Against players who bluff often, we'll call their bets more frequently for we have two ways to beat them. First, we can win for we have a better hand. Second, our hand can improve enough to be a winner. However, before calling, we must make sure our hand is strong enough on its own merits to make a stand or has potential to improve to be a winner if our opponent is not bluffing.

When we have strong hands, we'll bait bluffers and loose players alike into building up the pot and then lowering the boom at the showdown.

c. How to Play Against Tight Players. We'll play a looser game against a **tight player**, a player who makes and calls bets only when he's got good hands. We'll respect his bets, for he's generally betting on solid situations.

We'll take advantage of his tight play by always figuring him for a good hand. In borderline situations, we'll give him the benefit of the doubt and call his bets less often. When we do call his bets, we'll call with cards we figure can win, and if he raises our bets, we'll make sure the pot odds and the strength of our hand justify a call.

d. Against Players Who Don't Bluff. When in doubt, we'll give the non-bluffer the benefit of the doubt and fold marginal calls. We'll save money against this type of player by calling less with questionable hands and by not having our good hands bluffed out by his scare cards.

We love this type of player for he's predictable, and that gives us a big edge in poker.

Bluffing

The bluff! The beauty, romance and drama of poker lies in the bluff. Bluffing is an integral part of poker and is an art which matures with experience. There are two advantages to successful bluffing.

The first and most obvious reason is that a player can "steal pots" from better hands and win money he otherwise would not have seen. The second reason is that when a player is caught bluffing, he is more likely to get called on the occasions when he does have the goods, and will therefore win bigger pots.

The more opponents are kept guessing, the better off we are. A player who is never known to bluff will win smaller pots, for when he's got a strong hand, players with weak and marginal hands will not challenge him for the pot.

Here are a few pointer on bluffing:

Five Pointers on Bluffing

1. Avoid bluffing in low limit games. The bluff may be too small to scare anybody out.

2. Don't bluff for small pots with overly large bets. The small gain possible isn't worth the large risk. (However, do bluff for small pots. There is money to be made by stealing the antes - just keep the bluffed bet within reason.)

3. It's easier to bluff a good player than a weak one. Good players respect scare cards, weak players tend to call on garbage and almost nothing will get them out of a pot.

4. Bluffs are most effective against one player. The more players in the pot, the greater the chance that at least one player will call the bet.

5. Pick your spots carefully. Successful bluffing is a matter of proper timing and circumstance.

CALIFORNIA POKER

California has close to 500 licensed card clubs, with the highest concentration of clubs in Gardena, a Los Angeles suburb. The California poker clubs, unlike their Nevada counterparts, the casinos, do not supply dealers. Instead, the players take turns dealing and pay an hourly rental rate to the club. The rate varies according to the stakes played and is due every hour. Each participant is charged an equal amount - the larger the stakes, the greater the amount charged.

The club's main function is supplying the venue for the game and it has house employees who can be called upon to arbitrate in the event of a dispute. The maximum number of players allowed per table is eight and the minimum is three.

Previously, a bizarre law restricted the clubs to offering only draw poker, high and low (lowball: draw poker) to their patrons. These games, once the only games in town, are rarely played now. Recent legislation opened up the playing field for other forms of poker, and now games such as seven card stud and hold'em dominate the action at the tables.

A LAST WORD

Poker is one of the greatest and most exciting gambling games ever invented, and one sure to challenge you. In this section, we've given you a very brief introduction to the strategies of play; if you're interested in becoming a stronger poker player, we suggest you further your studies by reading more about the poker variations you enjoy playing.

To continue growing and improving as a poker player, you'll

need to reevaluate your play at the tables on a constant basis, learning from both your mistakes and strong moves, and from the play of your opponents.

Poker is a constant learning process for the good players; every hand a challenge and a classroom with gems of knowledge to be stored away for future hands. Be smart, and keep your eyes open, and you won't be able to help from being a better player every time you sit down at the poker table.

SPORTS BETTING

INTRODUCTION

The urge to gamble on sports is a fervent passion in the United States and fuels a tremendous underground economy that runs into the billions of dollars yearly. Sports games are exciting, and for many people, putting their money where there mouths are makes the games that much more intense.

Football, baseball, basketball and boxing all have their share of aficionados, and in this section we're going to show you just what goes into the making of the sports lines, how to read them, the odds involved, and finally, how to get an edge on these lines so that you can be a winner at sports betting!

THE BETTING LINES

There are two types of lines in sports betting, the money line, which is used in baseball and boxing, and the pointspread, the line used for football and basketball.

The **money line** penalizes bettors wagering on the favorite by making them lay money, that is bet more money than they hope to win back. For example, if a bettor had to lay 6 to 5 odds, it means he would have to lay $6 to win $5.

Underdog bettors, on the other side of that coin, would receive back more than they bet as compensation for betting on the "dog." If the odds on a contest are listed as 8 to 5, a $5 bet on the dog would pay back $8 if the bet is won.

The **pointspread** tries to equalize betting money by awarding the underdog extra points and creating what is called a **spread**.

Thus, if the bookie creates a spread of 7 points in a football game and you bet the underdog, you can win the wager even if your team doesn't win the game. Either a loss by less than 7 points or an outright victory affords the underdog bettor a winning wager. An underdog defeat by more than 7 points loses the wager.

If you bet the favorite in this example, your team must win by more than seven points for the bet to be won. A three point victory by the favorite is all well and good for the team itself. A win after all, is a win. But not for those who bet the favorite. The favorite did not cover the seven point spread, and therefore, all bets on the favorite are lost.

If the favorite wins by exactly seven points, the bet is a **push**, a tie, and both favorite and underdog bettors receive their wagers back.

Thus, you see that the concept of winning at football and basketball betting, sports where the pointspread line is used, is based on winning against the spread and not necessarily on the raw outcome itself.

How the Line is Made

The main purpose of the betting line is to divide public opinion in such a way that money gets bet equally on both sides of an event. As such, the important consideration in setting a line is figuring how the public will perceive an upcoming contest.

This is a very important concept to understand. The book-maker, whether run legally or illegally, is a business that makes its money by handling bets and taking a commission on the money wagered. Bookmakers really don't care which contestant wins a match - they only care that money is bet equally on both sides so that they can collect their **vigorish** or **vig**, the bookmakers built-in commission, no matter which side wins.

Thus, the betting line represents how fans perceive the game and how they will bet - not the actual match-up of the teams.

For example, a number of years back, the aging Ali, in another of his comeback tries and clearly over the hill, faced his former sparring partner, Larry Holmes who at 30 years old, was fighting in his prime. This match, clear to many prizefight experts, was really no contest. The betting public on the other hand, were still enamored with the mystique of the once great Ali, and this had driven the odds down to 8/5 in favor of Holmes.

If the betting line was made on the basis of Ali's real chances of winning, Ali would have been fighting as an overwhelming underdog, and most of the money would have come in on Holmes.

This would have created a situation called being **sided** - when most of the money gets bet on one side of a gambling proposition and comparatively little on the other.

Being sided is a tremendous risk for bookmakers for it makes them gamblers and that is not their business. Their business is to collect commissions on gambles other people take. If the bookmakers had not adjusted the line in the Ali-Holmes fight to reflect how the betting public would bet, an Ali win would have taken them to the cleaners.

As businessmen, bookmakers attempt to form a line such that they can collect profits regardless of who wins.

This same principle of the bookmakers trying to divide the betting money holds true in the betting lines for all the sports - football, hockey, basketball, baseball, boxing and other sporting events which attract gamblers.

An astute bettor who realizes this and who follows his sport carefully, can use this information to make money at sports betting.

The First Principle of Beating the Bookie

Now that you understand how and why the line is made, we can clearly outline the foremost principles of winning money at sports betting. First of all, we're going to look for games and sporting events where public opinions, for one reason or another, distort the line, and therefore give the sharp and ready bettor an edge in the game.

But having an edge is not enough, the edge must be sufficient enough to overcome the built-in vig that the bookie's have, and we'll discuss each sport in turn to show the exact odds you face with each betting proposition, and how best to overcome those odds.

Sports Betting Comparison Chart

Sport	Type of Line	Payoff	Winning % Needed to Break Even
Baseball	Money Line	Variable	Variable
Basketball	Pointspread	10-11	52.38%
Boxing	Money Line	Variable	Variable
Football	Pointspread	10-11	52.38%

FOOTBALL BETTING

Introduction

Every year, as constant as the seasons, sports fans gear up for the gala opening of NFL and collegiate football. Even before opening day, football fever spurs the frantic analysis and heated discussions that accompany every season, and helps fuel the mammoth underground economy of football betting. When it's that time of year, football owns the weekends and Monday nights for many Americans, a good portion of who could not conceive of life without this staple of excitement.

Betting is very much a part of football for fans, and the wagers that many bettors make add a lot of spice and enjoyment to the gridiron wars they see waged out on the field.

Let's see just what is involved in making the line, what odds you're up against, and how best to play ball.

The Football Line

Football betting, whether college or pro, works according to the pointspread. The bookmakers handicap opposing teams so that they can get equal betting action on both teams, and earn their vigorish without risk. As such, football contests have a pointspread, with one team playing the favorite, and the other, the underdog.

Bettors wager according to these lines, giving points when betting favorites, and taking points when betting the underdog.

Here is how a typical line may look.

> **San Francisco - MIAMI +3**

You may also that line listed as follows, but either way, means the same thing.

> **San Francisco -3   MIAMI**

The lines, however shown, will always list the favorite first and show the home team in capital letters. In the above example, San Francisco is listed first and is the favorite and Miami, listed in capital letters, is the home team.

The number shown indicates the amount of points that the favorite, listed first, is favored over the underdog, the team listed second. So whether the number shows up as a + next to the underdog or a - next to the favorite, doesn't make a difference.

In the above examples, we see the San Francisco 49ers listed as three point favorites over the Miami Dolphins.

The Bookmakers Vigorish

To bet on NFL or college games you have to lay 11 to 10 on all bets, whether betting the favorite or the underdog. To win $10, you have to give the bookie $11. Thus, for example, if you want to bet $50, you must give the bookie $55.

This difference between the 11 to 10 wager bettors must lay with the bookmaker and the true odds of 10-10, even-money, is the bookie's profit margin, his vig, and what allows him to conduct business.

For example, if you lay $11 to $10 on a game and win the bet, you'll get paid $21 back - the $11 bet, plus the $10 in winnings. If you bet $110, you'll get back $210 from the bookie, your original $110 bet plus $100 in winnings.

Let's see what happens when you win one game and lose one game laying 11 to 10 odds and betting $110 per game.

First Game: Win	+$100
Second Game: Loss	-$110
Net	**- $10**

You have an even win percentage, but yet have lost money. So you see, winning half your games isn't good enough to make money at football betting. If you win only half you're going to be a loser at a rate of $1 for every $22 bet, an edge to the bookmaker of 4.54%.

And this 4.54%, the bookmakers vigorish, or vig, is the figure you must overcome to show a profit on the gridiron.

Let's carry these figures over a 16 game season with a $110 bettor to see how a 50% win rate would work out. Remember, we have to lay 11 to 10 on every game.

8 Wins at $100 per win	+$800
8 Losses at $110 per loss	-$880
Net	**-$80**

Though we won 8 out of 16 games, not too bad in itself, the bookie's vig has eaten away at our stake, and we show a loss of $80!

What winning percentage is needed to overcome the bookie's vig?

52.38%. That's the magic number. As a football bettor, this is the figure that must be foremost in your betting mind. To be a winner, you must win greater than 52.38% of your bets.

Line Changes

As the week progresses, the line might change up or down a little to reflect the bets coming in. For example, if the Giants are playing the Cowboys and are favored by +3 points, and more money is coming in on the Cowboys than the Giants, the book-maker might move the line to +4, and then again if necessary, maybe +5 to encourage more money to be bet on the Giants.

However, once your bet is made, it is committed to the pointspread at which it was placed, regardless of how the line moves after. If your bet was placed when the line was +3, and the line moves to +5, your bet is committed to the +3.

Teasers

The **teaser** bet is an inducement for bettors to wager two games or more as a group with the condition that both teams chosen must win. If just one of the teased teams lose, than the whole bet is lost. Also, a tie against the spread on either game loses the teaser as well.

The bookmaker allows 6, 6 1/2 or 7 points, depending upon the wager made, as the tease incentive for the bettor to use any way desired on the match-ups chosen.

On a two team tease, a six point bonus gets an even money bet, instead of the usual 11 to 10 lay. If 6 1/2 points is taken, than the regular 11 to 10 bet is laid, and if a 7 point tease is chosen, than the bettor must lay 6 to 5.

Let's look at a tease with the following two teams:

> Chicago Bears - New England Patriots +6
> New York Giants - Green Bay Packers +3

On a six point tease you may elect to take the underdog Patriots at 6 points more for a +12 spread and the favorite Giants who now have a 3 point spread with the 6 points added.

You could also choose those games the other way around, or play both favorites or both underdogs. Wagering any of these 6 point tease combinations allows your bet to be made at even money instead of the usual 11 to 10.

You could also play the tease taking 6 1/2 points and lay 11 to 10, or take 7 points and lay 6 to 5.

Parlay Bets

A **parlay** bet is similar to a teaser in that the results of more than one game's results are tied together. With a parlay bet, you must pick a minimum of three teams, and all of these teams must win. A loss or tie in any of the contests spells a loss for the entire bet.

However, unlike a teaser, your teams are not given extra points - they must beat the spread straight out. The payoffs are big and that attracts a lot of bettors, but the odds are so atrocious that you would be better off throwing your money away, for more or less, that is what you'll be doing on a parlay.

A typical parlay card might pay as follows:

Typical Parlay Card		
Teams	**Payoff**	**True Odds**
Three	$6 for $1	7 to 1 (8 for 1)
Four	$11 for $1	15 to 1 (16 for 1)
Five	$20 for $1	31 to 1 (32 for 1)
Six	$40 for $1	63 to 1 (64 for 1)
Seven	$80 for $1	127 to 1 (128 for 1)
Eight	$150 for $1	255 to 1 (256 for 1)
Nine	$300 for $1	511 to 1 (512 for 1)
Ten	$500 for $1	1023 to 1 (1024 for 1)

You may notice the **"for"** in the Payoff column which is a subtle gambling term telling you that you're getting less. A payoff of $6 for $1 means that you get back $6 total on a won bet, your original $1 plus $5 in winnings as opposed to the word **"to"** as in $6 to $1, meaning you win $6 for every $1 you bet, and will get back a total of $7.

As you can see by the chart, parlays are sucker bets, and we advise you to avoid them, unless you happen to be the one booking other people's parlays, in which case, you'll be making lots

The Over & Under

There are also over and under bets in football, where you bet that the two teams combined will score more than a prescribed amount of points set by the bookmaker, **over**, or you can bet that they will score less, or **under**. The over and under betting works just like that of the pointspread betting in football. You still have to lay 11 to 10 on all your bets and will need a 52.38% winning percentage to beat the bookie.

Touts

One must be careful with the tout services for generally speaking, they're scam operations. These businesses are often started by gamblers who went belly-up with their own money and are now passing their worthy experience onto others at just $50 a pop or more.

You might see an advertisement, "65% win against the spread" for example or "3 out of our 4 best bets won last week," or any of a myriad of other enticing numbers. The problem is that these figures represent only a small slice of the truth. How about the week before or last year, facts which conveniently go unmentioned.

It's easy to describe a slice of the truth and make it sound appealing, which is what most of these services do. Let's say I run a two man race and my opponent beats me out at the finish line. Well, I comment, "I finished second, right behind the winner while my opponent finished next to last." Little does the listener know that only two people ran in the race.

In any case, be careful with tout services. I recommend instead, putting your money into learning more about winning and into your bets.

BASEBALL

The Baseball Line

Betting on major league baseball is done according to the money line. In baseball, whenever you bet the favorite, you must **lay odds**, bet more that the amount you hope to win, while when you bet the underdog, or dog, you will win more than you bet.

Let's see how a game may be listed and show how the money line will work.

> **YANKEES - Tigers 6 1/2 - 7 1/2**

The favorite, in this example the Yankees, is listed first, and is capitalized because it is the home team.

The line in baseball is listed to reflect all payments to $5.00. The first number, 6 1/2 represents the amount a Detroit bettor, the underdog, will win for every $5.00 bet. Thus, on a won bet, the Tigers bettor will receive back $11.50 - the original $5.00 wager plus $6.50 in winnings.

The second number, 7 1/2, is the amount of money a Yankee fan must lay to win $5.00. A Yankee win will return to New York bettors $12.50 - the original $7.50 wager plus $5.00 in winnings for every $7.50 wagered.

This style of listing can be confusing, however, we'll show you an easy way to remember what number goes with what team and just what the line means to you as a bettor.

The favorite, which is always listed first, belongs to the larger number - what the bettor must lay to win $5.00, while the underdog, listed second, belongs to the lower number - what the bettor will win with a $5.00 bet.

Just word-associate - favorite, larger number; underdog, smaller number. And remember, all bets are to $5.00.

You might also see that same line on the Yankee-Tiger game expressed as follows:

> **YANKEES -1.30 Tigers +1.50**

It is the same exact line, just written differently to reflect bets based on $1.00 as opposed to $5.00 above. Casinos will usually list the line this way.

If you bet on the Yankees, you need to lay $1.30 to win $1.00, and on the Tigers, a $1.00 bet will win $1.50. Multiply these numbers by $5.00 and you have the same numbers as the 6 1/2 and 7 1/2 figures discussed above.

This line is called a **20¢ line** for the 20¢ difference between the underdog and favorite's bet when worked out to the dollar and it represents the bookie's take on each set of bets. This 20¢ line is the standard baseball betting line, the one most bettors will face when betting on the "bigs."

The following chart shows the bookie's edge on the various lines.

20¢ or 1 Point Line

		Bookmaker's % Edge	
Quote	True Odds	Underdog	Favorite
11-10	1-1	4.55	4.55
5-6	11-10	4.76	3.97
5 1/2-6 1/2	6-5	4.55	3.50
6-7	13-10	4.35	3.11
6 1/2- 7 1/2	7-5	4.17	2.78
7-8	3-2	4.00	2.50
7 1/2-8 1/2	8-5	3.85	2.26
8-9	17-10	3.70	2.06
8 1/2-9 1/2	9-5	3.57	1.88
9-10	19-10	3.45	1.72
9 1/2-10 1/2	2-1	3.33	1.59
10-11	21-10	3.23	1.47
10 1/2-11 1/2	11-5	3.13	1.36
11-12	23-10	3.03	1.26
11 1/2-12 1/2	12-5	2.94	1.18
12-13	5-2	2.86	1.10
12 1/2-13 1/2	13-5	2.78	1.03

Quote - The line quoted by the bookmaker.
True Odds - The actual odds between the quoted numbers for favorite and underdog which would give the bookie no edge at all.
Bookmaker's % Edge: Underdog - The bookie's edge on under- dog bets at the line quoted.
Bookmaker's % Edge: Favorite - The bookie's edge on favorite bets at the line quoted

You'll notice that in all cases the edge is lowest when betting favorites, except in the 11-10 quote where the edge is equivalent for underdog or favorite bettors. This does not necessarily mean that favorites are the best bets. This is the bookie's edge against what he figures the true odds to be. That doesn't translate to a superior wager. We get a different view in this next chart.

The Payoff Chart

The Vegas Line	Take Odds	Profit to $1.00
+220	11-5	2.20
+200	2-1	2.00
+180	9-5	1.80
+170	81/2-5	1.70
+160	8-5	1.60
+150	71/2-5	1.50
+140	7-5	1.40
+130	61/2-5	1.30
+120	6-5	1.20
+110	51/2-5	1.10
Even	1-1	1.00
-110	5-51/2	.91
-120	5-6	.83
-130	5-61/2	.77
-140	5-7	.71
-150	5-71/2	.67
-160	5-8	.62
-170	5-81/2	.59
-180	5-9	.55
-200	1-2	.50
-220	5-11	.45
-240	5-12	.42
-260	5-13	.38
-280	5-14	.36
-300	1-3	.33

The Vegas Line - The line coming out of Vegas, though it could represent any standard line.
Take Odds - The first column equivalent in a different format.
Profit to $1.00 - The amount a won bet will return for every $1.00 bet.

On **The Payoff Chart**, we see the profit you make every time you wager $1.00 and win your bet. The + numbers on the top half of the first column indicates the payoff amount for underdogs, while the minus numbers below show the payoff on favorites.

Thus, a Vegas line of +220, means that a winning underdog bet of $1.00 pays $2.20 while a Vegas line of -220 indicates the opposite, that a winning $2.20 bet pays $1.00 to a favorite bettor.

Let's go back to our Yankee-Tiger game where the line reads +130 - 150, and see what **The Payoff Chart** shows to us as bettors.

If we bet on the Yano bearing on the Yankees, the favorite, we'd have to lay $1.50 to win $1.00. Looking at the column "Profit to $1.00", we see that we'd win only 67¢ for every dollar bet.

If instead, we bet on the Tigers, the dog, we'd get $1.30 for every dollar bet, for a net profit of $1.30.

Betting on the favorite, and laying $1.50 forces you to win 60% of the time just to break even. There's a big penalty betting favorites, and at a certain point, the winning percentage needed to show a profit on big favorites becomes too high to realistically show a profit.

The next table is very important for it shows the break even point for all bets in which odds are being laid as a favorite bettor or taken on the underdog side.

	Break-Even Point Against the Line		
The Line	**Underdog Percentage Needed To Win**	**The Line**	**Favorite Percentage Need To Win**
110 Pick	52.4	110 Pick	52.4
Even	50.0	-120	54.6
+110	47.6	-130	56.5
+120	45.5	-140	58.5
+130	43.5	-150	60.2
+140	41.7	-160	61.7
+150	40.0	-170	62.9
+160	38.5	-180	64.5
+170	37.0	-200	66.7
+180	35.7	-220	69.0
+200	33.3	-240	70.4
+220	31.3	-260	72.5
+240	29.4	-280	73.5

You can see that the bigger the favorite, the greater and more intimidating a win percentage will be needed just to break even. Let's say that a series of 100 bets is made laying -1.50/1 on the favorite at $7.50 a crack, and 60 of these wagers are won.

Here's how it would look.

```
60 wins   x $5.00 = +$300
40 losses x $7.50 = -$300
             Break-Even
```

There's no gain and no loss. The bets have broken even exactly. To win 60% of the time is a gargantuan effort. If you could sustain that winning percentage in football betting you'd be virtually minting your own money. But against very big favorites as in the above example, you don't even make a penny!

For a big-league team to win 60% of its games in a 162 game schedule, they must win 97 games! That's usually enough to take a division title. Anything less than a 60% win ratio while laying -1.50/1 will show losses in your wagers.

The question is, how many teams that you bet on will be good enough to do that for you? And that's the real problem betting big favorites in baseball.

So you see, that even though the bookie's edge is lower when you bet on favorites, your chances of winning are not necessarily less, for you have to score a big percentage of wins just to cover the odds you lay.

Let's now look at an example where you're pursuing an even bigger favorite, at -1.70/1. As you can see on our chart, you now need to win at a 63% clip just to break even. If you win 58% of the time, it's not good enough at a -1.70/1 line, for you'll be a loser.

Let's see how this looks. Laying -1.70 equates to 81/2-5 or in dollars, betting $8.50 to win $5.00.

> 58 Wins   x $5.00 = +$290
> 42 Losses x $8.50 = -$357
> **Overall**   **-$67**

That's a rough loss to take, especially when you've scored 58%, a pretty good win rate.

Let's now look at the previous betting situation from the other side of the coin. We'll assume a 100 $5.00 bets are made on the underdog half of the +1.30/-1.50 (6 /2 - 7 1/2) odds. 44 of those bets win and 56 lose.

Here's how it looks:

```
44 wins   x $6.50 = +$286
56 losses x $5.00 = -$280
Net Win              +$6
```

Obviously, it's a whole different smoke betting on underdogs. Even with a terrible losing percentage, a profit was shown betting the underdog position at +1.30.

But then again, don't be running out to the bookie's with your hands stuffed with betting money - it's not so easy. Big underdogs are big underdogs for a reason. Favorites can be good bets just as underdogs can be good bets as well. Each situation must be looked at separately and judged on its own merits.

Betting Strategies

We feel that you should avoid betting favorites calling for a line of -150 or more. A winning percentage of 58%, which would show you good profits in football or basketball, and get your baseball team pretty close to a pennant, would leave you in the hole betting against a +150 line.

On the other hand, you may find some good spots betting as the underdog part of a 1.50/1.00 line, for, as the chart shows, you need only a 40% win rate to break even.

However, you must pick your games carefully, for when a team is listed as a big underdog, there's a reason. For example, a pitcher like Randy Johnson of the Seattle Mariners who was virtually unbeatable when he was on his game, in fact going more than 20 straight decisions without a loss, may be a matchup you wouldn't want to bet against.

What we've shown you are the cold hard numbers you face in baseball betting. Now use your baseball knowledge and handicapping skills combined with prudent money management to come out of the season as a winner at baseball betting!

BASKETBALL

Betting on the hoops is done according to a point line. If you bet on the favorite, you need to give points, and if you take the underdog, you receive them. As in football, which also works according to a pointspread, you really don't care if the team you're betting on wins or loses, only that it covers the spread.

For example, if the Los Angeles Lakers are favored by 5 points over the Boston Celtics, the Lakers must win by 6 points to cover the spread. Even if Los Angeles wins the game by 3 points, it is still a loss for Laker bettors - the team has not covered the spread.

On the other hand, Celtics bettors can lose the game by 4 points and still win the bet, for the line has given them 5 points.

If the Los Angeles Lakers win the contest by exactly five points, then the game is a push, and nobody wins or loses the bet. The bookmaker will return underdog and favorite wagers without any loss at all. No commission is made on tie bets.

Following is an example of a basketball line:

KNICKS - Bulls +3

As in football and baseball, the favorite is listed first and the underdog second, while the home team is listed in capital letters. The points listed show how many points the underdog, Chicago in this example, is being given.

Thus, we see the Knicks, listed first, are the favorites by 3 points, and that they're playing in New York since their heading is capitalized. Or if you want to look at it the other way, Chicago is a three point underdog and is playing an away game.

The Betting Odds

As in football, you have to lay 11-10 on all bets, regardless of whether you're betting the favorite or underdog. The bookie's profit comes from the difference between the 11 and the 10, which works out to a vig of 4.54%.

As a bettor trying to beat the odds, the break-even point against the bookmakers vig is 52.38% no matter who is bet on, favorite or underdog. Anything less than the 52.38%, you're in the red, anything better, you'll have profits to show.

Basketball can also be bet as an over/under bet. The bookmaker sets a number and bettors can wager whether the total points in the game will exceed the listed number or go below. The final winner is unimportant in this type of bet - it's only the total point count that matters.

Thus, if the Chicago-New York game has an over/under number of 195, and the final score is 95 to 93, bettors wagering under will win, for the total points equal only 188. Should the score be 100-95 for a total of 195 points, than the bet is a push, nobody wins.

Over/under bets are also laid at 11-10 and the break-even point for bettors, as in the regular bets against the spread, is 52.38%.

Teaser Bets

The bookmakers offer teaser bets in basketball, where two or more team are chosen and both must win for the wager to pay off. Bettors are usually given 4 points extra per game as an inducement to bet the teaser, however all games wagered in the tease must be won. If just one game is lost or tied, the wager is lost.

The extra points can be used to bet on the favorite or underdog and are added to the current pointspread at the time of the wager. Thus, if the Knicks are 5 point favorites at home against the Bulls, you can take the 4 point tease to bet the Knicks as 9 point favorites. Or maybe you feel that the Bulls with those extra points are a great bet against the Knicks and will take them as a 1 point underdog using the teaser points against the spread.

The teaser bet is laid at 11 to 10 odds like the regular wagers. The main problem with teasers is that it's tough enough to win one game at a time against the spread without having two games tied together where both contests are must wins. One win and one loss won't do here - that's a loser on the tease. Both bets must be won.

If you're a pretty tight handicapper, those extra points may make the difference and turn good bets into very good bets.

Certainly though, stay away from teasers involving more than two games. It's just too difficult to call three wins. Keep your chances of winning within the stadium.

Recordkeeping

The most important part of winning at basketball betting as in the other forms of sports betting, is to keep good records. All handicappers stress this point, and with good reason. To know what is going on, you need the facts at hand and also, if you're a serious bettor, there is no better way to actually see, black and white, just what is happening with the calls you are making.

BOXING

The big marquee fights create tremendous excitement and betting not only in the United States, but worldwide as well. Great bouts such as Ali-Frazier, Leonard-Duran, and Hagler-Hearns, were anticipated by millions of people, many of whom were ready to splash down some major cash if the odds were right. Fights such as Tyson-Holyfield, or ones involving some of the many recent retreads fighting in the 90's would occasionally generate some excitement. And of course, new stars are always emerging and drawing interest among the betting public.

Prize fight betting is based on the money line, as in baseball, but at a greater disadvantage to the bettor. While baseball bettors wager against a 20¢ line, in boxing, the betting fan is generally up against a **40¢ line**, a bigger hurdle to overcome.

As in baseball, the boxing quotes are based on a $5 bet. The bigger number is the amount you must wager to win $5 while the lesser number is the amount you will win if $5 is wagered.

A fight listed at 6-8 means that you must lay $8 to win $5 if you bet the favorite, odds of 8-5, and that you will win $6 on a $5 bet if you take the underdog. The $2 difference between the $6 and $8, when taken to the dollar - we divide by 5 since the above line is based on $5.00 - $2.00 divided by 5, gives us 40¢ and hence, the term "40¢ line."

Of course, you can bet any amount permitted by the book-maker. Thus, a $100 bet on the underdog wins $120 if the underdog comes through, while the favorite bettor must lay $160 to win $100.

The money line in boxing can vary, depending upon where you place your wager and sometimes, the size of that wager as well. The following chart shows the 40¢ line.

		Bookmaker's Edge	
Quote	True Odds	Underdog	Favorite
"6-5 Pick"	1-1	8.33	8.33
5-7	6-5	9.09	6.49
6-8	7-5	8.33	5.21
7-9	8-5	7.69	4.27
8-10	9-5	7.14	3.57
9-11	2-1	6.67	3.03
10-12	11-5	6.25	2.60
11-13	12-5	5.88	2.26
12-14	13-5	5.56	1.98
13-15	14-5	5.26	1.75
14-18	16-5	9.52	2.65
15-20	7-2	11.11	2.78

40¢ or 2 Point Line

As the chart clearly indicates, underdog betting gives better odds against the bookie and if one was to think of prizefight betting on a long term basis, betting on the dog would seem to be a superior way of wagering looking at that factor alone.

However, boxing matches should be viewed on a fight by fight basis, as each match presents an interesting call and must be judged on its own merits. Over the years, betting on prizefights has lost some of its lustre as a wary public tires of the unpredictable and questionable quality of the scoring and of the ever-present undertones of tainted fights.

Too many times, a boxer has been robbed of a clear victory in the ring by judges working on questionable motives who seemed to watch a different fight than what fans saw in the ring.

And fights such as the Buster Douglas-Evander Holyfield match of 1990 that virtually saw Douglass lay down and close his eyes, don't help the picture any as well.

With all these problems, boxing is fairly tough to pick, but now and again some real doozies come along and allow the astute bettor to pick up some good action.

I would look for fights where an aging but popular champion who should by all rights be retired, is coming back for a last hurrah against a young, proven star. By popularity alone, the old champion gets a lot of money bet in his corner, but really has little chance anymore - as in the Ali-Holmes example earlier.

One may often find profitable spots near fight time when a contender shows himself to be clearly without motivation. For example, sharp bettors made some money betting against Douglass in the Holyfield fight when the one-fight champion showed up for the weigh-in looking like a beached whale and clearly out of shape.

These type of fights won't come often, but when they do, they're good opportunities to pick up a little in winnings. But remember, don't bet the ship - its poor money management to put all your eggs in one basket, and you never know what might happen.

PRINCIPLES OF WINNING AT SPORTS BETTING

1. Find situations where emotions run high for a particular contest and drive up (or down) the odds beyond what the real odds should be. Generally speaking, home town fans bet with their heart and will willingly bet against lopsided odds to support their team. Excellent bets can be found here for fans tend to ignore realities and bet blind. A good example was the Ali-Holmes matchup discussed earlier. Ali was every bit as much the people's champion as he billed himself and his fans supported him right to the end. Fine as a fan, foolish as a bettor. Smart bettors made lots of money on that fight. Look for those situations.

This lead us to the second principle.

2. Don't bet on games you're emotionally involved with. If your game plan is to win money, and it better be if you're reading this section and betting money, than you can't be wagering as a fan. Betting emotionally clouds your judgment and allows one to make stupid and costly mistakes.

If you're a diehard fan, you could probably watch your team lose six out of seven and feel that the eighth game shows promise for the team knowing full well that your team this year just doesn't have what it takes. Lay off those games - find other ones where you can see the game for what it is.

3. Always bet within your limits. Remember, no game or situation in life is a lock. You never know what can happen no matter what the situation appears to be. Of course, if you feel strongly about a bet, by all means, make that bet. However, and we go over this in our money management chapter, never bet above your means or way out of line from your normal betting.

It would be quite silly, to use kind language, to have one bad loss destroy a whole season of steady wins. Many foolish and greedy gamblers know that story. If greed takes over, then you're ripe as a sucker or a fool. It's a fact of life.

For those of you who believe in locks, the game that can't miss, think of the Oakland A's - Los Angeles Dodger world series of baseball in 1988 where nobody gave the Dodgers a chance and they rolled over the big, bad A's. There are many examples in baseball, basketball, football, hockey, boxing, and in fact any sport where competitors line up against one another to compete.

Or even more illustrative, in boxing, the Buster Douglas - Mike Tyson upset fight of 1990. That was a "lock" if ever there was a sports lock. Basically, you had to be crazy to bet against Tyson, who until then, was seemingly invincible. Nobody gave Douglass a chance and yet he pummelled Tyson all over the ring. Perhaps a few insiders knew something, perhaps not, but in any case, the public viewed this bout as a non-event, another walk for Tyson.

If you find betting situations you really like, by all means take advantage of them and make a bet. But always keep money management principles foremost in mind whenever money is at stake.

4. Bet only on games you think you have the edge. Stay away from marginal games which don't fit your winning formula. Many good handicappers get brought down by making bets on teams they don't feel strongly about. Cut out the bad bets, ones you know you shouldn't make, and your good bets may keep you a winner.

5. Make your own rating system of teams. Most professional handicappers advise you to really study your game and keep your own personal rating system of teams comparative strengths. When there's a significant difference between a way you would handicap a game and the bookie's line, then you may have a good bet.

6. Bet on consistency. Don't let one bad week in a teams performance or one excellent week cloud a teams true ability. Every team has good and bad days just as individuals do, but one day doesn't make a team or a player.

If a proven consistent winner looks bad in one game, you may find a great betting opportunity the following week as public perception sours on that teams capabilities. Visa-versa with bad teams having good days.

7. Be flexible in your winning approach. There is no one tried and true way of beating the bookie, and don't be conned into thinking there is one. There are many angles which can give you an edge. Look at them all before making the proper decision.

THE WHEEL OF FORTUNE

INTRODUCTION

The big spinning wheel, also called the **"Big Six"** or sometimes the **"Money Wheel,"** is only infrequently found in casinos outside the United States, and even within the U.S., the wheel barely gets much play. But apparently it gets some action, for the Big Six is still operating in numerous casinos.

The Money Wheel though, is fairly popular at county fairs, "Las Vegas Nights," carnivals and other such events, and generally, due to a lack of competition from other gambling games and a beer drinking and festive crowd, they get pretty good play - and I might add, very few winners.

The wheels vary in the amount of slots that could be landed upon, generally around 54. They're filled with $1, $2, $5, $10, $20 and sometimes other denominations that could be won. Some wheels might even put prizes in the slots.

Almost without exception, this quick and I think, boring game, has poor odds, and very little to cheer about. In Nevada casinos, the odds range from 11% against the player on the $5 bet to as high as 24% on others. Very steep.

PAYOFFS AND ODDS

Following are the typical odds of a Nevada-type 54 slot wheel on a $1 bet.

Wheel of Fortune · Payoffs and Odds

Wager	# of Winning Spins	# of Losing Spins	Payoff	Casino's Advantage
$1	23	31	$1	14.81%
$2	15	39	$2	16.67%
$5	8	46	$5	11.11%
$10	4	50	$10	18.52%
$20	2	52	$20	22.22%
$40*	1	53	$40	24.07%

*The $40 bet is usually indicated by a joker or "flag". In Atlantic City, the payoff on this bet is generally 45 to 1, which drops the odds on the wager to 14.81%

The overall average of all the bets combined comes out to just under 20%, not the most enticing figure for the discriminating bettor.

The odds can be even worse in carnivals and fairs, depending on how the payoffs are set.

In any case, don't lose any sleep if the "Wheel of Fortune" isn't offered next time you're in a gambling situation, unless of course, Vanna White is the one operating it!

MONEY MANAGEMENT

INTRODUCTION

To be a winner at gambling, a player must not only gamble intelligently, but must also make proper use of one's bankroll and keep his or her emotions under control. The tendency to ride a winning streak too hard in the hope of a big killing or to bet wildly during a losing streak attempting a quick comeback, have spelled doom to many a session which otherwise may have been a good win. Wins can turn into losses, and moderate losses can turn into a nightmare.

Winning and losing streaks are a very real part of gambling. It is how one deals with the inherent ups and downs at the tables that determines just how well a gambler will fare at the tables. In this section, we're going to present the sage advice every gambler should and must take to heart, for money management is a vital part of the winning formula.

You may be playing at an advantage or disadvantage to the house, but just because you're playing at an advantage doesn't mean you'll win in the short run, and conversely, just because you're playing at a disadvantage doesn't mean you'll lose. Anything can happen in the short run.

And that's why money management is so important. When you're winning, you have to stretch those winnings to the maximum safe level and make sure you finish a winner. And when things go the other direction, you must restrict losses to affordable amounts and protect yourself from ever really getting hurt at the tables.

If you follow the advice in this section, you'll be following the advice of professionals, and making the best use of your monetary resources. You'll always keep losses under control - and control is always a key concept in gambling - while winning sessions always end up as winning sessions.

You'll be on your way to successful gambling and when your luck falls right, you'll be a winner!

THE RISKS OF OVERBETTING

Astute gamblers have one thing in common - they know how to manage their money. Superior playing skills alone does not make one a winning player. The concept here is self control, the ability of a player to keep the game in check and never to lose sight of the winning strategies.

Let's show a simple example of how overbetting can quickly change a big winning session into a disaster. Let's say a bettor starts out with a bankroll of $250 and has been betting $5 - $20 a shot and after 2 hours of skillful play has ridden a surge of luck to $225 in winnings. Now he has $475 in front of him.

Getting greedy and caught up in the excitement of the game, the gambler now really wants to put the squeeze on and fast, so he goes against his pre-planned strategy, if he even has one, and now goes for $50 -$100 a bet. With a little luck and a few big wins in a row, he's on easy street.

However, after three straight losses at $100 a pop, he gets frantic, and goes for one more play at $175, pushing all his money on the wager. Make or break. Another loss.

Suddenly, a careful strategy that netted $225 got metamorphosed into "if I can get lucky on this play, please" strategy, and the player is out $250!

Madness. Here was an example of perhaps a technically skillful player losing control, betting over his head, and taking what by all rights was a tremendous winning session and finishing four bets later out all his bankroll!

And what if the sequence went a little differently, and more of those big bets were won rather than lost, so that instead the player sat with $500 in winnings. We all know that type of player, and know that he wouldn't have left until the game broke him. Bets would have been raised again and then he would have been bankrupted. Or the next session would have done the job.

To win, you must want to win, and want to win bad enough that you won't give that money back to the casino. I'm going to present a very important concept.

Once you have won money from a casino, that money is yours, and not the casino's. If you have $150 in winnings in front of you, you are not playing with the casino's money. It is your money now! If you think of your winnings as the casino's money, you won't feel bad giving it back. That's a dangerous attitude. Think of the money as your's now, and you won't be wanting to hand it back. And now maybe you'll walk away from the table with those winnings.

Let's move on the most important concept in money management.

NEVER GAMBLE MONEY THAT YOU CANNOT AFFORD TO LOSE, EITHER FINANCIALLY OR EMOTIONALLY.

Do not gamble with needed funds no matter how "sure" the bet seems. The possibilities of taking a loss are real, and if that loss will hurt, you're playing with fire. Don't be coming into town, as they say, in a $20,000 Cadillac and leaving on a $100,000 Greyhound.

Gambling with needed funds is a foolish gamble, for gambling involves chance, and the short term possibilities of taking a loss are real, no matter how easy the game may appear, or how well the odds are stacked in your favor. Unexpected things happen in gambling, that's what makes it so interesting. But if you never play over your head, you'll never suffer.

Gambling is a form of entertainment and if you can't afford the possibility of losing - don't gamble at the stakes you were considering. Either play at lower levels or don't gamble at all. If the larger wagers of your gambling game make your adrenalin rush too hard, you're over your head and need to find a game with lower limits.

But don't overlook the emotional side as well. If the playing of the game becomes a cause of undue anxiety, for whatever the reason, than it ceases to be a form of entertainment and you need a break. Take some time away from the game, be it a coffee break or a month's rest.

Playing under anxiety not only ruins the fun of the game but also adversely affects play and can influence you to make decisions contrary to what smart strategy dictates.

Your goal in gambling is not just to win, but to get satisfaction out of the game. Keep that in mind and you can never go wrong.

THE NATURE OF THE GAMBLE

In any gambling pursuit where luck plays a role, fluctuations in ones fortunes are common. It is the ability of the player to successfully deal with the ups and downs inherent in the gamble, that separate the smart gamblers from the losers.

You can't always win - even when the odds favor you - and you won't always lose, even when the odds are against you. In the short run, anything can happen and usually does. But over the long run, luck evens itself out, and it is skill, in the bets one makes and how one plays the game, that will determine if a player is a winner or a loser.

The smart player bides his time, is patient, keeps the game under control and as a result can win when the odds are in his favor.

PROPER BANKROLLING

Overbetting (or undercapitalization) leaves a player vulnerable in two ways. First, a normal downward trend can wipe out a limited money supply (as we saw earlier). Second, and equally important, the bettor may feel pressured by the shortage of capital and play less powerfully than smart play dictates.

For example, psychology and bluffing is an important part of poker, and if one is playing with "scared money," and the other players see it, they will have a field day forcing the under-capitalized player out of pots.

If the amount staked on a bet is above your head, you're playing in the wrong game. Play in a lower limit game - at levels of betting you feel comfortable with.

Know When to Quit

What often separates the winners from the losers is that the winners, when winning, leave the table a winner, and when losing, restrict their losses to affordable amounts. Smart gamblers never allow themselves to get destroyed at the table.

Minimizing losses is the key. You can't always win. If you're losing, keep the losses affordable - take a break. You only want to play with a clear head.

Minimizing Losses

The key concept in minimizing losses during a bad gambling run is to set a stop-loss limit. Before sitting at the table and making your bets, you must decide on the amount of money you'll put at stake, and should luck turn against you, restrict your losses to that amount only.

Do not go against this rule and you can never take a big beating. If things go poorly at first, take a break - simple as that.

When you're winning big, put a good chunk of these winnings in a "don't touch" pile, and play with the rest. You never want to hand all your winnings back to the casino. Should a losing streak occur, you're out of there - a winner!!!

Protecting Your Wins

Once you've accumulated a sizable win at the tables, the most important thing is to walk away a winner. There is no worse feeling than skulking away from a table after having lost all your wins back.

The general guidelines we recommend, is to put away half to two thirds of your winnings into a "**protected**" area that you won't touch under any circumstances. That money is bankable, for you won't play it. Keep playing with the rest of the winnings, putting more aside as the wins accumulate. Once the streak stops and the tides of fortune go against you, you'll leave the table a guaranteed winner for you've played it smart!

For example, let's say you're up 20 units. (A **unit** is the bet size you're using as a standard and could be $1, $5, $10, $25, $100, $500 or whatever value you want to assign.) Let's say your unit size is $5, so you're up $100. Put aside $50 (10 units) of your winnings into the protected zone and play the other $50 (10 units).

Set no limits on a winning streak. When you've got a hot hand, ride it for all its worth.

Increasing Bets When Winning

If you want to risk more to win more, go for it - but in moderation. Increase your bets gradually when winning, never getting overzealous as in the earlier example.

For example, if your bet size is a flat $10 in a game, and winnings are rapidly accumulating, jump up to $15, and if all goes well, to $20. This way if you keep winning, the wins get larger. If however, a sudden losing streak ensues, no problem, for you have protected yourself.

If you're playing in a game where you use a bet range, such as blackjack, take a $5-$20 range up to $10-$30 gradually, and then slowly higher if you're still winning.

And all the time, as you gradually increase bets in your gambling game, continually sock away won bets into your "don't touch" pile, so that by the time the streak ends, you've already got plenty in the bank and can walk away - **a big winner**!

CARIBBEAN STUD POKER

INTRODUCTION

Caribbean Stud Poker, which as the name suggests, caught hold and became popular in the Caribbean casinos first, has now spread and can regularly be found in Las Vegas casinos and other gambling establishments around the world.

While Caribbean Stud Poker is similar to standard poker in that both share the common rankings of the hands, it is dissimilar in most other aspects of the game. For one, Caribbean Stud Poker is played against a dealer, not the other players; for another there is none of the bluffing and skillful play inherent in regular poker.

The game is relatively simple to play. Like five card stud poker, five cards will be received by each participating player - there will be no draws. The player's only decisions are whether to call an additional bet after several cards are dealt, or whether to fold the hand and forfeit the original ante bet.

There is one other facet to the game that entices players to the Caribbean Stud Poker tables: There is a progressive jackpot that pays off as much as hundreds of thousands of dollars if a Royal Flush is drawn, and smaller bonus payouts for other winning hands.

Let's take a look now and see what the game is all about.

THE SETTING

Caribbean Stud Poker is played on a table that closely resembles that of a blackjack table, with the players seated around the oval side of the table, and the dealer standing along the flat side facing the players. In front of the dealer is a chip rack holding the table's bankroll. It is from this rack that the dealer will pay off winning hands, or deposit losing bets that he has collected.

The table is usually built to accommodate seven players, with seven seats placed around the oval side, along with corresponding betting areas on the layout to mark the locations where bets can be placed. The game can be played with just one player against the dealer or with the full complement of seven players. In either case, it doesn't affect the strategy or play of Caribbean Stud Poker, for players play against the house not against each other.

The standard 52 card pack is used in Caribbean Stud Poker, with 13 cards of each rank, Ace to King, and four suits, spades, diamonds, clubs, and hearts. The game is usually dealt from a single deck of cards using the Shuffle Master shuffling machine, an increasingly popular device used by the casinos that automatically shuffles the cards. The Shuffle Master machine is always found to the dealers left, or from the players vantage point, on the right side of the table.

In front of each player's position are three betting spots, one for each of the three bets a player can make. The first spot, closest to the player and in a circle, is marked "bet," the second spot, rectangular in shape, is marked "ante." The final betting area, closest to the dealer, is actually a drop slot, a "hole" in the table where a $1 coin or chip gets deposited to participate in the progressive jackpot.

THE OBJECT OF THE GAME

The players goal in Caribbean Stud Poker is to draw a five card poker hand that is stronger than the dealer's qualifying hand, and also, when good cards are drawn, to hold a hand that is strong enough to qualify for a bonus payout. The higher ranking the player's hand, the greater the bonus won, with the caveat that the dealer must possess a qualifying hand for the bonus to count. We'll see what this means later on.

When placing the $1 optional progressive wager in Caribbean Stud Poker, the player's goal for that bet is to draw a flush or better to receive additional bonus payouts. In particular, the player would like to get a Royal Flush, a hand that can win him hundreds of thousands of dollars.

Before we look at qualifying hands, and how that affects the game, we'll review the poker hands for players unfamiliar with their rankings.

RANKS OF THE HANDS

Following are the valid poker hands used in Caribbean Stud Poker. Hands are listed in order of strength, from the most powerful, the royal flush, to the least powerful, the hands less than A K high, which are all of equally poor value in this game.

All hands are poker hands recognized in regular high poker.

Royal Flush

An A K Q J 10, all of the same suit is called a royal flush. For example, A K Q J 10 of spades is a royal flush. The odds of being dealt a royal flush, the best hand possible in Caribbean Stud Poker, is one in 649,740.

Straight Flush

Five cards of the same suit in numerical sequence, such as the J 10 9 8 7 of clubs, is called a straight flush. This particular example is called a jack high straight flush since the jack is the highest ranking card. The ace must be used as either the highest card in the straight flush (an ace high straight flush is actually a royal flush) or the lowest card, as in A 2 3 4 5 of diamonds, to be valid. The hand of Q K A 2 3 of clubs is not a straight flush, simply a flush only.

Four of a Kind

Four cards of identical rank, such as the hand 6 6 6 6 3, is called a four of a kind. The odd card in the above example, the 3, is irrelevant and has no bearing on the rank of the hand.

Full House

A full house consists of three cards of identical rank along with two cards of an identical but different rank. 8 8 8 J J and K K K 7 7 are two examples of a full house.

Flush

Any five cards of the same suit constitutes a flush in poker. A K 7 3 2 of spades is an ace high flush in spades and Q 10 7 5 3 of hearts is a queen high flush in hearts.

Straight

Five non-suited cards in sequential order, such as 10 9 8 7 6, are a straight. When straights contain an ace, the ace must serve as either the highest card in the run, such as the ace high straight A K Q J 10, or the lowest card, as in the five high straight, 5 4 3 2 A. The cards Q K A 2 3 is not a straight. It is merely an ace high hand and will be beaten by any pair.

Three of a Kind

Three matched cards of identical value along with two odd cards (unmatched) are called a three of a kind. 7 7 7 Q 2 is an example of three of a kind.

Two Pair

Two sets of equivalently valued or "paired" cards along with an unmatched card, is a two pair hand. 4 4 3 3 A and K K 3 3 J are examples of two pair hands.

One Pair

One set of identically valued cards along with three unmatched cards are called a pair. The hand 2 2 8 4 A is referred to as "a pair of twos". Pairs are ranked in order of value from Aces, the highest, down to the deuces, the lowest. Thus, a pair of aces beats out a pair of kings, and a pair of nines wins over a pair of sixes.

Ace-King Hand

The next ranking hand in Caribbean Stud Poker is the hand lacking all above combinations but led by an Ace and a King, such as the hand A K J 5 3. This is the minimum strength hand that would be deemed a qualifying dealer hand. If both the dealer and the player hold this hand, then the highest-ranked of the remaining odd cards ranks supreme.

All Other Hands

Any hand not including any of the above combinations is a non-qualifying hand and has no value in Caribbean Stud Poker.

ODDS OF DRAWING HANDS

Following is a table showing the odds of getting dealt winning hands in Caribbean Stud Poker. These are the same odds of course, as those in regular draw poker.

Royal Flush	649,739 -1
Straight Flush	72,192 -1
Four of a Kind	4,165 -1
Full House	693 -1
Flush	508 -1
Straight	254 -1
Three of a Kind	46 -1
Two Pair	20 -1
One Pair	1.37 -1

RESOLVING TIED HANDS

Should both the dealer and player be dealt equivalently ranked hands, then the normal rules of poker rankings would apply to determine the more powerful hand, and therefore the winner. This typically involves using the higher ranked odd cards to determine the better hand, or in the case of flush and straight type hands, the highest cards leading those hands. We'll look at all these situation below.

Resolving Pair and AK Ties

If the player and the dealer hold the same pair or Ace King led non-pair hand, then the highest comparative odd cards would decide the winner. Should those odd cards be identical in rank, then the next highest ranking cards would be compared. If all cards are identical in value, then the hand is a push, a tie, neither side wins. For example, if the dealer has a 9 9 K J 5 and the player 9 9 K Q 4, the player wins by virtue of the Queen beating the Jack. Similarly, A K Q 7 2 beats out A K J 10 9.

Resolving Two Pair Ties

The same holds true for two pair hands. J J 7 7 K beats out 10 10 9 9 A and 8 8 4 4 10 loses to 8 8 5 5 9. When both pairs are evenly matched, the higher ranking fifth card, the odd card, determines the victor. If all cards are equally ranked, such as 5 5 3 3 2 and 5 5 3 3 2, then the hand is a tie.

Resolving Flush Ties

When the dealer and the player both hold flushes, the flush led by the highest card wins, or if that is tied, by the next highest card and so on down to the fifth card if all others are equal. In the unlikely event that both flushes hold identically valued cards, than the outcome is a push, neither side wins.

Resolving Straight and Straight Flush Ties

The winners of mutual straights and straight flush hands are also determined by the lead card. An Ace high straight beats any other straight, and ties against another Ace high straight. Similarly, a King high straight is stronger than a Queen high or any other lesser straight.

Resolving Three of a Kind and Full House Ties

When two players hold three of a kinds or full houses, it is the hand holding the higher ranking three of a kind that wins the pot. K K K 7 7 is a higher ranking full house than Q Q Q A A, and 9 9 9 3 4 beats out 8 8 8 Q 5.

THE PLAY OF THE GAME

Before any action can take place, participating players must make their initial bets. To begin the betting, each player must place at least the minimum bet in the area marked ante. The minimum and maximum bets allowable will usually be posted on a small placard in the corner of the table. In the typical casino, $5 will be the minimum bet allowed as ante. Players may also choose to make the Progressive Bet by dropping $1 into the drop slot. For now, no money can be wagered in the area marked "bet".

Once all players are ready to go and have placed their bets in the area marked ante, the dealer is ready to get the action going. The dealer's first action is to push a button that will automatically collect the $1 progressive bets that were made. These bets will drop out of sight into the bowels of the table and a red light will go on in front of each player who made the bet to indicate that that bet was made. The ante bets will still remain as before.

The dealer is now ready to distribute the cards. Five cards will be dealt face down to each participating player. The dealer will also deal himself five cards, four face down and one face up to be viewed by all players. This face up card is known as the upcard.

Players now have a decision to make about their hand. If they feel it is good enough to beat the dealer or qualify for a bonus payout, they can call, and do so by placing an additional wager in the box marked bet. This wager must be double the ante bet. Thus, if $5 was bet as an ante, then $10 would be placed in the bet area. Similarly, if $25 was the ante, then $50 would be the additional wager placed in the bet area. In the first case, the player would have total ante and call bets of $15, and in the second case, adding $25 to $50, $75 would be the total.

To indicate that the player wishes to make this additional bet, the player places his cards face down on the table. Players that do not wish to place this additional bet must fold, and do so by returning their cards to the dealer. While their ante bet is forfeited and collected by the house, no additional money is at risk for the hand. Players that have folded no longer participate in the hand.

Each player in turn will make the decision to play on by placing the additional double bet in the "call" box, or to fold and forfeit their ante bet. This is the only playing decision players will make once the cards are dealt. Play will proceed clockwise, beginning with the player at the dealer's left (the players right side) and continuing on to the third base position, the player positioned at the dealer's far right.

Once all players have made their decisions, the dealer will turn over his remaining four down cards to reveal his final five card hand. This hand will determine whether players have won or lost on their bets. The dealer first sees if he has a qualifying hand, the minimum hand required by the rules of the game to determine if bonuses and extra payouts will occur to players with stronger hands.

A qualifying hand is one in which the dealer has at least an Ace and a King, or a higher total such as a pair or better for his five cards. For example, A K 4 3 2 (Ace-King high), 3 3 7 9 Q (pair of threes), and 7 8 9 10 J (straight), are all qualifying dealer hands, while A Q 3 4 7 is not.

Why is a qualifying hand so important? We'll take a look at that now.

When The Dealer Does Not Have a Qualifying Hand

If the dealer does not have a qualifying hand, then all players who have remained in the game win their Ante bet, regardless of whether that hand is stronger than the player's. For example, if the dealer holds A J 10 8 2, a non-qualifying hand, and the player holds Q 9 8 6 2 or even 7 6 4 3 2, the player wins. The dealer cannot win if his hand doesn't contain at least a hand of A K strength. Players who folded however, have already conceded defeat and lost their bets. But for players who made call bets (anyone who didn't make a call bet had to have folded), a non-qualifying dealer hand spells an automatic winning hand.

That's the good news.

The bad news is that if the dealer does not have a qualifying hand, players win only the Ante bet. Their call bets, the ones placed in the bet area, are returned to them. They are not eligible for any Bonus payouts or even 1-1 payoffs regardless of the hand drawn. Thus, if $5 was wagered on the Ante and $10 in the Bet circle, and the player happened to hold three Jacks, the total win would be only $5, the $5 paid at even money for the won ante bet. The non-qualifying dealer hand negates the 3-1 bonus that would have been paid for the three of a kind if that player's hand was stronger than the dealer's. In the above example, the $10 wager in the Bet circle would be returned.

If the dealer does have a qualifying hand, there is no automatic win. Now, the stronger hand between the dealer and the player is the deciding factor. Let's see how this works.

When the Dealer Has a Qualifying Hand

When the dealer does have that qualifying hand though, that is at least an A K or better hand, than he'll compare his hand to each of the players to see who has the stronger hand. As opposed to the non-qualifying situation, both the ante bet and the call bet (the wager in the "bet" area) are at stake now. The player will either win both bets or lose both, depending upon whether he has a stronger total, which would be a winner, or a weaker total, which would be a loser.

For example, if $5 were bet on the ante and $10 on the call bet, and the dealer held two jacks to the players two deuces, than the player would lose both bets for a total $15 loss since, of course, two jacks are a stronger hand than two deuces.

However, if the player has the better hand, than both bets are won instead. Each wager, the ante bet and the call bet is paid differently. Ante bets are paid at even money, 1-1, while call bets are paid according to a bonus schedule which we'll show below.

Bonus Payouts on the Call Bet	
Royal Flush	100-1
Straight Flush	50-1
Four of a Kind	20-1
Full House	7-1
Flush	5-1
Straight	4-1
Three of a Kind	3-1
Two Pair	2-1
One Pair	1-1

We'll look at an example hand to make the bonus payouts perfectly clear. Let's say we have a $5 Ante bet, and of course, our call bet, which is double, is $10. We receive Three of a Kind and the dealer holds a pair of Aces. We'll win $5 for the Ante bet, plus $30 on the $10 call bet (three of a kind paid at 3-1) for a total win of $35. This would be in addition to the original $15 in bets that were made, $5 on the ante and $10 on the call. Thus, $50 would be returned to us.

We would not qualify for the bonus payout in the unlucky event that the dealer doesn't hold a qualifying hand. Only the ante bet would be won. We also don't qualify for bonus payouts if the dealer holds a stronger hand than our hand. In that case, not only is there no bonus payout on the call bet, but both the ante and call bets are outright losers.

Note that the dealer only wins at even money, regardless of the strength of his hand and that bonus payouts for the players are made only on the call bet itself and not on the ante.

THE MAXIMUM BONUS PAYOUT

Players must be aware that casinos have a limit on the maximum amount they'll pay winners on the Bonus Payouts. Some limits may be as low as $5,000 (even lower one might be found), while others might go as high as $50,000 or more. This limit will be posted on the table and may read, "Bonus payout's may not exceed table's maximum payout."

How does this affect the player? Well, not in a good way if the player gets a big hand and is denied the full payout because it exceeds the maximum posted table limit. Let's look at an example. Say the player has wagered $150 on the call bet and draws a Straight Flush in a casino with a $5,000 Bonus Payout. Normally the player would be entitled to $7,500 (50-1 x the $150 bet). However, since the maximum bonus payout is only $5,000, the player loses out on the extra $2,500 - a big hit to take. The "penalty" would be even worse if that hand was a Royal Flush paying 100-1 on the bonus; now the player would only get $5,000 of the $15,000, losing out on the extra $10,000!

To protect against losing out on the full amount that should be paid on a bonus payout, players must always make sure that the maximum call bet multiplied by 100 does not exceed the bonus payout. We use the number 100 because the largest bonus, on the Royal Flush, pays at 100-1. If 100 multiplied by a player's call bet is greater than the casino's limit, then the drawing of a royal flush would not get the full payout. As we've just shown, it will exceed that limit.

To easily come up with the maximum bet that won't be penalized if a Royal Flush is drawn, divide the casino's maximum payout by 100. For example, if the maximum payout is $5,000, dividing it by 100, the player's maximum call bet should not exceed $50. And of course, if the call bet is $50, the ante, which is always half that amount, would be $25.

Or, if a player likes to think in terms of the ante, which is half of the call bet, then the maximum casino payout limit should be divided by 200 to find the largest ante bet that should be made. Using the $5,000 casino limit example above, and dividing by 200, gives us an answer of a $25 maximum ante bet that should be made, and of course, a maximum $50 call bet since that bet is always double the ante bet.

No surprise; that's the same $25 ante and $50 call bets we

figured before, but came to from a different direction.

If a player likes to bet at much higher numbers, then casinos should be sought out that provide their patrons with higher maximum payouts.

THE PROGRESSIVE JACKPOT

The optional wager we spoke about earlier, the Progressive bet, is made by placing $1 in the drop slot or progressive slot as it is also known, before the cards are dealt. The goal of this bet is to draw a flush or higher ranked hand to receive additional bonus payouts. While flushes, full house and other powerful hands would be great, what the player really would like to get is a Royal Flush, a hand that will win the full progressive amount.

Near each Caribbean Stud Poker table is a Jackpot Meter that goes up in value each time $1 is placed into the drop slot by any table linked up to that meter within the casino. This jackpot can be as little as $5,000 or $10,000, the starting point after a Royal Flush is hit, depending upon the casino, or as high as hundreds of thousands of dollars, or even more.

The amount each progressive bet increases the jackpot varies from casino to casino. Some casinos put in only 49¢ of each dollar played, while others, particularly larger casinos with more forward thinking minds who understand the value of larger jackpots to draw players, may put in as much as 75¢ per dollar played. Thus, every time prior to dealing the cards that the dealer pushes the button which collects the progressive bets, the jackpot will go up that percentage in value, and get that much sweeter.

As that jackpot grows, so does player interest. It's just like the lottery. The larger the jackpot, the greater the players appetites to try and win that prize.

What does it take to win the full amount of the progressive? Why, nothing less than the big sandwich with all the dressings itself - the Royal Flush. While drawing this hand would certainly be nice, a player shouldn't hold his or her breath - it's a longshot. As we saw in the earlier chart, the odds of hitting the Royal is 1 in 649,739.

But playing longshots is what much of gambling is about anyway.

There are other paying hands as well in the Progressive Jackpot. The charts below show two payout schedules that a player might find. The first schedule, which might be found at a few larger casinos aggressively going after Caribbean Stud Poker players, is a liberal payout schedule that works for the benefit for the player. The second schedule, which is more commonly found, pays much less on the four of a kind, full house, and flush hands, and that of course, is to the detriment of the player.

Liberal Payout Schedule - 500/250/100

Royal Flush	100% of the Jackpot
Straight Flush	10% of the Jackpot
Four of a Kind	$500
Full House	$250
Flush	$100

Common Payout Schedule - 100/75/50

Royal Flush	100% of the Jackpot
Straight Flush	10% of the Jackpot
Four of a Kind	$100
Full House	$75
Flush	$50

There are other payout schedules you'll find. In between the 500/250/100 liberal schedule shown above, and the 100/75/50 also shown, you may find 500/150/75, 500/100/75, 500/100/50, 500/75/50, 300/100/50, 250/100/50, and 150/100/50. The three numbers for each group stand respectively for the four of a kind, full house and flush payoffs. This designation is similar to video poker jacks or better machines which are known by the payoffs on the full house and flush respectively (9-6 and 8-5 machines).

Players should keep in mind that the progressive is a separate bet and is not affected by the results of the ante or regular call bet. For example, if the player draws a full house and the dealer miraculously (or is it disastrously?) has a four of a kind at the same time, the player would still win $250 on the $1 progressive bet (assuming the more liberal payout schedule shown) even though the call and ante best are losers.

By the same token, the player gets the full bonus payout on the $1 progressive bet even if the dealer doesn't have a qualifying hand. Thus, players must be careful to alert the dealers to their flush or better hands when the dealer has a non-qualifying hand in case the dealer accidentally removes the cards before checking for progressive winners.

There is no maximum limit on a progressive payout as there is with the bonus payout. If the Royal Flush is hit, players will get paid the full amount of the progressive meter.

THE AGGREGATE PAYOFF ON PROGRESSIVES

One other casino rule comes into play on the Progressive payout. The Bonus Payout is limited to an Aggregate payoff on the Straight Flush and the Royal Flush. What this means is that on a Straight Flush hand for example, a total of 10% will be paid out. Thus, if two players hold a straight flush on the same deal, they would split that 10%, in effect, getting only 5% each.

If the meter showed $12,000, the total pool of $1,200 for the Straight flush would be divided evenly between the two winners at $600 each. This applies only to straight flush and royal flush hands on progressive wagers, not to the bonus payouts on the Four of a Kind, Full House and Flush hands, where each player will receive the full amount listed.

The chances of two players holding a straight or royal flush on the very same hand is so unlikely, quantum degrees more than one hundred million to 1 against (the exact odds depending upon how many other players are at the table), that this casino rule shouldn't be of great concern to you.

HOUSE PERCENTAGE

The odds in Caribbean Stud Poker are similar to American double zero roulette, which is to say, they are not kind to the player. With proper strategy, the player is trying to buck a house edge of about 5.25%, difficult odds to overcome for players trying to beat the game. If we compare these odds to baccarat, craps, and blackjack, games which offer much superior odds - no worse than 1.36% in baccarat, .08% or .06% in craps if the proper bets are placed, or even an outright advantage in blackjack with correct play - and you'll understand why I'm not so hot on this table game.

At more than a 5% disadvantage, players will see their bankrolls steadily bleed dry as the hours tick on and the hands get dealt. It's a relatively large house edge the way I see it, and if players try their hand long enough, they'll start to see things the way I do.

However, if players enjoy the game, and are excited by the possibilities, well, that's what gambling is all about. Gamblers could do much worse at keno, Big Six and the slots machines. As long as players realize that they're up against a big take compared to the other table games, then the game can be approached with open eyes.

On the good side, Caribbean Stud Poker is like all other gambling games; players will have their good streaks and bad streaks. With a little luck and smart money management, players can emerge with winnings in the short run.

WINNING STRATEGIES

In this section, we'll go over the playing and betting strategies that optimize a player's chances of winning at Caribbean Stud Poker. We'll discuss the ante, call and progressive bets, the best way to approach the playing decisions when it's time to call or fold, and an overall approach that gives players the best chances of walking away a winner.

We'll start with the playing strategies.

Playing Strategy

There is one crucial decision to make in Caribbean Stud Poker and that is whether to make the call to bet wager at double the ante size, or to fold and forfeit the ante without exposing additional money to risk. In some cases, as when players have a strong hand such as three of a kind or two pairs, the strategy is fairly obvious - we want the additional money out there. On the other hand, when our cards are weak and we don't even have an A and a K, cards that will at least compete with a qualifying dealer total, the strategy is also clearcut - we'll want to fold.

The basics strategy we show below will have players playing at a near optimal level. Playing the absolute perfect optimal strategy will gain players so little as to be negligible; only a few hundredths of a percent can be gained with perfect playing strategy. It is so tiny a gain, especially when we're dealing with a negative expectation of over five percent to begin with, that the extra effort needed to learn a semi-complicated playing strategy is not worth it by any stretch of the imagination. Players need not even worry about it; the strategy presented here is all that a player needs to know..

The correct playing strategy divides hands into those which are stronger than the dealer's qualifying total of A K, which we'll generally keep, and hands which are weaker than the minimum A K, which we'll throw away and surrender the ante.

We'll look at the details below starting with the strongest hands, and work our way down to the weakest hands.

Two Pair or Higher

Two pair, three and four of a kind, straights, flushes, full houses, and straight and royal flushes are all very strong hands that not only are heavily favored to win, but which pay bonus payouts. The strategy for this grouping of hands is very clear even to beginning players - make the call bet!

Pairs

Pairs are dealt 42% of the time in five card poker, so this is a hand players will see on a regular basis. The correct strategy when holding a pair, any pair, is to call, regardless of the dealer's upcard. This is a clear gain in all situations.

Note that this doesn't mean players win money in the long run in all pair situations. For example, when holding 2's, 3's, 4's, 5's, 6's, and 7's, players long term expectations are negative, that is, they will show a loss. However, except for the lowest of pairs, the 2's-4's, players will always have a positive expectation of winning when their pair is greater than the dealer's upcard. For example, if we hold a pair of 9's, and the dealer shows an 8, we have a long term expectation of winning. We already know that the dealer's 8, if paired and not improved with a further 8 or second pair, is a loser to our 9's.

Our strategy with these low pairs is to minimize losses, just as in blackjack when we are dealt inferior hands like 12-16 - the bust hands. In Caribbean Stud Poker, it is a mistake to throw away small pairs just because they're weak. Yes, they may be weak, but keeping them is a lot stronger play than discarding them and forfeiting the ante. Players that throw away small pairs give up anywhere from 5-10% depending upon the pairs they discard. That's a bad loss to take.

Remember that the general strategy in Caribbean Stud Poker is to minimize losses in bad situations, as when we're dealt a small pair and play it for lesser losses, and to maximize winnings when our situation is strong, as when we're dealt two pair or higher. To again use a blackjack analogy, when there is a doubling down situation, which means we have the edge, we want to get more money on the table.

The strongest pairs are 10's, J's, Q's, K's, and A's. These pairs have a positive expectation of winning against all dealer upcards.

A K vs. Dealer

When we hold A K, we have a borderline hand whose strategy depends on the other three cards we hold, and the dealer's upcard. This is a special situation based on the qualifying dealer rules of the minimum A K hand. Following are the two break-downs for playing A K hands.

a. *When our third highest card is a J or Q, we call the dealer.* For example, the hand A K J 9 4 should be played against all dealer upcards including the A.

The thinking here is that if the dealer makes a qualifying hand of A K x x x, x standing for any other non-pairing (or cards which form a higher hand), the A K J or better hand is strong enough to win, thus making the call bet a profitable play.

b. *When our third highest card is less than a J, we call the dealer only if his upcard matches one of our five up cards; otherwise we fold.* Examples: Call with A K 10 5 2 vs. A, and vs. 2, but fold A K 10 5 2 vs. Q, and A K 8 7 6 vs. 5.

The Ace-King hands are close plays that, percentage wise, are almost 50-50 for the player in terms of long term gain. To make calling a correct play, that is, a theoretical gain over not calling and folding, we need the little extra edge that favors our hand. In the situation where one of our cards matches the dealer's upcard, the dealer is that much less likely to have a pair and defeat us. There is now one less card that can help the dealer's chances. Therefore, under those circumstances, the correct play is to call. We use the extra piece of information (of holding a card the dealer needs) to gain that slight edge in this marginal situation.

A Q or less vs. Dealer

Any hand that doesn't have at least an A K or better should be folded. Examples: Fold A Q J 10 9, A Q 8 7 6, K Q J 10 6, and 10 8 4 3 2.

The problem with these hands are that in essence, they're worthless. A Q led hands are no better the J high or even 8 high hands. In all cases, if the dealer qualifies, these hands are losers. Obviously, since a qualifying dealer hand, by definition, contains an A K or better, it beats all the hands in this category.

The Disadvantage of Playing A Q or Less Hands

There is one constant in Caribbean Stud Poker that will make the playing of A Q or less hands disastrous: The dealer will make a qualifying hand approximately 56% of the time. At first glance, you might think that the loss is $12 for every $100 bet - 56 losses less 44 wins. That's a very convincing argument not to make this play. Giving up 12% is enormous and a foolish play. But the loss is much worse! It's equivalent to being more than ten times worse than that, about 125% when based on the ante bet!

Here's how the math breaks down. We'll use a $10 ante bet for this example. Of the 44 times the dealer doesn't qualify, we win a total of only $440. Since the dealer didn't qualify, only the ante bet is paid off. The $20 call bet is returned. That's $10 for each winning hand at 1-1, even money. Of the other 56 times that the dealer qualifies, we not only lose the $10 ante bet, but the $20 call bet as well! That's $1680 in losses against only $440 in wins for a net loss of $1240. Thus for every $1,000 made in Ante bets, a loss of $1240 is 124%, actually closer to 125% (we rounded down the 56% number to show the math easier).

Making these kind of plays will destroy us at the table. Players should never, ever think about playing these hands. These horrible plays are worse than any other play that can be found in the entire casino!

PROGRESSIVE $1 BET STRATEGY

Generally speaking, unless the progressive jackpot is in the hundreds of thousands, the progressive $1 wager is a complete sucker bet giving the house an edge that hovers around 50% in most cases and goes as high as almost 75% in the worse case. Ouch!

Even when the jackpot is say $250,000, the player still may be giving the casino an enormous edge by making this bet. The exact edge the casino enjoys is a function of several factors - the actual bonus paid on four of a kinds, full houses and flushes, which as we've seen, varies from casino to casino; the size of the jackpot itself; and equally important, the size of the ante bet.

This last factor, the size of the ante bet, is important because the progressive bet cannot be made as an independent wager by itself. At a minimum, to play Caribbean Stud Poker, the player must place an ante bet, and then optionally, if desired, he or she can make the progressive bet as well. Since each bet gives the casino roughly a 5.25% edge, the larger the average bet, the higher the jackpot must be to compensate for these bets. Thus, if $5 were wagered on the ante, a break-even for the progressive would be far lower than if $10 were the average ante bet.

For example, if we're playing in a casino with more liberal payouts, paying 500 for four of a kind, 250 for a full house, and 100 for a flush, and have an average $5 ante bet, then the break-even on a progressive jackpot would be around $200,000. However, if we had the less liberal payout of 100 for four of a kind, 75 for a full house, and 50 for a flush, the payout schedule found at many casinos, the break-even progressive jackpot is closer to $350,000 on that average $5 bet. But make that $5 average ante $10, and the break-even jackpot on the more liberal rules jumps almost $100,000!

A $1 average ante bet would afford overall better odds when making the $1 progressive and hoping to land a big jackpot, but that will rarely be found. Most casinos have a $5 minimum ante bet.

Thus, as we see, these three important factors - average ante size, jackpot size, and bonus payout schedule - all influence the actual disadvantage a player faces at Caribbean Stud Poker. Or, in the rare cases where we do find a monster payout that has built up, the progressive bet may actually be advantageous.

It's always nice to dream of the big hit, hence the millions and millions of players who play the lottery consistently, and the many players who donate the $1 to the progressive pool in Caribbean Stud Poker. However, the way I approach gambling, I would rather stick to the bets that offer me the best chances of winning in the long run. And unless the progressive jackpot is in the hundreds of thousands of dollars, we would be better off avoiding the progressive bet altogether. If a player feels the pressing need to make that $1 "dream" bet, he might consider the lottery. Lousy odds, but if the player does hit, the payout is not a few measly tens of thousands of dollars, it's a two year cruise around the world, a dream home, instant retirement, and the most expensive cigars money can buy.

But then again, my advice is always to play with grounded rationale. Make the best bets the games can give you, and if winning, make sure to walk away with the casino money in your pocket.

BETTING STRATEGY

In Caribbean Stud Poker, there is no particular betting strategy to pursue in terms of gaining an advantage as there is in blackjack, except to bet intelligently according to one's bankroll. A bettor should never risk money that he cannot afford to lose. That is the first rule for any betting proposition.

Occasionally, the progressive jackpot may get into the hundreds of thousands of dollars, and the bettor will be looking at a positive expectation on the progressive $1 wager. In these instances, when we're chasing a very large progressive jackpot, a situation which actually gives us the edge, our strategy is to keep the ante bet as small as possible so as to minimize the effect of the 5.25% house edge on the ante and call bets.

OVERALL WINNING STRATEGY

The main thing to keep in mind with Caribbean Stud Poker is that the game is a negative expectation gamble. The casino has an advantage of 5.25% on the regular ante and call bets. Theoretically, the longer a bettor plays, the closer to the 5.25% "tax" that will be extracted by the inevitable house edge built-in to the game. On the progressive bet, as we discussed earlier, the house edge can soar to almost 75%, or in exceptionable cases, where the progressive jackpot is in the hundreds of thousands of dollars, can actually favor the player.

But as we all know, there are up and down swings in gambling. Anyone can walk away from the table a winner. But to maximize one's chances of winning, bettors must play their cards correctly and make only the best bets available to them.

A player's first order of business is to avoid the progressive bet. Unless the jackpot is enormous, at least $200,000 or more, depending upon the circumstances, this bet gives too much away to the casino. Avoiding this wager will avoid a constant drain on a player's bankroll. Secondly, bettors must study the playing strategy so that the correct moves are made and the chances of winning are optimized. As we saw earlier, there is not much to learn, but one must learn the strategies and use them all the time, not just when the mood strikes There is no substitute for correct play. Hunches only build the casinos bigger and make the players poorer.

Finally, intelligent money management decisions must be employed at the tables. When things are going poorly, which they sometimes do, we must limit our losses. We will never take a bad beating in any one session. And when we're on a hot streak, we'll make sure that we leave a winner. We'll never give the casino back all our winnings once we've got a big winning streak going. That's not only the key in Caribbean Stud Poker, but in all gambling pursuits.

LET IT RIDE®

INTRODUCTION

Let it Ride® was first introduced to the Las Vegas casinos in August, 1993, and immediately became a rousing success. The game has continued to grow in popularity and can now be found in hundreds of casinos across the country as well as in international casinos as well. The Shuffle Master company, developer of Let it Ride® and Let it Ride®, The Tournament™, has really hit paydirt with this game.

Why the big fuss? Well, for one, Let it Ride®, The Tournament™, offers players millions of dollars in prizes if the optional $1 tournament bet is made and a big hand is hit. And as we all know, big prizes usually translates into big interest. Second, Let it Ride®, like Caribbean Stud Poker, draws some of it's popularity from its similarities with poker, a game very familiar to the gambling public. Thus, players find Let it Ride® easy to learn and play. Third, the unique feature of the game that lets players remove two of their three bets when they're unhappy with the cards they are dealt, is an attractive feature that strikes a responsive chord among players.

Let it Ride® is a simplified version of five card poker. Players get dealt three cards, and use these in combination with the two community cards shared by all players to form a final five card hand that either qualifies for a payout, which is a winner, or is of lesser value, which is a loser. There are no draws of additional cards, bluffing of opponents, or strategy decisions other than deciding whether to take down two of the three mandatory starting bets in the game, or whether to let them ride.

That said, let's take a closer look at Let it Ride® and see how the game works.

THE EQUIPMENT OF PLAY

Let it Ride® is played on a blackjack-style table with a standard pack of 52 cards. On the flat side of the table is the dealer who performs all the functions one would expect; the dealing of the cards, the paying off and collection of won and lost bets, and the overall running of the game. In front of the dealer will be the chip rack, where the bankroll of the table sits in long colorful rows in full view of the players.

Across from the dealer, along the oval edge and facing him, are as many as seven participating players, trying their hand with lady luck.

On the layout itself, where the game is played and all bets are made, are three betting circles in front of each player's seat. These circles are laid out next to each other, horizontally, in front of each player's position. Going left to right, they are marked 1, 2 and $ respectively. These are the spots where the three mandatory bets are placed by each participating player.

There is one additional bet spot as well, a red button located in front of each player, where an optional $1 wager can be made on Let it Ride®, The Tournament™.

Another item on the table might be the Shuffle Master shuffling machine, an increasingly popular device that automatically shuffles the cards.

THE OBJECT OF THE GAME

The player's goal in Let it Ride® is to draw a hand that is strong enough to qualify for one of the winners in the payout schedule. These payoffs range in value from even money wins, 1-1 on a tens or better pair, to 1000-1 when the Royal Flush is hit.

When placing the $1 optional wager on Let it Ride®, The Tournament™, a player's additional goal is to get a straight flush or a royal flush, hands that not only pay $2,000 or $20,000 respectively, but enter that player in the big tournament which has a grand prize of one million dollars.

There is no competition against other players as in regular poker, or against the dealer as in Caribbean Stud Poker. In Let it Ride®, the goal is solely to draw a hand strong enough to qualify for a payout.

HANDS THAT QUALIFY FOR PAYOUTS

As we mentioned above, the player's goal is to draw a hand that qualifies for a winning payout. The higher the rank of the hand, the greater the payout. At a minimum, a player must have a tens or better payout to be a winner. Any lesser hand fails to qualify for a payout, and the player's bets will be lost.

The following chart shows the winning hands and the payoffs.

The Payoff Schedule	
Royal Flush	1,000-1
Straight Flush	200-1
Four of a Kind	50-1
Full House	11-1
Flush	8-1
Straight	5-1
Three of a Kind	3-1
Two Pair	2-1
Pair of 10's or Better	1-1

THE WINNING POKER HANDS

For players unfamiliar with poker or who want to brush up on their knowledge of poker combinations, we've listed the categories of valid poker hands recognized in Let it Ride®. Hands are listed in order of strength, from the most powerful, the royal flush, to the least powerful, the hands which don't qualify for a payout at all.

Royal Flush

An A, K, Q, J and 10, all of the same suit is a royal flush. For example, A, K, Q, J 10, of spades is a royal flush.

Straight Flush

Five cards of the same suit in numerical sequence, such as the J 10 9 8 7 of clubs, is called a straight flush. The ace must be used as either the highest card in the straight flush (an ace high one being a royal flush) or the lowest card, as in A 2 3 4 5 of diamonds, to be valid. The hand of Q K A 2 3 of clubs is not a straight flush, simply a flush only.

Four of a Kind

Four cards of identical rank, such as the hand 6 6 6 6 3, is called a four of a kind. The odd card in the above example, the 3, is irrelevant and has no bearing on the rank of the hand.

Full House

A full house consists of three cards of identical rank along with two cards of an identical but different rank. 8 8 8 J J and K K K 7 7 are two examples of a full house.

Flush

Any five cards of the same suit constitutes a flush in poker. A K 7 3 2 of spades is called an ace high flush in spades and Q 10 7 5 3 of hearts is a queen high flush in hearts.

Straight

Five non-suited cards in sequential order, such as 10 9 8 7 6, are called a straight. When straights contain an ace, the ace must serve as either the highest card in the run, such as the ace high straight A K Q J 10, or the lowest card, as in the five high straight, 5 4 3 2 A. The cards Q K A 2 3 of mixed suits is not a straight. It is merely an ace high hand.

Three of a Kind

Three matched cards of identical value along with two odd cards (unmatched) are called a three of a kind. 7 7 7 Q 2 is an example of three of a kind.

Two Pair

Two sets of equivalently valued or "paired" cards along with an unmatched card, are called two pairs. 4 4 3 3 A and K K 3 3 J are examples of two pair hands.

Tens or Better

One set of identically valued cards along with three unmatched cards are called a pair. The hand J J 7 4 2 is a pair of jacks. In Let it Ride®, the minimum hand that qualifies for a payout is a pair of tens or higher. Thus, tens, jacks, queens, kings, and aces, are all winning totals with the 1-1 payout. Pairs of nines and lesser strength pairs don't qualify for payouts.

All Other Hands

Any hand not including any of the above combinations is a losing hand with no payouts, and thus, has no value in Let it Ride®.

THE BASICS OF PLAY

Before any cards are dealt, participating players at the table must make a bet on each of the three betting circles in front of them. These bets must be made in equal amounts. For example, if $5 were to be bet on the circle marked "1", then that same $5 must be bet on the other two circles, the one marked "2", and the one marked "$".

Additionally, a $1 wager may be made on the tournament spot, an optional bet that makes the player eligible for the big Let it Ride® tournament. We'll go over this bet in a little bit.

There is normally a minimum $5 bet on each circle, though smaller casinos may offer minimums as low as $3. In the first case, a minimum of $15 total would have to be bet among three bet circles, $5 per spot, and in the second case, a minimum of $9, $3 per spot, would be required.

Once all players have completed betting, and the cards are shuffled and ready to go, the dealer will deal three down cards to each player. The dealer will also deal two face down cards and place them in the two rectangular boxes imprinted on the layout in front of his position. These cards are called community cards, and will be shared by all active players to form their final five card holding.

The rules of the game disallow players from showing their cards to their fellow players at the table. The casinos don't want players to gain any untoward advantage that may help them make better playing decisions. (This is unlike regular poker where sharing card information actually hurt's a player's chance of winning since he plays against the other players at the table.) At Let it Ride®, players strategize only their own hand's winning chances. The relative strengths of other players hands has no bearing on a player's own chances of winning, though the cards those hands contain may help provide information to a player's own playing decision.

Beginning with the player on the dealer's left and proceeding in a clockwise direction, each player in turn has the following options:

THE PLAYER'S FIRST OPTION

Each player in turn, after looking at his or her three down cards, has the option of playing for the bet in circle "1", that is, letting it ride, or withdrawing that bet from play and having it returned to his or her bankroll.

Letting a bet ride is done by placing the cards under or in front of the cards in the circle marked "1". The dealer will understand this motion to mean that the player wishes to keep his or her bet in play, and will move on to the next player.

A player that wishes to remove his or her bet from play, does so by simply scraping the table with the cards. This motion will prompt the dealer to remove that player's bet from the first circle and return it to the player.

Thus, any player who is unhappy with the cards dealt to him, is able to remove his or her bet from the circle marked "1".

Players should not physically take back their own bets; they should let the dealer perform that function.

Once all players have made their decision, going clockwise from the dealer's left all the way around the table to the "third base" position, the seat at the dealer's extreme right, play will move on to the next round.

THE PLAYER'S SECOND OPTION

After all player's have made their decisions on bet circle "1", the dealer now turns over one of the two community cards in front of him so that each player knows four of the five cards that will be used to form his or her final hand.

Again, just like in the first round, players are faced with the decision to let their bet in circle "2" ride, or to take it down and put it back into their bankroll. The motions are the same. Players wishing to let their wager ride slide their cards under their bet in circle "2". And those wishing to remove their bets, scrape the table with their cards. Players that elect to remove their bet in circle "2" from play will have it returned to them by the dealer.

All players may remove their second bet, the one in circle "2", even players that chose to let the bet in circle "1" ride. Each bet is independent of the previous bet. For example, one player may remove the bet in circle 1 and let the bet in circle 2 ride; another may Let it Ride® in circle 1 but remove it in circle 2; a third may remove bets in both circles; and a fourth may let both bets ride. All these combinations are permissible.

When all players have completed their playing decisions on their bets in circle "2", it is time for the showdown.

THE SHOWDOWN

The dealer will now turn over the second and last community card. By combining the two community cards with the player's three individual cards, each player will know his or her final five card hand. All cards are now exposed and each player can see how they fared on this deal.

Unlike the previous two rounds, the bet in circle "3" cannot be removed. This bet is for keeps and will now be settled by the dealer along with any other bets that the players have in the other betting circles, if any.

Going from his right and proceeding to his left, the dealer will turn over each player's cards and settle the wagers.

SETTLING THE BETS

Players who hold at least a pair of 10's or higher ranked poker hand qualify for payouts according to the payout schedule we showed earlier.

Winning hands pay out on all spots which still contain bets. For example, a player holding a pair of Jacks, which pays 1-1, and having $5 bet on each of the three spots, would win $15 total, $5 for each of the spots. Thus $30 would get returned to the player, $15 in winnings plus the original $15 wagered. If only spots 2 and 3 contained $5 bets, then $20 would be returned to the player, $10 in which would be winnings ($5 each on circles 2 and 3).

By the same token, players whose hands didn't qualify for the payoff will lose on all spots where they had bets. At the very least, that would be one losing spot, the third circle whose bet cannot be removed, and at a maximum, three spots if the player let all bets ride. Thus, if a player bet $5, and let all bets ride, but lost, then $15 would be lost, $5 on each circle. However, if the player had removed the bets from circles 1 and 2, then only $5 would be lost.

Let's now see how the other wager, $1 Progressive bet works.

LET IT RIDE®, THE $1 TOURNAMENT BET

Players have the option to make an additional $1 bet which will earn entry into the big money Let it Ride® tournament if the player draws a straight flush or royal flush hand. While this is the big draw of this bet, there is an additional attraction to this wager - the $1 tournament bet also qualifies the player for the following cash bonuses if a straight or better hand is drawn. The following chart shows these bonus payouts.

Let it Ride® - $1 Tournament Payout - Bonus Payouts	
Royal Flush	$20,000
Straight Flush	$2,000
Four of a Kind	$200
Full House	$75
Flush	$50
Straight	$20

The tournament bet is made by placing $1 on the red button located in front of the three betting spots. Note that while a pair of tens or higher pair, two pair, and three of a kind hands will win on the regular betting circles, they don't qualify for the bonus payouts on the $1 bet. The minimum bonus payout for this bet, as we see on the chart, is a straight or better.

We'll go over a sample bonus win for both the three betting circles and the $1 Tournament bet to make the payoffs in Let it Ride® perfectly clear. Let's say the player had $5 bet, let the bets ride in all three betting spots, and drew a flush for his five cards. Each of the three betting circles would receive an 8-1 payoff (for the flush) on the $5 bet, for a $40 win per circle, or $120 total on those bets. Of course, if only one bet circle contained a bet, that win would be only $40. In addition to this win, the player earns $50 for the bonus payout on the $1 tournament bet. Thus, the total win for that round would be $120 plus $50, for a grand total of $170.

If that hand was instead a straight flush, the picture would be a whole lot sweeter. Each spot now would win $1,000 (the $5 bet at 200-1) for a total of $3,000 on the three spots, plus the bonus win of $2,000 for a grand total win of $5,000. And the really good news is that the player would automatically get entered into Let it Ride®, The Tournament™, where $1,000,000 could be won!

However, to receive the bonus payouts and possible entry into the tournament, the player must have made that $1 tournament wager.

LET IT RIDE®, THE TOURNAMENT™

The Let it Ride® Tournament is an exciting concept which allows participating players the chance to win a million dollar jackpot. There are four qualifying rounds a year, each one lasting for a period of three months. These exciting and lucrative events are only open to players who paid the $1 "entry fee" and were lucky enough to hit a straight or royal flush on that hand.

All players who receive a straight flush or royal flush during the three month qualifying period (and who had the $1 bet on the red button for the tournament bet) will be asked to fill out a tournament registration form at the time of winning. When the three month qualifying period is up, these players will be invited by the Shuffle Master Corporation to participate in the Tournament Playoffs.

And here is where the really big money can be won. At the very minimum, participants get guaranteed cash prizes beginning at $1,000. And for the lucky player who goes all the way, the grand prize of one million dollars will be the reward.

There are four rounds in the playoffs. Each player in this first qualifying round, as in every succeeding round, is given an equal amount of chips to start. Players are pitted against each other with the goal of trying to win more chips than their opponents so they can move on to the following rounds. These chips have no cash value and are only used for the purpose of determining winners on a round by round basis.

The first round gives each player a guaranteed $1,000 bonus just for playing. The top 100 winners in this first round will move on to the second round and receive an additional $1,000 bonus for their efforts, while the losers will have to settle for their original $1,000 and their "what ifs".

In this second round, players start fresh again with an equal amount of non-redeemable chips. No winnings are carried over from round one. Again, players make their best efforts to build up the winnings, hoping to be among the top winners so they can move on once again, one step closer to the million dollar grand prize.

Only the top 25 players from round two move on to round three, accompanied by another $1,000 bonus. These 25 players have now earned $3,000 in prizes, but their sights are set on going one more round, to round four where the big money prizes await. Again, chips are divided up with an equal number going to the 25 competitors.

When the dust settles, it will be only the top six players who move on to the fourth and final round and the big prizes. These six players now play for the banana split with all the fixings - three scoops, two toppings, whip cream, sprinkles, and cherry.

In this final round, players are playing for a one million dollar prize! While the losers may be disappointed in not coming in first, they don't do too shabby either - there are $450,000 in prizes for the runners-up.

The prize schedule for the top six finalists is shown below.

Finish	Tournament Prize
1st	$1,000,000
2nd	$200,000
3rd	$100,000
4th	$75,000
5th	$50,000
6th	$25,000

Quick Summary of Play

Players have a choice of removing or letting their bets ride on the first betting circle after seeing their three cards, and then on the second betting circle after the dealer exposes the first community card. All player decisions are now finished - the bet on the third betting circle cannot be removed - and the dealer will turn over each player's cards to see who won. The player's final hand, composed of his or her three down cards and the two community cards, must be at least a pair of 10's or higher to qualify for a payoff. Hands of lesser rank than a pair of tens are losers, and the dealer will remove the lost bets. Winning hands will be paid on each circle where there is a bet.

Players who made the $1 tournament payout bet and drew a straight or better, will get paid their winnings according to the bonus payout schedule. And if the hand is a straight flush or royal flush, that player earns entry into the big tournament.

THE WINNING STRATEGIES

In this section, we'll go over the third and fourth card playing strategies for Let it Ride®, the house percentages inherent to the game, and the overall strategy for winning at Let it Ride®.

The main strategy considerations in Let it Ride® center around the bets that have been made in the first two betting circles, 1 and 2, where the player has a choice of letting these bets ride or bringing them down and playing only for the mandatory bet in the third circle. Thus, there are two decisions to make, one for each circle.

The first decision occurs when we've looked at our three cards and decide on letting the bet ride in circle 1 or bringing it down. We'll call this the Three Card Betting Strategy. The second decision occurs when the dealer has exposed a community card, the player's fourth known card, and we must now decide the fate of the bet in circle 2. Since this occurs when we have knowledge of four of our cards, we'll call this the Fourth Card Playing Strategy.

We'll start our strategy discussions with the third card playing strategy.

THIRD CARD BETTING STRATEGY

Our first three cards give us a good indication of where the hand may be headed. We already know three fifths of the cards that will comprise our final hand and can make a clear determination on the best way to play the bets.

Sometimes, as in the case of three of a kind or a pair of tens or better, the strategy decision is obvious - we're already sitting with winners and should let the bet ride. A payout is already guaranteed and with a little luck, that hand may improve to a stronger rank and larger payoff. We'll also play strong hands that don't yet have a guaranteed payoff but which give us a positive expectation of winning.

On the other side of the coin, weak hands with negative expectations of winning will dictate a strategy of minimizing losses and the correct play will be to take down the bet in circle 1.

Below are the seven categories of Let it Ride® poker hands where the optimal play is to let the bet ride in circle 1. Hands are listed from the strongest to the weakest.

Hands that We Will Play

We'll let our bet ride with the following three card hands:

1. Three of a Kind - This is fairly obvious. We've got an automatic winner guaranteeing us at least a 3-1 payoff on all our bet spots.

2. Pair of 10's or Higher Pair - Another obvious play. We already have a 1-1 payoff, and can't lose. Improving the hand will give us an even larger payout..

3. Three to a Royal Flush - We have all sorts of shots here for a payoff; a flush, a straight, a high pair (and even three of a kind), and of course, the hand we would really like to get, a Royal Flush.

4. Three to a Straight Flush - Ditto above. There are good possibilities for improvement. We should let the bet ride.

5. Three to a Flush with Two Cards 10 or Higher and a Straight Possibility - It is not enough to have the flush chance, for there are two additional suited cards that must be matched up. We must also have the value of the two high cards, which can pair, and the possibility of the straight. The combination of all the above factors make this hand a profitable one to let the bet ride. An example of this hand is Q J 9 of clubs, or K J 9 of hearts.

6. Three to a Flush with J 9 8, 10 9 7 or 10 8 7 - Unlike the above grouping, which can be played with a two gap straight possibility, these three hands have only one high card and are thus more marginal as a playable combination. They need the greater straight possibilities of the one gap hand (compared to the two gap straight in category 5 to make letting the bet ride a profitable play.

7. 10 J Q or J Q K - These hands, the most marginal of the seven categories, but still profitable enough to let the bet ride, provide two good possibilities for payoffs. First, any of the three cards, if paired, gives us a payoff with the added outside chance of trips on the fifth card; and second, both hands are open-ended straight possibilities that can fill into a winner paying 5-1.

Hands that We Won't Play

Similar hands to the seventh group of hands above that we won't play are A K Q, which is only a one-way, and therefore more difficult straight possibility to fill, and J 10 9, which has only two high cards that can pair into a payoff. On these marginal hands, we just don't have enough juice to justify the bet in circle 1, and the best percentage play is to take the bet down.

Other specific hands that should not be played are low pairs, that is, pairs less than 10's. For example, on the hand 7 7 Q, we should take down our bet. While you'll sometimes catch the third 7 or another Q, the times that you don't will more than over-shadow the times you do, with a net long term result of a losing wager. That's exactly what we're trying to avoid.

And there you have it. Unless you have one of the hands in the seven categories listed in the above section, you should remove your bet from the first circle. While there are always winning possibilities with any three starting cards, the cost of playing low percentage hands is too costly to justify letting the bet ride.

Where you have a chance to remove a bet with inferior cards, you should always do so. That's the smart way to play.

Let's now move on to the strategy for the next round.

FOURTH CARD BETTING STRATEGY

After the dealer exposes one of the two community downcards, each player knows four of the five cards that will make up his or her final hand. We're faced with our final strategy decision: Should we let our bet ride, or should we reclaim it back into our bankroll?

As with the third card betting strategy, we'll play hands that give us a positive expectation of winning, and take down our bet in the second circle when our expectation of winning is negative. In the obvious cases where we already have a winning combination, the clear-cut play of course, is to let the bet ride. However, in many cases, we won't be quite as thrilled with our prospects, and would like nothing better than to take down our bet with our lousy cards.

Below, we'll look at the full strategy for letting bets ride or taking them down on circle 2.

Hands that We Will Play

We'll let our bet ride with the following four card hands.

1. Three or Four of a Kind - These are obvious winning hands paying 3-1 and 50-1 respectively. Let 'em ride!

2. Two Pair - A clear-cut play. We already have a guaranteed 2-1 payoff with possibilities of improving to a full house for an 11-1 yield.

3. Pair of 10's or Higher Pair - We've already got a winner paying 1-1 and can improve to a two pair or three of a kind hand with a good draw on the final card.

4. Four to a Royal Flush - One more card, and we're there with a big payoff. There are also the possibilities of making a flush or straight, and an excellent chance of catching a high paying pair since any of our four high cards, if matched, becomes a winner.

5. Four to a Straight Flush - This is not as strong as a four to a royal flush, but it is still holds excellent possibilities.

6. Four to a Flush - The payoff of 8-1 should the flush be drawn is greater than the odds of filling the flush, and is therefore an excellent bet. Of the 48 unseen cards in the deck, nine of them will make the flush, and 39 will not, odds of 4.33-1. Being paid 8-1 on odds of about 4.33-1 is always a great bet in my book.

*7. **Four to an Open-Ended Straight** - When there are no high cards held, this bet is a wash. Of the 48 unseen cards, eight of them will make the straight, and 40 will not, odds of 5-1. Since the payoff is exactly 5-1, we have an even chance - there is no theoretical loss or gain on the play. We could choose to let our bet ride, or take it down.

If there is at least one high card as part of the open-ended straight, we now gain the advantage on the four card open end straight draw, for the last community card may pair with our high card for a winner.

Hands that We Won't Play

We don't let our bet ride on circle 2 when holding a one way or inside straight, such as A K Q J or J 10 9 7, for the chances of making these one way straights climb to 11-1. Being paid at only 5-1 if the straight is made is clearly a terrible percentage bet. Small pairs, those 9's or under, are not worth chasing anymore. Our winning expectation is negative, and since these hands promise no payoff as a 10's or better does, the best play in the long run is to take down the bet in circle 2.

Lacking any of the seven combinations listed above, in other words, holding hands of various degrees of junk, gives us a negative expectation on this fourth card and the strategy is clear - take down the bet and have it returned to your bankroll.

HOUSE PERCENTAGES

The best percentage that can be achieved at Let it Ride® is about 3.5% against the player. This is assuming that the player uses the optimal basic strategy we present here and that the $1 bet is not made on the tournament spot. Less than optimal play at the table can cost the player multiple percentage points, the severity of which depends on the degree of ineptness or even outright blundering. For example, a player who doesn't let his bets ride on automatic winning hands or who lets his bets ride on terrible starting cards, will increase the house edge precipitously.

Also, players who make bets on the optional $1 tournament spot are giving the casino a very large edge and that would raise the overall house edge higher than 3.5%. The smaller the average bet, the higher that house percentage would be. For example, a poor percentage $1 bet has a greater overall negative effect on an average $5 bettor than an average $25 bettor.

OVERALL WINNING STRATEGY

While the house edge at Let it Ride® is less than the approximate 5.25% at Caribbean Stud Poker, the 3.5% nut on the three bet circles is still higher than other table games such as blackjack, baccarat and craps, when those games are played properly.

The big draw for Let it Ride® is the $1 tournament bet and the hope of hitting a monster hand. However, this wager is even worse than the 3.5% edge of the other bets. For my taste, I don't like making high percentage negative bets, and if I do, I might be more apt to go for the multi-millions of the lottery with that same $1 bet. But then again, as opposed to the lottery, Let it Ride® lets players participate in the action, make decisions that effect the outcome of the game, and of course, be part of the casino experience.

It is my recommendation to stay away from the $1 tournament bet due to its terrible odds, but since this wager is one of the allures of the game, players will have to draw their own conclusions.

For players to give themselves the best chances of winning at Let it Ride®, they'll need to study the third and fourth card playing strategies, keeping only the bets which give them a positive expectation of winning, and taking down those bets where the hand doesn't justify the extra money wagered. It is always best to play the optimal strategy so that the casino edge is brought down to the bare edge possible.

Let it Ride®, like all gambling pursuits, is subject to the ups and downs of winning and losing streaks. Players must make sure to keep their losing streaks to reasonable and acceptable levels, and when winning, to walk away with the casino's money.

THE GRI MASTER KENO STRATEGY

David Cowles Professional Winning Strategy

Finally! David Cowles, the *world's foremost expert on keno*, and the publisher of the *Keno Newsletter*, has released his **powerhouse strategy** on winning money at keno **exclusively** to Cardoza Publishing. This strategy is now available for the **first time** and is only available through us!!!

TIRED OF LOSING? LEARN HOW TO WIN! - Learn how to bet the tickets that provide the **highest payoffs** and push the percentages in your favor, how to increase winning tickets **tenfold** using way, combination and king tickets, how to set goals and plot a winning course, how to parlay small bankrolls into large fortunes by **playing smart** instead of betting haphazardly, and how to stretch your bankroll so you have **more winners** and chances for **big jackpots**!

WIN MORE PLAYING KENO! - Cowles reveals, for the first time, the magic *wager-to-win ratio* - a quick way to determine if a keno ticket is playable; also how to find the most **profitable** tickets, the *real scoop* on how to **pick winning numbers**, tips from the pros on **winning** keno tournaments and contest prizes.

THE SECRET TO THE MOST PROFITABLE BETS - Many keno tickets are blatant ripoffs. Learn to avoid the sucker bets and how to **slash the casino edge** to the bone. You can't change the odds, but you can get the best deals once you learn the *secrets* revealed here.

FREE ROOM, FOOD & DRINKS? - You bet! They're yours for the taking. You just have to know *who, how* and *when* to ask - and then *how much*.

DOUBLE BONUS! - With your order, **absolutely free**, receive two insider bonus essays: *12 Winning Tips From the Pros* - the 12 master jewels that can increase winnings drastically; and *The 10 "Don'ts" of Keno*, mistakes made by both novice and experienced players. You'll never make these mistakes again. Be a winner!

To order, send $50 by check or money order to Cardoza Publishing

SUPER SYSTEM - A COURSE IN POKER POWER
by World Champion Doyle Brunson

This is the **classic** book on every major no-limit game played today and is considered by the pros to be one of the **best books ever written** on poker! **Jam-packed** with **advanced strategies**, theories, tactics and money-making techniques - no serious poker player can afford to be without this **essential** book! Hardbound, and packed with 605 pages of hard-hitting information, this is truly a **must-buy** for aspiring pros. Includes 50 pages of the most precise poker statistics ever published!

CHAPTERS WRITTEN BY GAME'S SUPERSTARS - The best theorists and poker players in the world, Dave Sklansky, Mike Caro, Chip Reese, Bobby Baldwin and Doyle Brunson, a *book by champions for aspiring pros* - cover the **essential** strategies and **advanced play** in their respective specialties. Three world champions and two master theorists and players provide non-nonsense winning advice on making money at the tables.

LEARN WINNING STRATEGIES FOR THE MAJOR POKER GAMES - The important money games today are covered in depth by these **poker superstars**. You'll learn seven-card stud, draw poker, lowball, seven-card low stud (razz), high-low split (cards speak) and high-low declare; and the most popular game in the country today, hold'em (limit and no-limit). Each game is covered in detail with the **important winning concepts** so that anyone can become a **bigger money** winner.

SERIOUS POKER PLAYERS *MUST* **HAVE THIS BOOK** - **Mandatory reading** for aspiring pros, tournament and no-limit players. **Ideal** for average players seeking to move to higher stakes games.

MASTER POKER PLAYER'S STRATEGY
Almost $40 in Savings with this Exclusive Professional Offer!!!

The foremost authority on poker strategy, psychology, and statistics, Mike Caro, the *Mad Genius of Poker* has put together the **best winning strategy** available anywhere and at **tremendous savings**!!! You'll receive four hard-hitting and inspirational audio cassettes, a strategy-filled book and 4 powerful insider reports (10,000+ words!) for **serious** poker players. **Exclusive** to GRI - *not available anywhere else!* For just $95, receive $132.55 in Mike Caro's winning materials !!! Here's what you get:

A. Strategy-Filled Book ($12.95) - Caro's Fundamental Secrets of Poker (128 page) Unique blackboard teaching style helps illustrate most profitable concepts, tips and tactics.

B. Four Powerful Audio Cassette Seminars ($9.95 each) - **Pro Poker Secrets I** - Diverse but powerful Caro advice for all forms of poker. **Pro Hold'em Secrets I** - Selected and powerful advice specific to Hold 'em. **Positive Poker** - Based on over 100 motivational seminars, with Mike's actual narration. Learn how to stay tough and play your best game - always. **Real-Life Strategy**. Shows how to apply proven poker strategies to success in real life.

C. Professional Poker Reports ($19.95 each) - **11 Days to Seven-Stud Success** - 11 strategy missions are taken one day at a time. One advantage is gained each day. Powerful method to 7 stud winnings. Essential. **12 Days to Hold'em Success**. 12 strategy missions, a day at a time. Guaranteed to improve play. Very popular. **Professional Seven-Stud Report** - Tells how to read an opponent's starting hand, plus sophisticated advanced strategies. Signed, numbered. **Professional Hold'em Report** - Describes controversial system used successfully by thousands. Charts. Signed, numbered.

BACCARAT MASTER CARD COUNTER
New Winning Strategy!

For the **first time**, Gambling Research Institute releases the **latest winning techniques** at baccarat. This **exciting** strategy, played by big money players in Monte Carlo and other exclusive locations, is based on principles that have made insiders and pros **hundreds of thousands of dollars** counting cards at blackjack - card counting!

NEW WINNING APPROACH - This brand **new** strategy now applies card counting to baccarat to give you a **new winning approach,** and is designed so that any player, with just a **little effort**, can successfully take on the casinos at their own game - and win!

SIMPLE TO USE, EASY TO MASTER - You learn how to count cards for baccarat without the mental effort needed for blackjack! No need to memorize numbers - keep the count on the scorepad. Easy-to-use, play the strategy while enjoying the game!

LEARN WHEN TO BET BANKER, WHEN TO BET PLAYER - No longer will you make bets on hunches and guesses - use the GRI Baccarat Master Card Counter to determine when to bet Player and when to bet Banker. You learn the basic counts (running and true), deck favorability, symmetrical play vs. non-symmetrical play, how and when to increase bets and much more in this **winning strategy**.

PLAY SCIENTIFICALLY TO WIN - Drawing and standing advantage, average edge, average gain, total gain, win-loss and % of occurrence are shown for every relevant hand. You won't need to know these numbers or percentages, but we've included them here so you can see exactly how the strategy works and how you can use it to your advantage.

LEARN TO WIN IN JUST ONE SITTING - That's right! After **just one sitting** you can successfully learn this powerhouse strategy and use it to your advantage in the casino. Be the best baccarat player - the one playing the odds to **win**! Baccarat can be beaten. The Master Card Counter shows you how!

To order send just $50 by check or money order to:
Cardoza Publishing, P.O. Box 1500, Cooper Station, New York, NY 10276

INTERNET CASINO BETTING?
Yes - You Can Now Bet From Your Home!

The Era of the New Casino! - www.cardozacasino.com

Yes! It's happening now from internet casinos around the world. You can now can play all your favorite gambling games – blackjack, roulette, slots, keno, video poker, craps, and more – right from your home computer and go for the big winnings, just as if you were in the casino.

Real Play & Free Play

At some sites you can play for free, but if you want to gamble for real from your home or office, internet gambling–the new casinos – has become a reality. Are you dealt a square deal? Is casino gambling on the internet legal? We'll talk about these isues and more.

Find Out More!

Our web site will keep you up to date and informed with the latest developments on this exciting new technology. Check out our site anyway, there's no charge!

FREE GAMBLING INFORMATION
www.cardozapub.com

You'll also want to check out the new web site for Cardoza Publishing. Here, you'll find out the latest information on all our publications, receive the inside privy on the debut of our **free** online **gambling magazine**, and be kept up to date on internet gambling, the latest gambling strategies, the tip of the week, hotel specials in Las Vegas, and other gambling meccas. It's all coming soon right at our web site, **www.cardozapub.com.**

We'll see you there!

AVERY CARDOZA'S 100 SLOTS
THE ULTIMATE SIMULATION FOR SLOTS FANATICS!
For CD-ROM Windows 3.1 & 95 - Requires 486 or better, 8MB RAM

100 SLOT MACHINES - 22 VARIETIES!

GET READY FOR A GREAT TIME! Enter Avery Cardoza's incredible 3D slots world where *you're really part of the action*. The ultimate in realistic slots simulations, gives you Las Vegas style action at **100 incredible machines** (actually 101!) - so many that you'll be playing and **having fun for hours and hours!**

WIN 5 MILLION DOLLARS! If you play big, you can win big - if you're lucky. Our **monster jackpot** payout gives you the chance to beat the game for all it's worth.

TONS AND TONS OF MACHINES! This game has it all! **Three reel machines** with one, three and five payout lines, **four reel machines** with one and three payout lines, plus **bonus payout machines**, seven **progressives**, lots of big **suprises**, the huffin, puffin, incredible **Big Bud**, and choices of $1, $5, $10, $50, $100, $500 and $1,000 machines for the big players, and nickel, dime and quarter pulls for the old time feel!

FREE BONUS BOOK! ($15.00 VALUE)! Receive the bonus, *Slots For Serious Players*, by gambling guru **Avery Cardoza**. This $15.00 strategy guide shows you how to win money at slots and is included **free** to you!

STATE-OF-THE-ART GRAPHICS! Individually hand-enhanced **3D animation frames**, full casino sound with tunes written specifically for **winning** pulls on every machine, 3D artwork, and **complete realism** put you right at the helm of victory and in the **heart of the action**!.

SUPER FEATURES! In addition to the strategy guide, there is a **complete player record** that tracks every conceivable stat for every machine in every denomination.

GRI'S PROFESSIONAL VIDEO POKER STRATEGY
Win Money at Video Poker! With the Odds!

At last, for the **first time,** and for **serious players only,** the GRI **Professional Video Poker** strategy is released so you too can play to win! **You read it right** - this strategy gives you the **mathematical advantage** over the casino and what's more, it's **easy to learn!**

PROFESSIONAL STRATEGY SHOWS YOU HOW TO WIN WITH THE ODDS
This **powerhouse strategy,** played for **big profits** by an **exclusive** circle of **professionals,** people who make their living at the machines, is now made available to you! You too can win - with the odds - and this **winning strategy** shows you how!

LEARN TO PLAY FOR A PROFIT
You'll learn the **key factors** to play on a **pro level**: which machines will turn you a profit, break-even and win rates, hands per hour and average win per hour charts, time value, team play and more! You'll also learn big play strategy, alternate jackpot play, high and low jackpot play and key strategies to follow.

WINNING STRATEGIES FOR ALL MACHINES
This **comprehensive, advanced pro package** not only shows you how to win money at the 8-5 progressives, but also, the **winning strategies** for 10s or better, deuces wild, joker's wild, flat-top, progressive and special options features. All strategies shown in **easy-to-read charts** for ease of play..

BE A WINNER IN JUST ONE DAY
In just one day, after learning our strategy, you will have the skills to **consistently win money** at video poker - with the odds. The strategies are easy to use under practical casino conditions.

FREE BONUS - PROFESSIONAL PROFIT EXPECTANCY FORMULA ($15 VALUE) -
For serious players, we're including this free bonus essay which explains the professional profit expectancy principles of video poker and how to relate them to real dollars and cents in your game. This is bound right into the strategy.

To order send just $50 by check or money order to:
Cardoza Publishing, P.O. Box 1500, Cooper Station, New York, NY 10276

Win at Blackjack Without Counting Cards!!!

Multiple Deck 1, 2, 3 Non-Counter - Breakthrough in Blackjack!!!

BEAT MULTIPLE DECK BLACKJACK WITHOUT COUNTING CARDS!

You heard right! Now, for the **first time ever, win** at multiple deck blackjack **without counting cards**! Until I developed the Cardoza Multiple Deck Non-Counter (The 1,2,3 Strategy), I thought it was impossible. Don't be intimidated anymore by four, six or eight deck games - for **you have the advantage**. It doesn't matter how many decks they use, for this easy-to-use and proven strategy keeps you **winning - with the odds**!

EXCITING STRATEGY - ANYONE CAN WIN! - We're **excited** about this strategy for it allows anyone at all, against any number of decks, to have the **advantage** over any casino in the world in a multiple deck game. You don't count cards, you don't need a great memory, you don't need to be good at math - you only need to know the **winning secrets** of the 1,2,3 Multiple Deck Non-Counter and use but a **little effort** to be a **winner**.

SIMPLE BUT EFFECTIVE! - **Now the answer is here**. This strategy is so **simple**, yet so **effective**, you will be amazed. With a **minimum of effort**, this remarkable strategy, which we also call the 1,2,3 (as easy as 1,2,3), allows you to win without studiously following cards. Drink, converse with your fellow players or dealer - they'll never suspect that you can **beat the casino**!

PERSONAL GUARANTEE - And you have my personal **guarantee of satisfaction**, 100% money back! This breakthrough strategy is my personal research and is guaranteed to give you the edge! If for any reason you're not satisfied, send back the materials unused within 30 days for a full refund.

BE A LEISURELY WINNER! - If you just want to play a **leisurely game** yet have the expectation of winning, the answer is here. Not as powerful as a card counting strategy, but **powerful enough to make you a winner** - with the odds!!!

EXTRA BONUS! - Complete listing of all options and variations at blackjack and how they affect the player. ($5.00 Value!)

EXTRA, EXTRA BONUS!! - Not really a bonus since we can't sell you the strategy without protecting you against getting barred. The 1,000 word essay, *"How to Disguise the Fact That You're an Expert,"* and the 1,500 word *"How Not To Get Barred,"* are also included free. ($15.00 Value). These are bound right into the strategy.

To Order, send ~~$75~~ $50 (plus postage and handling) by check or money order to:
Cardoza Publishing, P.O. Box 1500, Cooper Station, New York, NY 10276

$25 OFF! (Only $50 With This Coupon!)

Yes! I want to be a winner at blackjack! Please rush me the **Cardoza Multiple Deck Non-Counter** (the **1,2,3 Strategy**). I understand that all the two bonus essays, and the "Options and Variations" Charts all will be included **absolutely free**! Enclosed is a check or money order for $50 (plus postage and handling) made out to:

Cardoza Publishing, P.O. Box 1500, Cooper Station, New York, NY 10276

Call Toll-Free in U.S. & Canada, 1-800-577-WINS

Fax Orders (718)743-8284 - E-Mail Orders: CardozaPub@aol.com

Include $5.00 postage/handling for U.S. orders; $10.00 for Canada/Mexico; HI/AK, other countries, $20.00. Outside U.S., money order payable in U.S. dollars on U.S. bank only.

NAME _____

ADDRESS _____

CITY _____ STATE _____ ZIP _____

HG 97

Order Today! 30 Day Money Back Guarantee!

THE CARDOZA CRAPS MASTER
Exclusive Offer! - Not Available Anywhere Else
Three Big Strategies!

Here It is! **At last**, the **secrets** of the **Grande-Gold Power Sweep, Molliere's Monte Carlo Turnaround** and the **Montarde-D'Girard Double Reverse** - three big strategies - are made available and presented for the **first time anywhere**! These powerful strategies are designed for the serious craps player, one wishing to bring the best odds and strategies to hot tables, cold tables and choppy tables.

I. THE GRANDE-GOLD POWER SWEEP (HOT TABLE STRATEGY)
This **dynamic strategy** takes maximum advantage of hot tables and shows you how to amass small **fortunes quickly** when numbers are being thrown fast and furious. The Grande-Gold stresses aggressive betting on wagers the house has no edge on! This previously unreleased strategy will make you a powerhouse at a hot table.

2. MOLLIERE'S MONTE CARLO TURNAROUND (COLD TABLE STRATEGY)
For the player who likes betting against the dice, Molliere's Monte Carlo Turnaround shows how to turn a cold table into hot cash. Favored by an exclusive circle of professionals who will play nothing else, the uniqueness of this strongman strategy is that the vast majority of bets **give absolutely nothing away to the casino**!

3.MONTARDE-D'GIRARD DOUBLE REVERSE (CHOPPY TABLE STRATEGY)
This **new** strategy is the **latest development** and the **most exciting strategy** to be designed in recent years. **Learn how** to play the optimum strategies against the tables when the dice run hot and cold (a choppy table) with no apparent reason. **The Montarde-d'Girard Double Reverse** shows how you can **generate big profits** while less knowledgeable players are ground out by choppy dice. And, of course, the majority of our bets give nothing away to the casino!

BONUS!!!
Order now, and you'll receive **The Craps Master-Professional Money Management Formula** ($15 value) **absolutely free**! Necessary for serious players and **used by the pros**, the **Craps Master Formula** features the unique **stop-loss ladder**.
The Above Offer is Not Available Anywhere Else. You Must Order Here.
To order send ~~$75~~ $50 (plus postage and handling) by check or money order to:
Cardoza Publishing, P.O. Box 1500, Cooper Station, New York, NY 10276

WIN MONEY PLAYING CRAPS!
$25 Off!
YES, I want to take advantage of this **exclusive** offer and learn these **newly revealed** strategies. Please **rush** me the **CSB Craps Master** and the **bonus**. Enclosed is a check or money order for $50 (plus postage and handling) made out to:
Cardoza Publishing, P.O. Box 1500, Cooper Station, New York, NY 10276
Call Toll-Free in U.S. & Canada, 1-800-577-WINS
Fax Orders (718)743-8284 - E-Mail Orders: CardozaPub@aol.com
Include $5.00 postage/handling for U.S. orders; $10.00 for Canada/Mexico; HI/AK, other countries, $20.00. Outside U.S., money order payable in U.S. dollars on U.S. bank only.

NAME _____

ADDRESS _____

CITY _____ STATE _____ ZIP _____
Order Now to Win at Craps! 30 Day Money Back Guarantee! HG 97

CARDOZA SCHOOL OF BLACKJACK
- Home Instruction Course - $200 OFF! -

At last, after years of secrecy, the **previously unreleased** lesson plans, strategies and playing tactics formerly available only to members of the Cardoza School of Blackjack are now available to the general public - and at substantial savings. **Now**, you can **learn at home,** and at your own convenience. Like the full course given at the school, the home instruction course goes **step-by-ste**p over the winning concepts. We'll take you from layman to **pro**.

MASTER BLACKJACK - Learn what it takes to be a **master player**. Be a **powerhouse**, play with confidence, impunity, and **with the odds** on your side. Learn to be a **big winner** at casino blackjack. *Lose no more.* Go to the tables with the goal of **winning money**.

MAXIMIZE WINNING SESSIONS - You'll **learn how** to take a good winning session and make a **blockbuster** out of it, but just as important, you'll learn to cut your losses. Learn exactly when to end a session. We cover everything from the psychological and emotional aspects of play to altered playing conditions (through the **eye of profitability**) to protection of big wins. The advice here could be worth **hundreds (or thousands) of dollars** in one session alone. Take our guidelines seriously.

ADVANCED STRATEGIES - You'll learn the *latest* in advanced winning strategies. Learn about the **ten-factor**, the **Ace-factor**, the effects of rules variations, how to protect against dealer blackjacks, the winning strategies for single and multiple deck games and how each affects you; the **true count**, the multiple deck true count variations, and much, much more. And, of course, you'll receive the full Cardoza Base Count Strategy package.

$200 OFF - LIMITED OFFER - The Cardoza School of Blackjack home instruction course, retailed at $295 (or $895 if taken at the school) is available here for just $95.

DOUBLE BONUS! - **Rush** your order in **now**, for we're also including, **absolutely free**, the 1,000 and 1,500 word essays, "How to Disguise the Fact that You're an Expert", and "How Not to Get Barred". Among other **inside information** contained here, you'll learn about the psychology of the pit bosses, how they spot counters, how to project a losing image, role playing, and other skills to maximize your profit potential. These bonuses are bound directly into the strategy.

To order, send $95 (plus postage and handling) by check or money order to:
Cardoza Publishing, P.O. Box 1500, Cooper Station, New York, NY 10276